Praise for
Ubiquitous Computing for Business

"Distilling research over a score of years, Bo nicely describes Ubiquitous Computing's tremendous business potential."

—**Gordon Bell**, author of *Total Recall: How the E-Memory Revolution Will Change Everything*; former Vice President of R&D at Digital Equipment Corporation

"In a field where there remains a surprising paucity of authoritative reference works in print, Bo Begole's detailed and comprehensive overview stands out. Alongside Kuniavsky's *Smart Things*, his book should form the core of any serious working library on Ubiquitous Computing and will challenge preconceptions of this technology's place in business for years to come."

—**Adam Greenfield**, Managing Director of Urbanscale; author of *Everyware: The Dawning Age of Ubiquitous Computing*

"Finally, a comprehensive and wonderfully clear articulation of Ubiquitous Computing—one that goes to the heart of Mark Weiser's original vision and explains just how powerful this vision was and still is. Indeed, this vision goes to the root of why we still feel so frustrated by today's technology, but also why the Ubiquitous Computing perspective will bring less stress and more productivity to us all."

—**John Seely Brown**, Former Chief Scientist of Xerox Corp. and Director of Xerox PARC; co-author of *A New Culture of Learning: Cultivating the Imagination for a World of Constant Change*

"*Ubiquitous Computing for Business* provides a blueprint for anybody in management who seeks better intelligence on the market, more actionable information without the overload, and instantaneous data for fast decisions. For innovating in an ever more uncertain world, Bo Begole shows us that computing power everywhere has emerged as the essential foundation."

—**Michael Useem**, Professor of Management and Director of the Leadership Center, Wharton School, University of Pennsylvania; author of *The Go Point: When It's Time to Decide*

"Few people on the planet know more about Ubiquitous Computing and context awareness than Bo Begole. Applying these two technologies to improve the way businesses interact with their customer is sure to be transformative."

—**Justin Rattner**, Intel Chief Technology Officer and Director of Intel Labs

"Ubiquitous Computing was coined at PARC decades ago, and the vision has continued to evolve here since. So it's wonderfully appropriate that Bo Begole, the current manager of this technology area for PARC and its clients, has authored a book that helps strategists—from CTOs to inventors—understand and exploit its disruptive business possibilities. This book will not only help readers map the various technologies to corresponding trends, but more importantly, help them sort hype from real value. The most valuable part, after all, isn't just ideas about what the future will hold, but actionable plans for turning these opportunities into products and services that people use."

—**Teresa Lunt**, Director of Computer Science Laboratory, Palo Alto Research Center

"Coming from the birthplace of Ubiquitous Computing at PARC, Dr. Begole's excellent introduction to this growing technology is approachable, interesting, well-informed, and humorous. His insightful treatment of the connection between Ubiquitous Computing and business is one of the few I have seen anywhere, and it goes deeply into what's coming and how businesses will be affected."

—**John Krumm**, Microsoft Research; Editor of *Ubiquitous Computing Fundamentals*

"*Ubiquitous Computing for Business* takes the potential value in Ubicomp technology and makes its value real. Its straightforward approach distills the experience of two decades of research and innovation to help executives and managers understand the business impact of pervasive computing technology in a way that no other business and technology book has tried. Every chapter is full of great ideas and practical advice from the thought leaders in the field."

—**Mike Kuniavsky**, author of *Smart Things: Ubiquitous Computing User Experience Design*

"On par with the business impact of laser printing, the Ethernet, and personal computing, this new paradigm of Ubiquitous Computing is revolutionizing the ways businesses exchange information and interact with customers. This book provides a practical view into the business opportunities enabled by embracing Ubiquitous Computing's capabilities."

—**Sophie Vandebroek**, Xerox Chief Technology Officer and President of the Xerox Innovation Group

Ubiquitous Computing for Business

Ubiquitous Computing for Business

Find New Markets, Create Better Businesses, and Reach Customers Around The World 24-7-365

Bo Begole

Vice President, Publisher: Tim Moore
Associate Publisher and Director of Marketing: Amy Neidlinger
Executive Editor Jeanne Glasser
Editorial Assistant: Pamela Bolan
Operations Manager: Gina Kanouse
Senior Marketing Manager: Julie Phifer
Publicity Manager: Laura Czaja
Assistant Marketing Manager: Megan Colvin
Cover Designer: Alan Clements
Managing Editor: Kristy Hart
Senior Project Editor: Lori Lyons
Copy Editor: Krista Hansing
Proofreader: Williams Woods Publishing Services, LLC
Senior Indexer: Cheryl Lenser
Senior Compositor: Gloria Schurick
Manufacturing Buyer: Dan Uhrig

© 2011 by Bo Begole
Pearson Education, Inc.
Publishing as FT Press
Upper Saddle River, New Jersey 07458

FT Press offers excellent discounts on this book when ordered in quantity for bulk purchases or special sales. For more information, please contact U.S. Corporate and Government Sales, 1-800-382-3419, corpsales@pearsontechgroup.com. For sales outside the U.S., please contact International Sales at international@pearson.com.

Company and product names mentioned herein are the trademarks or registered trademarks of their respective owners.

All rights reserved. No part of this book may be reproduced, in any form or by any means, without permission in writing from the publisher.

Printed in the United States of America

First Printing March 2011

ISBN-10: 0-13-706443-8
ISBN-13: 978-0-13-706443-4

Pearson Education LTD.
Pearson Education Australia PTY, Limited.
Pearson Education Singapore, Pte. Ltd.
Pearson Education Asia, Ltd.
Pearson Education Canada, Ltd.
Pearson Educación de Mexico, S.A. de C.V.
Pearson Education—Japan
Pearson Education Malaysia, Pte. Ltd.

Library of Congress Cataloging-in-Publication Data:

Begole, James, 1963-
Ubiquitous computing for business : find new markets, create better businesses, and reach customers around the world 24-7-365 / Bo Begole.
    p. cm.
Includes index.
ISBN-13: 978-0-13-706443-4 (hardback : alk. paper)
ISBN-10: 0-13-706443-8
1. Marketing. 2. Globalization. I. Title.
HF5415.B4238 2011
658.8—dc22
                    2010041445

To Florence

Contents

About the Author xi

Chapter 1   Introduction: Reading the Waves 1

Section I: **Background and Capabilities of Ubiquitous Computing**

Chapter 2   Profound Technologies 7

Chapter 3   Harmless if Used as Directed 31

Chapter 4   Still Stupid after All These Years 53

Chapter 5   Missing Ingredients 83

Section II: **Business Opportunities**

Chapter 6   Making Choices 101

Chapter 7   The Soft Sell: Personalized Marketing 111

Chapter 8   Breaking Out of the Supply Chain Gang .. 137

Chapter 9   Discontinuous Connections 173

Chapter 10   Coordination 187

Chapter 11   Clear Sailing 201

Chapter 12   Ubiquitous Business 227

Appendix   Further Reading 239

Index 241

Acknowledgments

Most of the concepts here come from conversations and experiences I've had with many, many colleagues over the years. I rarely work alone, and I am always bugging other people about what they think about this or that.

I would like to thank a number of my collaborators with and from whom I first learned the concepts in this book: all current and past employees of the Palo Alto Research Center, particularly the Ubiquitous Computing researchers in the Computer Science Laboratory; colleagues at the former Sun Microsystems Laboratories in the Network Communities research group; and my dissertation advisor, Cliff Shaffer, who opened this marvelous field to me.

I would also like to thank my parents: my mom for teaching me adequate English in spite of my attempts to thwart her; and my dad for giving me a need to create.

I would also like to thank my children, who remind me daily of why I love life. It is my wife who has really made this book possible and has *always* been supportive of any endeavor. To her, I offer particular gratitude.

About the Author

Bo Begole is a Principal Scientist at the Palo Alto Research Center, the famed innovation center credited with inventing and commercializing many core information technologies, including laser printing, Ethernet, graphical user interfaces, the laptop, and more. He currently manages the Ubiquitous Computing Area at PARC, a computer science team that invents and commercializes novel technologies like those in this book. Before joining PARC, he worked at Sun Microsystems Laboratories, where he created systems to facilitate global collaboration and sensor networks. Dr. Begole habitually collaborates with social scientists and others to create innovations that help people work together remotely, find information more rapidly with less effort, communicate more efficiently, and increase the performance of people using information technologies.

Dr. Begole has chaired committees of several research conferences crossing the fields of human–computer interaction and computer-supported cooperative work, and he has participated on organizing and program committees in Ubiquitous Computing, intelligent user interfaces, user interface software and technology, and pervasive computing. With colleagues, he has written dozens of papers that have appeared in peer-reviewed scientific conferences and journals. He holds several patents. He also hosts and participates in several Silicon Valley business technology special-interest groups and has spoken at several business and technology conferences.

Dr. Begole received a B.S. degree in Mathematics (*summa cum laude*) in 1992 from Virginia Commonwealth University, an M.S. degree in 1994, and a Ph.D. in 1998 in Computer Science from Virginia Tech. Before earning his degrees, he served in the U.S. Army from 1981-89 and during the Gulf War in 1991 as an Arabic language translator. He lives in Los Altos, California, with his wife, Florence, and three children, Brighton, Aiden, and Annecy.

1

Introduction: Reading the Waves

It's often hard to notice a sea change until it washes over you. You know one is coming—it's happened before—but it creeps up slowly and is hard to pay attention to. We see this effect often in information technologies: the web, personal computers, three-dimensional graphics, digital media, virtual worlds, smartphones, social computing, and more. We call such technologies "disruptive" because they seem to come from nowhere to wash over the established leaders.

For the most part, though, we could have seen any of them coming. Each had made a preceding beachhead: hypertext, workstations, animated sprites, cassette tape recorders, text-based multiuser domains, citizens' band (CB) radio, bulletin board services, and other forgotten predecessors of today's rich electronic media environment. At the time, those capabilities were mere novelties, prominent enough to take notice of but only actively used by devotees and geeks. In fact, the "flash in the pan" effect seen in the media causes us to sometimes dismiss later versions that actually *do* cause the sweeping changes prematurely predicted previously. Think back to when you first heard of hypertext; we had grand visions of universally interconnected information but dismissed Xanadu as providing marginal value,[1] unable to foresee the tremendous value of today's World Wide Web. Similarly, workstations preceded personal computers, bulletin board systems demonstrated community-generated content before Wikipedia, multi-user domains (MUDs) anticipated SecondLife and other virtual reality systems, and CB radio foreshadowed mobile phones. The rudimentary capabilities of the early versions of such technologies are easy to dismiss, making it difficult to imagine their ultimate success.

A sea change *is* hard to see—so many swells rising, merging, and dipping. It's the same with technologies. Gartner research uses the notion of a "hype curve" to describe the pattern in which a new idea creates inflated expectations that cannot be realized, leading to a crashing wave of disappointment and dismissal of the idea, which eventually does bring some measure of its initial promise to market. Gartner plots each idea at a point on the "hype curve," as an estimate of each idea's position in the rising and falling cycle. But the notion of just one "hype curve" along which all technologies rise and fall is misleading. In fact, each idea has its own swell and surge, and they all mix together to *cancel* or *reinforce* each other—like waves. This convergence of reinforcing concepts actually generates the enormous effects that overwhelm markets.

A champion surfer can "read the waves" to anticipate which rhythms of rips and sweeps will create that "fat wave" that comes once a day. But even champions know that the waves are not entirely predictable and that the *big ones* are very hard to see. The history of failed business projections and predictions of disruptive technologies makes the business strategist's job seem impossible. We cannot expect to see exactly what the changes will be, but we can at least see the general trends and estimate some prospective impacts both horizontally across and vertically within industrial sectors.

Who This Book Is For

This book aims to help business strategists, chief technology officers (CTOs), futurists, innovators, and entrepreneurs understand the mix of technologies that form the field of Ubiquitous Computing and to understand the opportunities and threats these imply. The business strategist's role is to foresee oncoming sea changes, to anticipate the ebbs and swells that will affect the ways in which they conduct their business, and to find the best ways of exploiting the positive while mitigating the negative effects. The aim of this book is to provide a map of the *capabilities* and *benefits* of Ubiquitous Computing technologies, not a map of the technologies themselves, and to help you identify which ones are reinforced or diminished by other trends in our society.

What This Book Is About

This book describes a long-coming trend in information technologies called Ubiquitous Computing ("Ubicomp," for short), first described in the early 1990s by Mark Weiser of the Xerox Palo Alto Research Center (Xerox PARC) as a research agenda for innovation. It's now seeing substantial commercial impact. I'll provide a more thorough description in Chapter 2, but the short description of Ubicomp is the use of technologies to bridge physical and electronic information spaces to increase efficiencies in our personal, school, and work lives. Ubicomp goes beyond simple mechanical automation, such as antilock brakes and automatic doors, by using sophisticated processes to proactively predict future needs, accurately target information to personal needs, help people reach one another at convenient times, conserve energy resources, remember meetings and encounters in our lives, provide personalized service, and coach us about healthy life choices.

Questions This Book Answers

Dozens of books cover the technologies and research in this area by addressing the question "How does it work?" but no one is answering the hard question of "How valuable is it?" The aim of this book is to describe the value of interweaving computing throughout our everyday activities across work, life, and education to create new business opportunities.

A term such as *Ubiquitous* Computing obviously covers a lot of ground, so it's important to identify the segments and technologies that can generate *breakout value*, as opposed to those that will simply grow as part of the natural progression of technology and business process refinement. Conversely, which technologies are not likely to live up to their hype, and why? Which technologies will reinforce each other, and which will cancel each other out? What steps should you consider to position your business for these transformations? What should you build, partner with, or buy? What barriers will your business need to overcome in adopting Ubicomp-based business models?

What if during the course of reading this book it seems that your business is likely to be on the *losing* side of coming transformations? In addition to taking comfort from the notion that a rising tide raises all ships, you'll also see points of weakness that you can leverage to slow or redirect the change elsewhere. Yes, I'm a proponent of Ubiquitous Computing, but we all need to protect our business position at least long enough to find a value position in the new order. What barriers can you erect against the competition? Can you erect impediments anywhere to cause the surges to expend energy prematurely?

How This Book Is Organized

The book consists of two parts. Chapters 2–5 provide background knowledge to identify technologies, general business opportunities, and threats related to Ubiquitous Computing. This part begins with some history, current trends, and future potentials.

Chapters 6–11 provide methods to exploit business opportunities or counter threats. Included are case studies of recent examples of business germination in this field. The book concludes with Chapter 12, "Ubiquitous Business," which includes an action plan to help you sketch out an approach for your business.

Endnotes

[1] Gary Wolf, "The Curse of Xanadu," *Wired*, June 1995. www.wired.com/wired/archive/3.06/xanadu.html

Part I

Background and Capabilities of Ubiquitous Computing

2

Profound Technologies

The most profound technologies are those that disappear. They weave themselves into the fabric of everyday life until they are indistinguishable from it.
—Mark Weiser, 1991

Ubiquitous Computing is the use of technologies to accomplish both simple and complex tasks throughout our work and personal lives. Ubiquitous Computing systems are embedded in the environment or carried on the body and adapt to the natural interactions of people. In contrast to terms such as *personal computing* and *mainframe computing*, which are derived from the type of computer used to do the work, Ubiquitous Computing is not intended as a description of the ubiquity of computer devices themselves; it's a description of how *computing* fits in our lives *ubiquitously*.

Repeating History for Profit

"Santayana taught us that those who do not know history are condemned to repeat it. That surely is true in design as in anything else, but in design there is a corollary: Those who do know history are privileged to repeat it at a profit." So said Ralph Caplan in his book *By Design*.[1] The history of Ubiquitous Computing provides several lessons from which we may all profit.

It's obvious now that computers have taken over our lives. They are ubiquitous. They permeate our work and home environments, transportation systems, entertainment and news media devices, payment and financial systems, and healthcare. But this wasn't *always* obvious and it hasn't happened by chance.

At one time in the history of information technologies, the problems were big and obvious and partitioned into easily recognizable technical categories, such as the following:

- **Performance:** Computations should be instantaneous, not take an entire day.
- **Storage:** Information should persist and be accessible as long as needed, without deteriorating.
- **Transfer:** Separate computing components should be able to get information from each other without requiring manual transfer.

The problems were apparent immediately to anyone using a computer and have been the focus of computer research and development for many decades. These problems persist today, although they are not nearly as acute, as a result of microprocessor advances, increasing storage density, and pervasive networking. We're not done yet. Computing systems are not 100% reliable or anywhere near instantaneous, and we'd like them to continue to become smaller, faster, and cheaper so that everyone can have access to the full range of computing capabilities, including weather prediction, artificial intelligence, and even biological simulation. On the other hand, outside of complex scientific investigation, today's technologies are well beyond "good enough" for the vast majority of information-oriented problems at work, home, and school.

Today's information problems are more subtle and are often related to the human biological processor in the loop, having less to do with unreliable electronics. Let's be clear: Computing has *always* been about creating results for human use, but in the past, the primary bottlenecks were in the limits of the technologies. Today the bottlenecks are primarily imposed by humans: *cognitive limitations* of human users, legal and policy constraints of data access, and the economic objectives of businesses. Today's innovations wrestle with fundamental questions that are not inherently technical at their core, but for which technologies can provide solutions. In addition to performance, storage, and transfer, today's problems are of the following nature:

- **Control:** Who owns the information and how can they control who can access it when
- **Overload:** How to find *pertinent* information
- **Interoperation:** How data from one system can be used by a complementary device or service

No progress can be achieved in solving such problems by making technologies that are simply smaller, faster, and cheaper than before. The problems are vague and ambiguous, the sort that stymied governments and businesses long before information technologies arrived. Who owns data? How do we control bits? What determines "pertinent information"? How and when should it be presented? Who decides? How do we anticipate that a device or service might be used by another device or service unless both are specifically designed for each other? Ground-breaking inventions today require deeper knowledge of human, social, business, and political problems than the key inventions of yesterday.

Foreseeing a Big Wave

In the late 1980s, the information age was just bringing personal computing into everyday business life. Rather than having to share time on big-iron mainframe machines, a personal computer allowed individuals to use computer power at their individual discretion. However, researchers at the Xerox Palo Alto Research Center (Xerox PARC)—where personal computing had been invented—and elsewhere foresaw a future in which there would be more than *one* computer for each person, but rather their environments would contain a *multitude* of computers.

In the 1970s, Xerox set up Xerox PARC as one of several research centers charged with the mission of creating technologies for the "office of the future" (sometimes envisioned as a "paperless office"), giving Xerox early access to new technologies that could revolutionize its business in paper copiers and printers. For centuries, paper or paper-like media and marking technologies had facilitated the transfer and storage of information, but the founders of Xerox PARC could see that the advantages of the then-emerging electronic forms of information storage and transfer (not to mention interaction and processing) would make paper and printing eventually superfluous. Toward that eventuality, Xerox PARC employed scientists from a wide range of disciplines: physicists, chemists, information scientists, designers, linguists, engineers, psychologists, anthropologists, and even artists. The lab was set up to cover the full spectrum of areas for innovation, "from atoms to culture," which led to new ways of making physical marks on paper (laser printing), creating content ("what you see is what you get" [WYSIWYG] word processing), enabling devices to communicate with each other (Ethernet), enabling devices and humans to communicate (graphical user interfaces), and improving the effectiveness of our life and work with technologies. We have yet to realize a fully paperless office and perhaps never will. In *The Myth of the Paperless Office*,[2] Sellen and Harper, researchers in Xerox's Cambridge, U.K., research center, outlined a variety of factors that keep paper alive, mostly attributable to the *ubiquity* and simplicity of paper throughout our lives today. From such insights across Xerox's research centers emerged a vision of Ubiquitous Computing that focused not on inventing technologies that were cheaper, smaller, and faster, but on inventing technologies that were pervasive and convenient, and that didn't require special training to use effectively.

Ubiquitous Computing emerged in the late 1980s, by which time Moore's law[3] was well accepted after several generations of continual miniaturization of computation had already been observed. The computational power that once required a warehouse of space could now be contained on a microchip. Mainframes had already given way to mini-computers, which personal computers soon displaced. Mobile computing devices were seen in the form of programmable calculators, and embedded microprocessors were controlling many electric appliances and automobiles. Just as the paradigm of personal computing had moved computation and storage out of centralized mainframe centers and into individual office workers' environments, many of the leading minds of the 1980s saw that computation would continue to pervade our lives such that we would interact with tens, if not hundreds, of computing devices throughout our daily routines. In the future, it was predicted, there would be too many devices in a person's life to be able to give each one the full individual attention demanded by the then-emerging personal computer.

A prominent spokesperson for a way out of the impending era of information overload was Mark Weiser, who coined the term *Ubiquitous Computing* (often shortened to *Ubicomp*) while heading the Computer Science Laboratory at Xerox PARC in 1988. In a seminal article in *Scientific American,* he described a vision of "calm computing" in which the computer did not require full attention to operate: Instead, information technologies would "disappear" and "weave themselves into the fabric of everyday life until they [were] indistinguishable from it." He wrote:[4]

> The idea of integrating computers seamlessly into the world at large runs counter to a number of present-day trends. "Ubiquitous computing" in this context does not just mean computers that can be carried to the beach, jungle or airport. Even the most powerful notebook computer, with access to a worldwide information network, still focuses attention on a single box.

Weiser's description of Ubiquitous Computing was in stark contrast to the then-popular notion that everyone would become a "power user," directing operations of the world from behind the console of their computer, like a fighter pilot. He also wanted to make clear that making the computer portable was not the solution. Rather, people would engage in life and work by using computing services scattered conveniently throughout their environment.

The main insight of this philosophy is that the best tools fit into the flow of one's work and that the work, not the tool, remains the central focus. Weiser pointed to many examples of "invisible" technologies that we take for granted, such as pens and pencils (we don't generally think about a "personal pencil"), electric motors (20–30 per vehicle), electricity itself, furniture, and other everyday objects. Consider a recent example when you had several productive hours (at work or leisure). The time passed unnoticed; you were not conscious of your surroundings; you were engrossed in the activity; you unconsciously used tacit skills, knowledge, and resources; and the situation included rich detail and subtleties that you unconsciously incorporated into the *flow* of the activity. Whatever tools you used may have made you more efficient, but your internal knowledge and access to resources were critical to the accomplishment and required your *personal* conscious effort. Good tools require attention only when they break down (for example, pen ink dries, pencil lead breaks, wiper blades fail, power cuts out, or a chair wobbles), implying that any technology that dominates the interaction as much as a personal computer today is, at best, a brittle tool and, at worst, creates more work than it solves.

Weiser's call for "calm computing" was a reaction to the increasing complexities that information technologies were creating. The promise of computing systems was that they would *simplify* complexities, not introduce new ones. Information explosion is both a blessing and a curse. We are surrounded by technologies that allow us to maintain knowledge of things that are not directly discernable by our human senses, as well as to take actions that go beyond natural human ability using sophisticated electro-mechanical devices. Controlling all of this is taxing to human cognitive processes that evolved to control our bodies within the immediate social and environmental situation. Weiser and other progenitors of the field of Ubiquitous Computing sought to create technologies that enhance people, allowing them to manipulate an environment *filled* with information and to control elements of the physical world *spontaneously* and *effortlessly*.

On the heels of creating laser printing, Ethernet, and the first personal computer, Xerox PARC researchers turned their attention toward realizing the new classes of computing devices that would be needed to support effortless, convenient, and pervasive computing. They created hardware and software prototypes spanning handheld, tablet, and wall-sized computers and displays, which they referred to as computing by the inch, by the foot and by the yard (see Figure 2-1).

The PARC Tab was a very early handheld computer with a touchscreen display. Xerox PARC researchers invented new interaction techniques for these devices, such as the Unistrokes character input in which each character of the alphabet could be written without lifting the pen.[5] The PARC Pad was an early tablet computer also with touchscreen input.

Both devices used wireless networking based on infrared, which requires line-of-sight communication between the device and the network hub. Although line-of-sight communication required that a hub be installed in each room of the building, it allowed the system to

Chapter 2 • Profound Technologies   13

know in which room each device was located. Indoor location led to the invention of several location-based and "context-aware" services that proactively provided personalized assistance such as supplying navigation; locating colleagues; locating nearby devices (such as printers and projectors); indexing information according to where, when, and with whom it was created; securely connecting nearby devices (for example, a handheld computer connected to a large display or projector in the same room); and appropriately routing incoming calls and messages depending on your activity. These kinds of context-aware services were early precursors to the location-based services

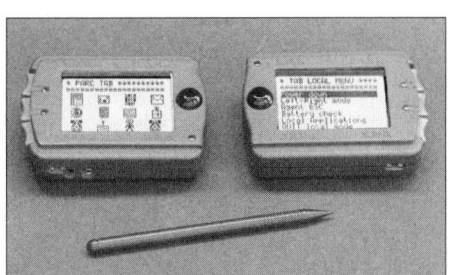
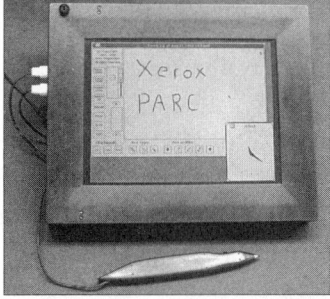

Figure 2-1 Early examples of Ubiquitous Computing devices circa 1991: PARC Tab handheld computer (upper left), PARC Pad tablet computer (upper right), and Liveboard wall-sized computer (bottom). © Palo Alto Research Center, Inc. Included here by permission.

that have now become popular on GPS-enabled smartphones. We explore context-awareness in more depth in Chapter 4, "Still Stupid after All These Years."

Japan

Beginning in 1984, before the term *Ubiquitous Computing* was coined, Ken Sakamura led The Real-time Operating System Nucleus (TRON) project at University of Tokyo. The project aimed to create a single unified operating system that could be used by every object that contained a computer and would allow interoperation and sharing of information across the network.[6] Versions of TRON have appeared in smart houses, intelligent buildings, and intelligent furniture. Versions of ITRON (Industrial TRON), an architecture for real-time operating systems for embedded systems, run on mobile phones, digital cameras, CD players and other devices; ITRON is said to be the most widely used operating system in the world.[7] Today organizations such as the TRON Association and the T-Engine Forum continue to advance the aim of developing a unified platform for Ubiquitous Computing. However, it seems that computing platforms are even more fragmented today than in the 1980s.

United Kingdom

In addition to the activities in Palo Alto and Tokyo, technologies that contributed to the vision of Ubiquitous Computing emerged in the United Kingdom. In investigating the creation of computer-telephony integration (CTI) technologies, researchers at Olivetti created the Active Badge Location System.[8] The Active Badge was a small battery-powered device with just one input button that was connected to a wireless infrared network and worn by the user like a badge. In an early example of "open innovation," Olivetti created a number of sets of the Active Badge systems for other research labs, including Xerox PARC, EuroPARC, Digital Equipment Corporation (later acquired by Compaq and, ultimately, Hewlett-Packard), and the MIT Media Laboratory, allowing others to experiment with indoor location-aware services.

The increasing computational power on personal computers led to an expansion of what was thought of as "information." Early business computers were able to handle information in the form of simple numbers and text strings, but new digital recording devices were generating multiple forms of media such as still images, audio, and video. The Active Badge was only one component of a larger Olivetti project called Pandora[9] that explored the creation of multimedia services over high-speed networks. Handling multimedia information involved revising the software of the day to support complex, multiformat data structures and repositories. In addition to mouse and keyboard input, multimedia documents used new kinds of input devices: cameras and microphones. Multimedia information is common today partly because of the value of the capabilities demonstrated by the early prototypes.

> ### Weiser Words on Ubiquitous Computing
>
> Over the years, Mark Weiser's description of Ubiquitous Computing evolved from an emphasis on the ubiquity of technology to an emphasis on invisible, natural, calm interaction. He published the following definitions of Ubiquitous Computing on the PARC web site (www.ubiq.com/hypertext/weiser/UbiHome.html).
>
> **Ubiquitous Computing #1**
>
> Inspired by the social scientists, philosophers, and anthropologists at Xerox PARC, we have been trying to take a radical look at what computing and networking ought to be like. We believe that people live through their practices and tacit knowledge so that the most powerful things are those that are effectively invisible in use. This is a challenge that affects all of computer science.
>
> Our preliminary approach: *Activate the world*. Provide hundreds of wireless computing devices per person per office, of all scales (from 1-inch displays to wall sized). This has required new work in operating systems, user interfaces, networks, wireless, displays, and many other areas. We call our work Ubiquitous Computing. This is different from PDAs, dynabooks, or information at your fingertips. It is invisible, everywhere computing that does not live on

a personal device of any sort, but is in the woodwork everywhere. (© Palo Alto Research Center, Inc. Included here by permission.)

Ubiquitous Computing #2

For 30 years most interface design, and most computer design, has been headed down the path of the "dramatic" machine. Its highest ideal is to make a computer so exciting, so wonderful, so interesting, that we never want to be without it. A less-traveled path I call the "invisible"; its highest ideal is to make a computer so embedded, so fitting, so natural, that we use it without even thinking about it. (I have also called this notion Ubiquitous Computing and have placed its origins in post-modernism.) I believe that in the next 20 years the second path will come to dominate. But this will not be easy; very little of our current systems infrastructure will survive. We have been building versions of the infrastructure-to-come at PARC for the past four years, in the form of inch-, foot-, and yard-sized computers we call Tabs, Pads, and Boards. Our prototypes have sometimes succeeded, but more often failed to be invisible. From what we have learned, we are now exploring some new directions for Ubicomp, including the famous "dangling string"[10] display. (© Palo Alto Research Center, Inc. Included here by permission.)

Ubicomp Stalls During the World Wide Web

At the dawn of the Ubicomp vision, the researchers who embraced it anticipated that it would be the next major wave of computing, following mainframe and personal computing. Ubicomp researchers at PARC and elsewhere foresaw the limitations of personal computing: lock-in on operating system and applications, emphasis on the *computer* and *data* rather than the *people* and *tasks*. At the time, other alternative paradigms were being proposed, such as virtual reality and agent-based interaction, but these also implied direct control and *management of the tool* itself instead of augmenting existing skills by providing information and services to help people gets things done. Weiser wrote:

> Perhaps most diametrically opposed to our vision is the notion of "virtual reality," which attempts to make a world inside the computer. [...] Although it may have its purpose in allowing people to explore realms otherwise inaccessible [...] virtual reality is only a map, not a territory. It excludes desks, offices, other people not wearing goggles and body suits, weather, grass, trees, walks, chance encounters and in general the infinite richness of the universe. Virtual reality focuses an enormous apparatus on simulating the world rather than on invisibly enhancing the world that already exists.

Prescient though they were, even the Ubicomp visionaries missed the really big wave on the horizon and the impending sea change of the World Wide Web. It wasn't that they didn't see it coming at all—most of those researchers were living in distributed computing environments—but they didn't realize that massive internetworking and the act of opening the world's databases to each other and to consumers would create such tremendous opportunities for new businesses. The technology industry and research communities have been largely consumed with the potentials (and fallout) of the dotcom era until recently. As a result, the advances in Ubicomp have received less attention than the early researchers anticipated. Timing is everything in innovation, as in surfing; even a champion surfer may pre-anticipate the biggest wave.

The network revolution alleviated some of the key issues that Ubicomp addressed. Information access has expanded beyond what is immediately physically at hand (hard drives, removable disks, flash memory), to vast information repositories on the network. Furthermore, we can reach these repositories from a wide range of networked devices, including mobile, wirelessly connected phones and other devices. However, we still access the information through brittle tools that require nearly as much knowledge and time to use as they alleviate. Web services and smartphones today still largely follow the point-to-point connections of a client/server architecture rather than the multipoint, multiservice interactions that ubiquitous technologies should certainly be capable of. Despite the vast interconnectedness of our networks and information technologies, we are still forced to manually copy and paste data from one place to another, or to print paper documents and forms that we or others manually re-enter.[11] I am reminded of the early complaints of iPhone users prior to version 3 of iOS, which enabled copy and paste: Why should we need to manually copy and paste? Why can we not invoke services and seamlessly transfer data from any representation of information we encounter?

Despite their certainty of long-term adoption of Ubicomp principles, Weiser and colleagues struggled to find near-term commercial success for these "calm" and "invisible" technologies. In an era when the complexity of computing systems was accepted, providing calm interfaces was seen as "nice to have" but not essential to creating value. In addition, the value of Ubiquitous Computing services occurs only after some critical mass of ubiquitous wireless networking exists, which has only started to be realized as wireless networking based on the IEEE 802.11 standard became popular after 2000.

Tragically, Mark Weiser died quite unexpectedly in 1999 just as Ubiquitous Computing was beginning to achieve commercial reality and reach into people's everyday lives: The World Wide Web connected machines across the globe; the first Blackberry from Research In Motion provided wireless two-way email; the Palm Pilot took a huge chunk of business from printed calendars, address books, and agenda notebooks; and the world awaited the imminent demise of mainframes as Y2K drew near.

Post-Web Ubiquitous Computing

Fast-forward 20 years from when Weiser first articulated the vision in the late 1980s and early '90s to 2011. Today Ubicomp is a major subdiscipline of computer science and electrical engineering research and innovation, to the point that at least two annual international conferences are held on the topic, and several periodical magazines and journals (listed at the end of the book) focus on it. Ubicomp research certainly has not sat stagnant while the web washed over everything. On the other hand, although exciting advances have emerged in these research venues, Ubicomp will not have arrived at its promise until it comes out of the labs and is realized in most people's everyday lives.

How far have we come toward achieving the dreams of seamless, effortless interaction with information? The reality is that Ubicomp commercialization has grown at different rates in different parts of the world. Broad adoption of Ubicomp-based systems, wireless digital services on mobile phones, and GPS-enabled phones has emerged in Japan and Korea. Considerable innovations in mobile and wireless technologies also have taken place in Europe. In the United States, we have only recently achieved the critical mass of digital technology adoption that is needed to reap the network-effect value of Ubicomp.

Why has the growth of Ubicomp been slower in the United States than in other parts of the world? The most likely explanation has to do with the key barrier for Ubicomp to provide value: interoperation. The usefulness of any digital device depends on the information it carries. To the extent that a device has everything it needs, such as a personal computer, interoperation is not needed. But as soon as the information needs to be updated, edited, or provided to some other service, the device needs to be able to exchange data with other devices and services. In some ways, because the United States deployed telephone networks and digital infrastructure earlier than many parts of the world, we are stuck with older technologies that are not as convenient as Ubicomp equivalents but that get the job done.

For example, in Japan, the Super Urban Intelligent Card (Suica) system provides fast and convenient electronic payment for transit services and is increasingly used for payments of other products and services. The Suica system was first deployed in 2001 and uses a form of near-field communication (NFC) radio-frequency identity (RFID) chip that is embedded in a card or in the body of a mobile phone. This system is so fast and reliable that commuters flow quickly through the payment turnstiles in mass-transit stations without pausing an instant. The technology is also being used to pay for products at kiosks and in small shops in transit stations throughout Japan.

Proponents of NFC payment systems for the U.S. and other parts of the world often point to the success of the Suica system. Unfortunately, the United States already has a widely deployed payment system based on magnetic stripes on cards. This magnetic stripe technology is primitive by comparison, much less robust, and much less secure than NFC, yet, frankly, it is good enough. Although NFC systems read cards in an instant, it takes only a second or two to swipe a card through a magnetic card reader. NFC readers have few moving parts and almost never fail, whereas magnetic strip readers wear out. On the other hand, the magnetic stripe readers work more than 95% of the time and are fairly inexpensive to replace. Good enough.

Fundamentally, though, no entity in the United States has the motivation to pay for installing NFC systems across the country or even across a local region. The United States does not have a nationwide organization to coordinate the various parties who would be involved. In Japan, the transit system is controlled by seven privatized spin-offs of the now-defunct government-run Japanese National Railways. Although the current transit companies are independent, they do not compete directly and they share a cultural history of top-down organization and consensus-based execution. Japanese transit is heavily used, running trains with such frequency that the rail lines are utilized at near-full capacity. To add capacity, the transit companies faced a hard choice: invest in more rail lines or pack the trains more densely. Installing a reliable high-speed NFC payment system allowed the companies to increase the passenger flow for much less than it would have taken to lay more track and to purchase and run more trains. For the Japanese rail companies, NFC payment is a necessity; in the United States, it would be a convenience.

Another example is in South Korea. I remember marveling at the integrated "smart" hotel room I stayed in at the Shilla Seoul. The lights and air were controlled by both my room key card and a panel of buttons next to the bed. The room even came with free mobile phones that were integrated with the room's voicemail box. In fact, those rooms are ten years old and are outdated by some of the more modern hotels and apartment buildings going up in Korea today.

A new city, Songdo International City, is being built in the Incheon region of South Korea. Construction for Songdo City, outside of Incheon about 40km from Seoul, began in 2000 with the buildup of 200 square kilometers (77 square miles) of land reclaimed from seabed. The city is being constructed using sustainable methods and materials, and includes plans for many technology marvels, including a theme park called Robotland. The city's infrastructure includes video connections between the residents, schools, government offices, business offices, and stores. The infrastructure further allows residents to remotely control all the appliances, security, and other electronic services in the residential units. These pervasive connections and advanced capabilities caused the organizers to refer to Songdo as a "ubiquitous city." People in Songdo will be able to connect with each other and services to live and get things done without even having to use transit or otherwise expend time, fuel, or energy.

Initiatives such as Songdo City require the kind of heavy investment and long-term commitment that only a national government can muster. Not since the creation of the city of Washington, D.C., has the U.S. political system allowed our government to come together on such a grand building scheme. Anyone voting in favor of such white-elephant spending would be thrown out in the next election cycle.

A further example of government enablement of interconnectivity is the seeding of Ubiquitous Computing research by the European Union (EU). In the late 1990s and early 2000s, the European Community created the Disappearing Computer initiative that funded a large number of research projects to explore the invention and application of technologies beyond desktop, laptop, and conventional computers of the day. In 2005, the EU committed to further research in Ubiquitous Computing technologies on the order of $216 million U.S. dollars over a number of years.[12] In the United States, Ubiquitous Computing does not garner direct research funding, although advances do occur under funding for other objectives, such as those for the military or healthcare.

An All-Too-Ubiquitous Reality

As illustrated in Figure 2-2, the technology trends that spawned Ubiquitous Computing in the 1980s continue today. Regardless of the differences in rates of adoption, growth in the ubiquity of technologies throughout the world has been steady, particularly with regard to wireless networking for communication and data services. Digital devices exist in a wide variety of sizes and capabilities; wireless networks permeate the airwaves at work, school, and home; and complex machines contain embedded processors that simplify how humans control them (such as antilock brakes). We are well past the early dream of many

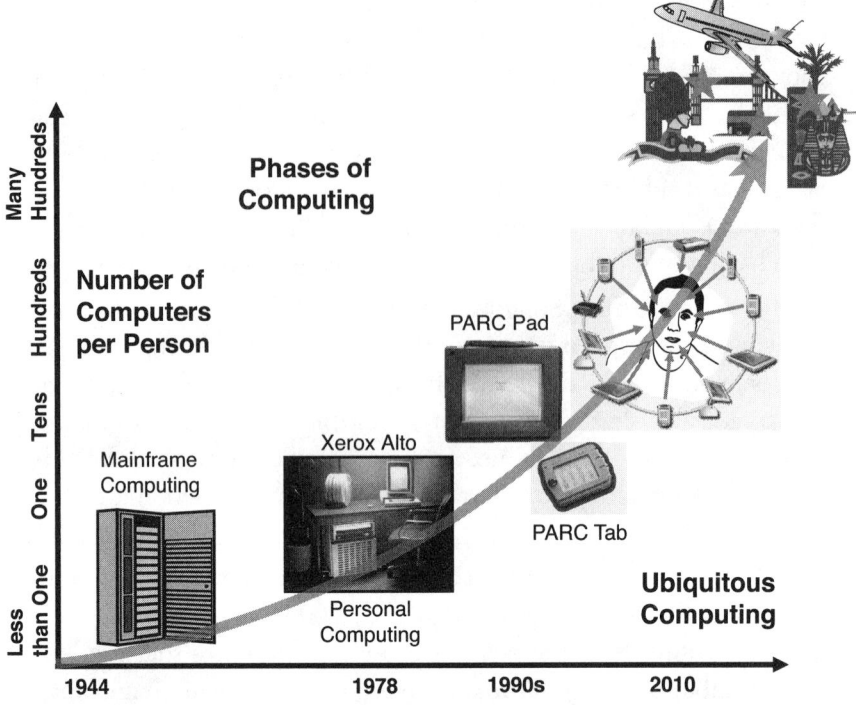

Figure 2-2 Although a personal computer was a lofty goal in the 1970s, researchers in the '80s saw that the proliferation of devices would quickly surpass one computer per person. See Figure 4-1 for the exact growth of number of devices per person in the United States.

computers serving each person and well on our way to tens, hundreds, and someday thousands of computing devices per person.

Unfortunately, the proliferation of technologies has so far resulted in more complexity than simplicity. People often become frustrated as they are required to contend with many mundane details of system administration in interacting with multiple devices, multiple networks, multiple service accounts, multiple data formats, multiple digital rights mechanisms, and multiple inconsistent interfaces. Figure 2-3 illustrates that in many ways, yesterday's dream of Ubiquitous Computing (widespread computation, information, media, and communication) is no longer a dream, but *an all-too-ubiquitous reality* in which managing and controlling these many types of information services, devices, and applications is becoming increasingly impossible.

CHAPTER 2 • PROFOUND TECHNOLOGIES   23

Figure 2-3 Ubiquitous Computing is no longer a dream, but an all-too-ubiquitous reality. The many devices and services we manage are anything but "[woven] into the fabric of everyday life."

The ubiquity of technologies has created new complexities among devices, information, people, and networks.

Too Many Devices!

At the device level, many of us deal with multiple computers (home, work, school, volunteer organization), multiple mobile media devices (camera, music player, video player, game device), and one or more wireless phones; we are system administrators of home networks, we have multiple remote-controlled media devices, we have to program our home thermostats, and some of us have installed home-automation systems to control lighting and security. Soon our homes will be on the smart grid, with dynamically controlled energy pricing and consumption. Personally, even as a programmer, I dread the idea of having to debug my smart home. Something has *got* to be done.

Too Much Information!

Precisely measuring the growth of information is difficult. Should we count only new information? How much should we count "remixed" information? Regardless of whether it is new or old information, how much of it is actually consumed? And of what is "consumed," how much of that did someone actually pay attention to? Analysts differ on what metric matters most, but regardless of the metric used, they all point to explosive growth.

International Data Corporation (IDC) published a report in 2008[13] that estimated that the amount of information created in 2007 was 281 billion gigabytes (281 exabytes) and that the amount of data is growing at a compound annual growth rate (CAGR) of almost 60%. At that rate, the amount of data created will reach 1.8 zettabytes (1,800 exabytes) by 2011.

Researchers at the University of California, San Diego, published a report in 2009 estimating that the average U.S. household consumes as much as 34GB of information per average person in an average day. This sounds tremendous, but considering that each pixel in a video image is at least 1 byte, and taking into account the growth of video games and interactive web content, this number is not so surprising.

So what? There's a lot of data. Information is valuable, so isn't that good? The problem is that although a lot of information is presented in a form that humans can read and use, only 5% or less of it is "structured" in such a way that it can be reused by other information services. "Structure" here means that the information is tagged with "meaning."

A database is structured. In the classic model of a database table, each record is a row in the database, and the columns represent the fields of information. A typical example is an address record that contains fields such as `first_name`, `last_name`, `initials`, `address_line_1`, `address_line_2`, `city`, `country`, `region_state`, and `postal_code`. This structure is necessary so that a computer program, such as a billing system, can place the fields in the correct slots of a bill. However, more than 85–95% of the information that flows across our systems today does not preserve the field names of information because most information is formatted for human consumption. Because humans can easily parse an address label to learn what they want to know, preserving the structural metadata is not seen as necessary.

After the field labels are stripped, computer systems have a hard time determining how to parse information into chunks. That's why when you see an address on a web page, your computer cannot automatically import it into your address book or show it on a map.

Someone has to have made the explicit connection between an address (or the general format that an address takes) and a mapping service.

Actually, addresses are relatively straightforward to parse, and we are seeing more automatic recognition of addresses and phone numbers on mobile phones, for example. In fact, there have been tremendous advances in natural language technologies that can extract important types of information such as proper names, phone numbers, addresses, corporate names, monetary amounts, times, dates, and similar fields that are referred to as "entities." Unfortunately, today's entity-extraction techniques still miss many things that a human reader would easily see.

Although text parsing has come a long way, we now need to be able to parse information out of new types of media: images, video, and audio. Recognizing people and objects in images and video is an active area of research referred to as "computer vision." It is already possible to easily detect people's faces in scenes, along with some easily distinguishable objects (a house versus a car, for instance). However, computer vision cannot perceive many things with anything near the reliability that humans can, such as distinguishing an image of a cat from that of a dog. This is an active and exciting area of research, but we are probably at least a decade away from the reliability that text parsing is capable of today, which already falls short of human capabilities.

The upshot is that, along with having to deal with an exponentially expanding universe of information, we have to manually integrate information generated from one source into other sources. This is true of enterprise services, consumer web services (how many web accounts do you have to enter your personal info into?), and also digital home entertainment systems, in which owners have to teach their universal remote how to control devices they've purchased from other manufacturers. The ubiquity of devices is turning us all into part-time computer system administrators.

Too Many Social Connections!

All this connectivity has greatly increased our capacity to reach other people. Face it, the main purpose of computing systems and networks is really to communicate with other people, not to do complex computation. Whether the system is tallying monthly account statements, recording a purchase transaction, editing a document, creating a product plan, or calculating next quarter's budget, that work is intended to communicate the results to someone. Sometimes that someone is just your future self as you write down something so you can remember it later, but usually this is another person.

In the past, our ability to communicate was partly throttled by the necessity to convert electronic information to physical form such as paper in order to distribute the information. The cost of physical distribution kept a lid on how much was generated and distributed. Now with pervasive networking, the floodgates are open and it's easier to send an email to a hundred people across the planet than it is to physically talk to someone in the next cubicle.

And of course, social media networks such as Facebook, MySpace, Twitter, and LinkedIn expand the number of personal connections we can each maintain. Unfortunately, such systems increase others' expectations of how much we know about what's going on in their lives. We need something that gives a quick update of a person's life right before we run into each other.

Many statistics indicate high percentages of mobile phone penetration across the globe, approaching saturation. Combine those phones with the growing number of communication channels, such as email, Twitter, social networks, instant messaging, Short Message Service (SMS), and Multimedia Message Service (MMS), and it's no wonder that we seem to be always talking to each other. Yet somehow we still have trouble connecting to the people we need to talk to at the right time. They might be away briefly, or in a meeting, or driving their car, or helping their children with schoolwork—or the cellphone battery could be dead. Despite the huge arsenal of communication tools at our disposal, we still spend a large portion of time figuring out who to talk to and the best way to reach them.

Too Many Networks!

The Internet itself is another area of complexity. How many networks do we encounter during the course of a normal day? Workplace local area networks (LANs) are standard today, with 95% of U.S. workers having a broadband connection to the Internet.[14] Many workplaces have multiple networks (private intranet and a public guest network). More than 57% of U.S. homes have broadband network connections as well,[15] growing by 300% between 2001 and 2007.[16] Wireless networks are available in many public spaces, such as schools, cafes, hotels, and airports. Also keep in mind the growing number of network service providers, including cable and satellite television networks, and other forms of wired and wireless networks that carry digital traffic.

We all gain tremendous value from being able to connect to a broad wealth of devices, information, and people. Yet the proliferation of networks introduces a set of technical administrative tasks to contend with as we attempt to cross networks to access content that physically resides elsewhere. There are firewalls to cross using virtual private networks, and network addresses to resolve that change dynamically, along with many, many user accounts.

Fortunately, the problems Ubicomp has raised also provide the seeds of a solution. The proliferation of devices and services provides multiple points of interaction that can be recorded and mined for patterns to increase efficiencies. These patterns allow automated systems to proactively *assist* people and *provide knowledge* that they wouldn't otherwise encounter. I refer to this as "contextual intelligence," which is explored more fully in Chapter 4.

> ### What's the Difference between Ubicomp and Augmented Reality?
>
> Several terms overlap with Ubicomp: Pervasive Computing, Mobile Computing, Symbiotic Computing, Wearable Computing, Multidevice Interaction, Ambient Intelligence, Context-Aware Computing, Everyware. Those terms carry some minor distinctions but are practically synonymous. Augmented Reality, however, is quite different.
>
> **Augmented Reality** (AR) is the presentation of electronic information along with a real-world object, projected physically or as seen through an electronic display. **Ubiquitous Computing** (Ubicomp) is the seamless integration of information services as we accomplish goals throughout our work and personal lives.

Both have to do with the use of information services in conjunction with real-world objects. However, AR focuses on perceiving "reality," and Ubicomp focuses on the usefulness of a "computing" service to our goals.

The key point of overlap, and the source of confusion to some, is that both AR and Ubicomp utilize machine perception to detect the state of the real world and to supplement the physical state with digital information. AR systems typically use cameras, GPS, and electronic compass to detect the location and orientation of physical objects relative to each other. A Ubicomp system may also employ those same sensors, along with others such as switches, thermistors, microphones, chemical detectors, strain gauges, accelerometers, and more.

AR depends on machine perception technologies to project information alongside a physical object. Common examples are seen in television broadcasts of sports, such as the yellow "first down" lines during U.S. football games and the colored location tails of hockey pucks.

Ubicomp does not necessarily require that the information be displayed alongside one's perception of the real-world items. Ubicomp uses machine perception to incorporate inputs that are not necessarily explicitly entered by human operators—these include physical states of motion (such as running, walking, driving, or riding), attention demands of the situation (such as driving in traffic or sitting on a train), other people's attributes (such as their roles, demographics, or psychographics), and more. It further encompasses electronic information about things outside of one's physical environment, perhaps adapting the presentation based on the attention (driving in heavy traffic) and physical (arms full) demands of the user. A common example of a ubicomp system is a portable navigation device that tells a driver where to turn; some of these systems are integrated with an automobile's radio and reduce the volume of the music in the driver's side speaker when giving turn instructions. More sophisticated examples appear throughout this book.

Summary

Ubiquitous Computing (Ubicomp) describes the paradigm of information technologies embedded throughout our everyday work, home, and school environments that are designed to fit into natural practices of humans. Unlike most information technologies, Ubicomp systems should not require any training to use them and are designed to fit into and adapt to what humans need and do.

The vision was first described by Mark Weiser, then head of the Computer Science Laboratory at the Xerox Palo Alto Research Center (Xerox PARC) in 1988, where Ubicomp technologies and businesses continue to be created. Along with scientists and engineers in the United Kingdom and Japan, the early Ubicomp systems focused on creating prototypes of mobile, wirelessly networked devices along with sensors and other devices to perceive the state of the physical environment.

The rate of adoption of these kinds of solutions has varied across the globe. Japan and Korea have broadly adopted Ubicomp systems into their everyday infrastructures. Europe has seeded invention in the field by actively funding research programs. In the United States, political and business structures limit the kind of top-down coordination needed to achieve critical mass of value among ubiquitously interconnected computing devices. Nevertheless, the technologies have grown in the United States as well, with recent successes seen in smartphone adoption rates and location-based services.

Endnotes

[1] Ralph Caplan, *By Design: Why There Are No Locks on the Bathroom Doors in the Hotel Louis XIV, and Other Object Lessons* (New York, St. Martin's Press, 1982).

[2] A. Sellen and R. Harper, *The Myth of the Paperless Office* (Cambridge, MA, MIT Press, 2001).

[3] A long-term trend identified by Gordon Moore in which the number of transistors that can be inexpensively incorporated on a central processing unit has doubled approximately every two years since 1958.

[4] Mark Weiser, "The Computer for the 21st Century," *Scientific American* 265 (1 September 1991): 94–104.

[5] A variant of the Unistrokes technique was later developed for the Palm Pilot handheld.

[6] K. Sakamura, "TRON—Total Architecture," *Proceedings of Architecture Workshop in Japan '84* (August 1984), 41–50.

[7] Jan Krikke, "The Most Popular Operating System in the World," *LinuxInsider* (15 October 2003): www.linuxinsider.com/story/31855.html?wlc=1278642252.

[8] R. Want, A. Hopper, V. Falcão, and J. Gibbons, "The Active Badge Location System," *ACM Transactions on Information and System Security* 10, no. 1 (January 1992): 91–102.

[9] A. Hopper, "Pandora—An Experimental System for Multimedia Applications," *SIGOPS Operating Systems Review* 24, no. 2 (April 1990): 19–34.

[10] The "dangling string" hung from an office ceiling and was controlled by a motor that spun according to the amount of network traffic—the more traffic, the higher rate of spin. Artist-in-residence Natalie Jeremijenko designed the string as an ambient information display to provide peripheral awareness of current network activity without requiring direct attention, analogous to the way that the sound of leaves rustling in the breeze conveys current windiness subconsciously. Over time, as people peripherally learn the normal patterns of activity, impending network trouble is detected and anticipated just as changes in windiness are an indication of impending change in weather.

[11] One of the remaining uses for paper today is *interoperability* to communicate and transfer information from one data system to another. This use of paper will likely diminish with the advent of electronic medical records and other interoperation schemes, but paper will never entirely go away.

[12] T. Starner, K. Lyons, and R. E. Grinter, "Missing the Wave? Scattershot Funding Has Its Costs," *IEEE Pervasive Computing* 4, no. 1 (2005): 80–82.

[13] John F. Gantz, et. al., "The Diverse and Exploding Digital Universe: An Updated Forecast of Worldwide Information Growth Through 2011," IDC, March 2008.

[14] "US Broadband Penetration Drops to 25th Worldwide," *Optimization Week* Issue #113, April 13, 2010. www.optimizationweek.com/issues/113/

[15] "Broadband Penetration Grows to 57% in US Homes," *Optimization Week* Issue #94, April 22, 2008. www.optimizationweek.com/issues/94/

[16] Scarborough Research, "Scarborough USA+ Studies," Release 2, 2002–2007.

3

Harmless if Used as Directed

Perk up pouting household surfaces with new miracle Ubik, the easy-to-apply, extra-shiny, non-stick plastic coating. Entirely harmless if used as directed. Saves endless scrubbing, glides you right out of the kitchen.
—Philip K. Dick, *Ubik*[1]

By this point, it may have occurred to you that Ubicomp is simply a description of the state of information technology today: Computing is *everywhere, all the time*. How is Ubicomp different from other computing paradigms? This question reminds me of the metamorphic product at the center of Philip K. Dick's 1969 novel *Ubik*, which showed up as a different product for each chapter ranging from an electric vehicle to a pain reliever. Ubik was advertised as a cure for any and all ills (when used as directed), and its value was derived through the consumer's simple faith in its effectiveness. In some ways, a new computing paradigm can have a similar feel to Ubik: It can be anything you want it to be and can seem to solve any problem, yet it may actually be simply repackaging an existing set of capabilities (can you say "cloud computing"). Is Ubicomp (or should we say *Ubik*comp[2]) really a distinct category of information technology, a different paradigm for interacting with information systems?

Yes. A distinction exists between the ubiquity of information technology and the paradigm of Ubiquitous Computing. A Ubiquitous Computing system is generally one that interleaves information from physical and digital worlds. Desktop, mobile, web, and embedded computers are all examples of digital systems on one side of the information stream. The other side contains the physical elements:

location, paper, images, audio, or tactile information. In most cases, the person is trying to achieve a goal (which may be simply entertainment), and the Ubiquitous Computing system provides *assistance* or *knowledge* that the user needs, if not proactively, then at least conveniently.

Figure 3-1 shows the three key pillars of a Ubiquitous Computing system: *ubiquitous interoperation* among devices, information, and networks to create *interactive and proactive services* for *personal assistance and knowledge*. A successful Ubicomp system combines all three of these to serve the user's needs.

Mobile and Ambient Devices, Networks, Information

Ubiquitous Interoperation creates

Interactive and Proactive Services for **Personal Assistance and Knowledge**

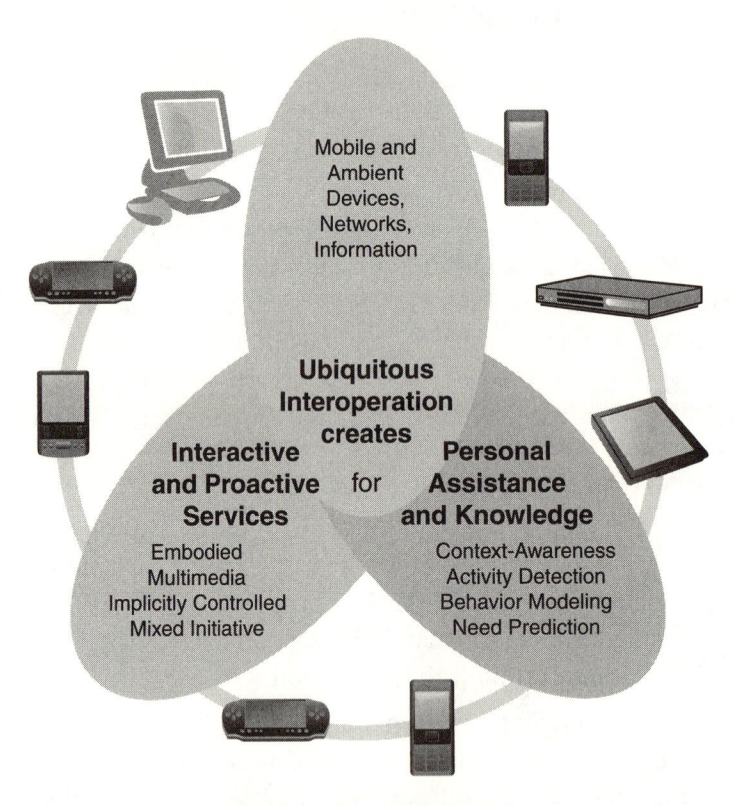

Embodied
Multimedia
Implicitly Controlled
Mixed Initiative

Context-Awareness
Activity Detection
Behavior Modeling
Need Prediction

Figure 3-1 Ubiquitous Computing innovation focuses on new technologies and practices to interweave digital and physical information sources when working toward an objective.

What Did the Car Say to the Home Heating System?

Nothing. And that's the problem. Why doesn't your vehicle tell your home heating system when you are headed home so that it can preheat the home? Why doesn't your thermostat setting at home get used to set the temperature in the car? Why don't all of my devices share the information that I enter into them?

The first dimension of advances in Ubiquitous Computing has focused on leveraging the increasing miniaturization of computation and proliferation of devices throughout our lives. At the inception of the field, research and invention centered on creating the hardware devices and software infrastructures for exchanging information that would be needed to realize the vision.

In the previous discussion of the history of the field, I described some of the early prototype devices and networks developed by researchers at Xerox PARC and elsewhere, such as the PARC Tab, PARC Pad, the Tab Network, and Liveboard. At the time (late 1980s, early '90s), wireless battery-operated computing devices were not commercially available, so researchers were required to implement the hardware. Today, of course, wireless battery-operated devices are common in the form of laptops, e-readers, tablets, and smartphones. Until recently, the research community focused on the integration of sensors with the devices, but even that has become commercially common, with examples such as accelerometers, GPS, gyroscopes, and digital compasses on more handheld computers. Certainly, Ubiquitous Computing will continue to advance the field of hardware devices, but at this point, we can be assured that the critical mass of pervasive devices, networks, and information does exist. The larger questions to address today involve leveraging this ubiquity into new services.

The Interoperability Barrier

Increasing computational power on personal computers has expanded what we conceive of as "information." Early business computers were able to handle information in the form of simple text and numbers, but new digital recording devices are generating multiple forms of media: still images, audio, and video. Today documents on the web and word processors can readily handle image, audio, and video media, so the focus of investigation in media technologies has shifted to issues related to the digital delivery of media content for consumer entertainment rather than to business users in the workplace. The same problems exist for consumers as they grapple with understanding how to compose a wide assortment of devices from multiple manufacturers that generate and consume multiple media types (text, photos, video, animations, music, and voice). It's easy to understand that technical difficulties would arise in translating from one media type to another, such as speech to text, but it's hard to understand why so much complexity surrounds the seemingly simple problem of encoding and transcoding content across the dizzying array of "standard" formats (JPG, RAW, WindowsMedia, Quicktime, RealMedia, DVD, Blu-ray, and MVI DVD), as well as exchange protocols (Universal Plug and Play, Digital Living Network Alliance) and media networking technologies (HDVI, Bluetooth, WiFi, and proprietary network protocols). The diversity and complexity is feeding a large segment of the media industry to help consumers understand the various tradeoffs to optimize fidelity, cost, and performance. This confusing array of formats, along with the risk that any new standard might become quickly obsolete, slows adoption of new technical capabilities The wise consumer waits for the standards wars to run their course before making a purchase.

The problems with multimedia are not entirely technological, of course. Some of the "standards" are owned by businesses that aim to optimize commercial benefit by exploiting some proprietary advantage or consumer lock-in to a standard that they own or control. The complexity of standards can keep small players out of a market. Even for the large companies that can afford to participate in standards consortia, the agreements require time-consuming negotiation and fail to accommodate unforeseen technical advances. A recent example is the unexpected growth in 3D video that the recently adopted video standard, H.264, does not cover. The limitations of existing standards give rise to new standards, but the fundamental problem with standards approach remains: standards lag innovation.

Despite the fact that the problem is not wholly based on technological issues, Ubiquitous Computing research has investigated solutions to these sets of problems, such as dynamic transcoding of media formats to match the rendering device's capabilities.[3] In a recent example, researchers at PARC (see sidebar PARC Today) devised technologies for "recombinant computing," called the Obje™ interoperability framework,[4] which uses the approach of dynamically transferring a media codec from a media source (such as a video library server) to a media renderer (such as a digital display). This approach not only solves the core problem of interoperability, but also enables new models of device interoperability, such as "recombinant" device networks,[5] in which end users can co-opt a device designed for one purpose to be used for a different objective (such as using an off-the-shelf digital camera as a page scanner to send a fax through a networked computer).

Under the Obje framework, a flexible security mechanism allows devices to alert each other of their presence and allow safe interconnectivity of trusted and untrusted devices all under the user's direct control. With this and similar approaches to interoperation, consumers can remain confident that their new and existing products will work together. Manufacturers also are free to introduce new and innovative devices, media formats, and networking options without depending on the sluggish creation of standards. As time-to-market cycles shrink, the need for faster iteration of interoperation is increasingly necessary.

PARC Today

Xerox's Palo Alto Research Center, founded in 1970, recently celebrated its 40th birthday. In 2002, Xerox PARC was transformed from a division of Xerox into an independent company. In its new form, PARC, Inc. is still owned by Xerox and now has the flexibility to create technologies with commercial impact outside of Xerox's traditional business domains (which itself has broadened from document scanning and copying into information services and business process outsourcing). Historically, some of Xerox PARC's

> technologies were inadvertently commercialized by companies other than Xerox. Today PARC deliberately commercializes technologies with partners across various industries, including solar energy, natural language search, biology, retail shopping, and water filtration. In addition to technology innovation, today's PARC is innovating in the business of doing research.

Keeping Control

Even if the problem of various digital media formats and protocols went away, we would still have two problems: making sense of what kinds of interconnections are possible, and then controlling the connections. Think about a typical home media system: The possible connections between TV, video library, music, speakers, and satellite or cable feed are endless—just look at the back of your components at home to see the tangle of complexity there from wires and terminals.

At least today you can see the wires that define the connections. Those wires are disappearing; wireless digital networks are supplanting wires throughout our environments. Sure, the wires are annoying and we will all be better off with fewer. On the other hand, the existence of a physical wire between two connected devices leaves no uncertainty that they are connected. When no wires exist, how will you know whether the media server in your living room is connected to the speakers in the kitchen (or the neighbor's speakers)?

Today's home media entertainment systems come with a remote controller for each device, each using the specific control codes and protocols for that model device from that particular manufacturer. These remote controllers quickly add up to too many to keep track of. A common solution is to use a "universal controller" that is capable of talking to several models of devices from several manufacturers. Thus, we might imagine extending the capabilities of such devices to include the ability to define the logical connections between media servers and players in a wireless network. However, today's universal controllers can control only a device that has been physically connected to another device; universal controllers are not currently capable of making connections, just controlling existing ones.

Let's think of the extension of universal controller as a kind of "universal connector." What would that look like? First, it would need to show a representation of all the media devices or services (sources of content and destinations for playback) that it knows about and allow direct control of each. Second, it would need to provide a way to define that two (or perhaps more) media endpoints should be connected without physical "hardwiring." These connection configurations should sometimes include simple instructions of what to do when some event occurs, such as to turn down the volume when the telephone rings. Finally, it should make the connections semi-permanent by recording the connection. Figure 3-2 shows an example of such an interface based on the Obje framework described earlier.[6]

The first market entry point for this capability is consumer media devices in the home, but it could expand to include interoperation with other electronics in the environment, such as smart conference rooms, smart stores, and others.

This first dimension of Ubiquitous Computing has become a reality. The devices that once required research scientists to construct can now be purchased at electronics stores. In this sense, Ubiquitous Computing is already upon us. As we have seen, however, users continue to struggle with how to make sense of the richness of technologies available to them, so the full vision of Ubiquitous Computing has not yet been realized. Fortunately, the continuing adoption of mobile and embedded devices and networks opens up two new capabilities that reduce user confusion and propel us toward the ultimate vision of technologies that weave themselves seamlessly into the fabric of our everyday lives: *interactive and proactive services* that address the needs of *personal assistance and knowledge*.

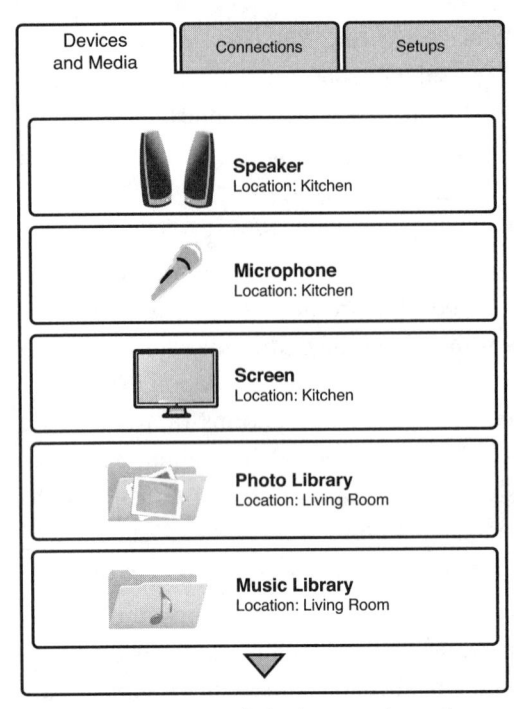

Discover and control devices and services

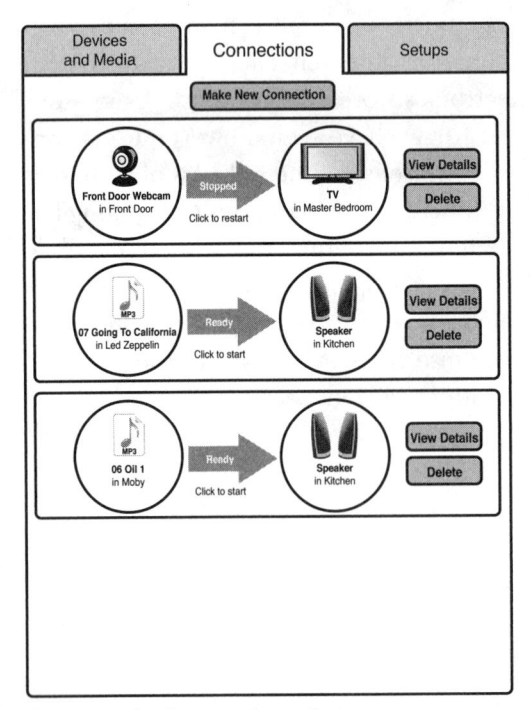

Connect devices and services

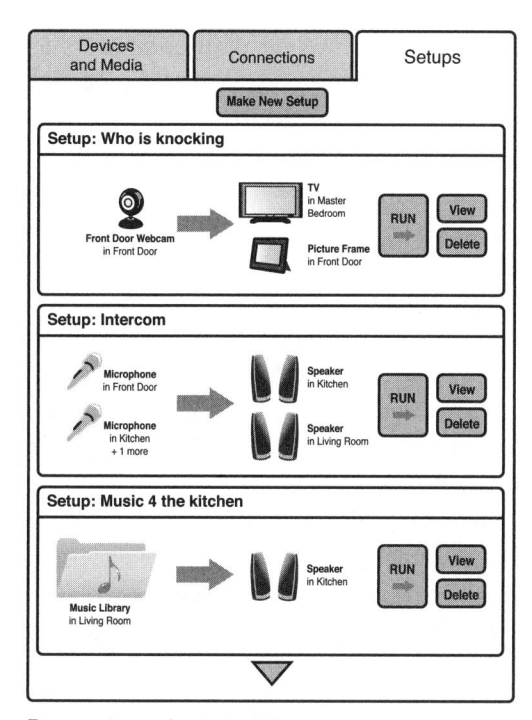

Figure 3-2 Obje Universal Connector simplifies defining connections in the absence of physical wires. The Universal Connector can dynamically learn about the existence and operation of a device/service because the control interfaces are served up by the devices themselves. (Figure credit: Mark Newman)

Preserve and reuse setups

Proactive Interaction

But if you're proactive, you don't have to wait for circumstances or other people to create perspective expanding experiences. You can consciously create your own.
Stephen Covey, *The 7 Habits of Highly Effective People*

It often seems that the world of electronic information is separate from our own; our PCs, handheld computers, and mobile phones provide tiny portals where people can peer through the screen at a sliver of the info-verse. People manipulate information and devices by poking buttons and pushing a mouse. Ubiquitous Computing adopts the philosophy that no distinction should exist between information space and physical reality, and that we shouldn't have to be trained on how to input data into a computer. Just as we are able to exchange information with humans without necessarily using a text-entry keyboard or mouse, we should have natural ways to interact with computers as well. The keyboard and mouse are recent inventions, but our bodies long ago mastered touching, grasping, speaking, moving, hearing, and interacting naturally with the world.

Act Naturally

Generally, a human operator *explicitly* directs what functions the system should take by deliberately generating commands that direct the operation of the system. Why is it necessary for us to direct every single operation of the computer? Human coworkers don't tell each other explicitly what to do (for the most part). Furthermore, why do we have to manipulate information by poking buttons, pushing pucks, touching graphics, and occasionally speaking to devices? Ubiquitous Computing adopts the philosophy that, just as we don't have to use a keyboard to talk to other humans (though my wife just sent me an email from the kitchen!), we should have *natural* ways to interact with computers as well.

What qualifies as "natural" interaction? *Natural* is a subjective term based on the perception and experience of each individual. A number of metrics are used in the field of human–computer interaction to evaluate the effectiveness of interactive systems: performance speed, number of errors, time on task, perceptions of quality, simplicity, and others. Perhaps the closest metric to the notion of "natural" interaction is ease of learning. A system that is simple to learn seems more natural. The simplicity of learning, however, depends on the skills of the person using the system: Someone who has not yet learned to use a mouse will find even the simplest graphical user interface difficult to use.

Let's use "natural interaction" in an extreme sense: An interactive system is natural if *any* human in the targeted user demographic (age, gender, education level, work type, and so on) will be able to use the system with absolutely no prior training. Examples of purely naturally interactive systems include automatic doors, motion-sensing light switches, antilock brakes, and traction control in automobiles. Anyone who functions normally in the world can use these systems with no training whatsoever.

Computer Perception

The oldest medium for exchanging information is speech. Despite ambiguities and imprecision, human language is the richest form in which to express concepts. Computers in the dawn of Ubiquitous Computing had some ability to recognize human speech, but researchers realized that wasn't enough. Speech is not the only means by which we interact; we point, gesture, draw, emote, write, gaze, and use other external cues to indicate meaning. Each of these communication modalities is better at communicating some types of information than another. Humans often combine modalities to emphasize and reinforce meaning. Similarly, human–machine interaction benefits from the use of multiple input/output modalities: text, mouse, voice, gesture, vision, and touch. Researchers have even done experiments with interaction technologies based on olfactory and taste sensing. The goal is to enrich human–machine interaction beyond the use of one or even two input mechanisms (keyboard and mouse) so that people can use the best communication modality to express their intent.

Touching, Moving, Grasping

"Direct manipulation" is a commonly used computer-interaction paradigm in which users "touch," "move," "select," and in other ways interact with objects that they want to perform operations on—physical objects or abstract objects such as information files and documents can be represented for users to manipulate. Direct manipulation is a more "natural" interaction style than the command-line interfaces that preceded it. On the other hand, direct manipulation interfaces are actually somewhat *indirectly* controlled through the movement of a mouse on a surface that moves a corresponding pointer on a screen. Modern touchscreens get closer to the intent of direct manipulation, but there again, the icons on the screen are usually indirect representations of objects.

An even more direct form of manipulation is present in tangible user interfaces (TUI), such as those created by the Tangible Media Group at MIT since 1996, in which the physical space where information is represented is also what the user manipulates.[7] One example of this approach is Illuminating Clay, a system that allows a landscape designer to manipulate a flexible clay landscape model. The system laser-scans the clay model and calculates heights, contours, water flow, and slopes; those are then projected onto the clay model in near–real time. The clay, a traditional tool for landscape designers, is used as both the input and output medium, providing direct support for the iterative process of design.[8] Certainly, such interfaces are quite "natural" to use, but most TUI-based applications require some user training to understand what actions can be performed on the tangible objects and what information will be delivered as a result of actions. TUI-based systems are easy to use after this information has been conveyed, but some amount of training is definitely required.

Natural interaction is one among a superset of interaction paradigms that has been referred to as Reality-Based Interaction (RBI).[9] This set covers a broad range of interaction styles "that diverge from the 'window, icon, menu, pointing device' (WIMP) or Direct Manipulation" interaction, including virtual, mixed, and augmented reality; tangible interaction; Ubiquitous Computing; context-aware computing; handheld interaction; and perceptual and implicit interaction styles, such as natural interaction. All of these interaction paradigms utilize people's tacit knowledge in the following four categories: simple physics (gravity, friction, persistence of objects, relative scale), body awareness (proprioception, range of motion, two-handed coordination, and whole-body interaction), environment awareness (navigation, depth perception, distance between objects), and social awareness and skills (presence of others, verbal and nonverbal communication). Systems that embody the paradigm of natural interaction leverage the user's knowledge in all four of these categories.

The same kinds of technologies that enable multimodal interaction can also detect user actions that *implicitly* indicate the user's goals and intentions without requiring deliberate direction from the user. A recent example of such a system is the PARC Responsive Mirror,[10] shown in Figure 3-3 and described in more detail in Chapter 11, "Clear Sailing." This is an implicitly controlled video technology for clothes fitting rooms that allows a shopper to directly compare a currently worn garment with images from the previously worn garment, matching the shopper's pose as she moves. When a shopper turns to look at herself in the mirror, she is indicating a need for information about how she looks from that angle. A camera detects the

CHAPTER 3 • HARMLESS IF USED AS DIRECTED 43

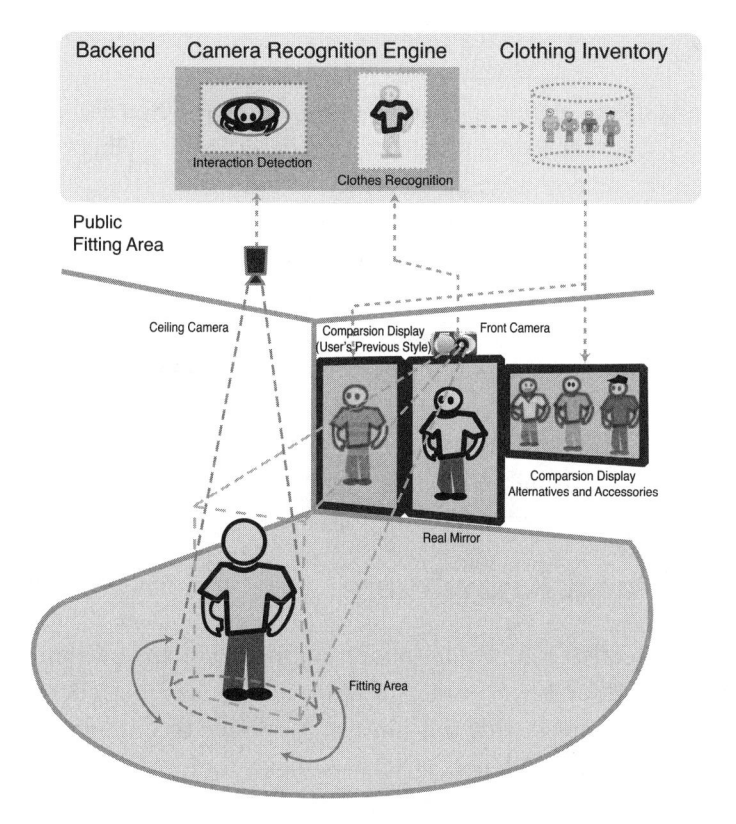

Figure 3-3 The responsive mirror is implicitly controlled: Images in the electronic display on the left match the angle of the user's view in the conventional mirror in the center. (Figure credit: Takashi Matsumoto)

shopper's orientation, and an electronic display shows images of previously worn garments in the matching orientation, providing the information that the shopper desires (how she looks in multiple garments from the same angle). People exhibit many other behaviors in retail settings that indicate their information needs: picking up and examining objects, searching for assistance, comparing products side by side, and more. As machine perception becomes more reliable and less costly to deploy, we will see the ability to deliver information based on implicit behaviors in other domains. Think about all the situations in which you can pretty much tell just by looking what people are trying to do at work, at home, or in kitchens, schools, airports, shopping districts, theaters, hospitals, and more.

Proactive Systems

Proactive systems span a spectrum from ones that automatically take anticipatory action to ones that merely detect and facilitate a potential need for action but that wait for the user to take action. The degree of proactivity depends largely on the appropriateness of taking action and the severity of being wrong. For example, automatic doors sometimes open incorrectly, but the cost of this error is low because little harm results if no one goes through an open door. On the other hand, although automatically printing to the nearest printer *usually* is the right thing to do, possible exceptions make it more prudent to ask the user which printer to use. It is safe and still helpful to sort a printer list according to the proximity to the user, allowing the user to quickly select the nearest printer but still search for others when desired.

Assistance and Knowledge

The main objective of Ubiquitous Computing is not any particular technology or interaction mode. Instead, it is to *assist* users in achieving their objectives with the most appropriate technology at hand. Certain aspects of Ubicomp systems make them particularly suited for such assistance.

Context-Aware Systems

Computing devices seem oblivious of the environment in which they are being used: mobile phones ring in the middle of meetings, email notifications pop up in the middle of presentations, speech-enabled navigation systems interrupt conversations in automobiles, and users cannot simply state that they want to connect to the "nearest" printer, display, or speaker, they have to pick it from a list. In the Ubiquitous Computing paradigm, devices are aware of the context in which they are being used and behave appropriately. Context includes the state of the physical environment (location, time, and weather), the state of the electronic environment (calendar appointments, contents of recently viewed documents and emails, phone calls) and the state of the people involved in the situation (talking, concentrating, laughing).

Context-awareness allows systems not only to react appropriately to the situation, but also to anticipate user needs and behave proactively *when appropriate*. It's not enough to simply have access to contextual information; effective proactivity requires understanding what the situation *means* to the person and what actions are appropriate and will be helpful. Some categories of proactive assistance are almost trivial to implement, requiring little or no analysis of tradeoffs or innovation. Automatic door openers are context-aware, proactive, and easy to implement—for example, a switch or motion sensor rigged to a door-opening actuator is all it takes (but do take care to design the passageway so that the door won't strike a person as it opens).

A grand challenge in artificial intelligence is that of a digital personal assistant. Although prototypes of such have been developed in laboratories, we are only now seeing the emergence of commercial products in this category. The ultimate personal assistant is one that knows your personal preferences, can tell how you would react in any given situation, adjusts for social/political objectives, and behaves proactively only when you would want it to. A combination of a Radar O'Reilly who presciently knows what you want done, a Passpartout who smoothes the way on your journeys, and a Jeeves who deftly extricates you from a jam—the ultimate executive assistant for us all! Between these two extremes lie a broad range of personal services requiring different levels of complexity and innovation to make them real.

The vision of intelligent agents is marvelous and shares many objectives with Ubicomp but takes the approach of doing as much as possible without you (see the accompanying sidebar for more). Do you really want something else to do the work for you? Have we not learned that a sedentary life is not healthy? Will our abilities to learn and think for ourselves atrophy? Ubicomp has publicized the notion of calm computing, but the calmness is intended to be with respect to how one thinks about the computers being used, not that the person is necessarily calmly, lazily existing but not achieving. In fact, while the early visions of Ubicomp espouse systems that anticipate and proactively satisfy needs, they just as equally describe people actively engaged in their lives and work.

Limitations of Agent-Based Interaction Metaphor

The notion of using computer intelligence in the service of users is also at the heart of a subdiscipline of artificial intelligence known as Agent-based Interaction. For the most part, Ubicomp and Agents are complementary notions that enable each other—the ubiquity of systems allows them to be more intelligent, which, in turn, spreads the systems ever more ubiquitously. However, the two have one fundamental difference. An intelligent agent is modeled after a human co-pilot and intended to be a centralized locus of control, handling all your needs in one place. Ask, and it responds. Command, and it performs. Relax, and it will alert you when trouble arises.

To get any particular job done, the agent may have to call on others to perform subtasks, usually in a hierarchically structured organization. Unfortunately, this mode of commanding an agent boils down to essentially the same problem as in using any single point of control. First, you have to be able to communicate what you want. However, we humans do not always have a clear idea of what we want—when we do, by the time we've articulated clearly the goals and the constraints, we might as well have done it ourselves. Speech recognition may help but is not a complete solution, either, as there is inherent ambiguity in human speech. How many times have you seen people in a conversation come away with different interpretations of the discussion? Text input is nearly error free, but does that make keyboard-based user interfaces easy? Second, as a single locus of control, an intelligent agent needs to be able to utilize other services to accomplish goals. Somehow, the agent will have to preserve your intention as commands are dispersed to other systems and actions are taken on your behalf. Generally, intentions blur and become reinterpreted with each link in a communication chain, resulting in inefficient iterations of command-response cycles and outright unintended results.

The Ubicomp paradigm is modeled after a flat business organization in which the leader connects directly with frontline employees and customers. Ubicomp systems are intended to work in the mold of artisanal tools that become extensions of the artisan's body.

Today, though, instead of using physical tools to construct physical artifacts, modern work involves complex information gathering, planning, and communication. Instead of subcontracting the work out to an agent, Ubicomp systems consist of controls, displays, workplaces, communication channels, authentication protocols, and other information tools arranged to facilitate the direct achievement of knowledge-oriented tasks.

At a symposium on User Interface Agents in 1992, Mark Weiser used a version of the following table to contrast the two philosophies.

TABLE 3-1 Distinctions between Intelligent Agents and Ubiquitous Computing Systems

Intelligent Agent	Ubiquitous Computing
Single locus of information about me	Distributed, partial information by place, time, and situation
Command the computer	What computer?
Personal, intimate computer	Personal, intimate people (whom I happen to access through a computer)
Filtering, blocking, re-routing	Breathing, living, strolling, engaging
User interface between person and computer	No boundary between you and the machine
DWIM (do what I mean)	WIWYHIAFI (when I want your help, I'll ask for it)
I interact with an agent. You reach me through my agent.	I interact with the world. You reach me.

To be fair, the idealized visions of personal assistants in fiction (Radar, Passpartout, and Jeeves) know when it is appropriate to intervene and when to get out of the way. The vision of humanlike interaction with an intelligent agent is not inconsistent with Ubicomp; it's just that the emphasis differs. An intelligent agent would do the work for you, calling on you only in extreme circumstances. In a Ubicomp system, you still do the work and conduct the interactions, but you have at your disposal a broad set of well-designed tools that extend and augment your own inherent personal abilities.

The concept of location-based services and context-aware systems began at PARC with the deployment of Olivetti's Active Badge and the PARC Tab, which were able to detect the room in which a person was located in the building. Although these prototype devices proved the viability and value of the concept, commercial success depended on the availability of location-tagged information and reached critical mass in the early 2000s with web-based mapping systems. Since then, a wide range of location-based services has emerged in the form of a variety of GPS-enabled navigation devices and smartphones.

Figure 3-4 shows that the time between the research concepts of context-aware services and the onset of commercial services was roughly ten years. Widespread adoption of location-based service did not occur until around 2007, largely due to the lack of commercial infrastructure for location awareness. Now that the infrastructure exists, the subsequent advances in research labs will become commercially viable at a *much* faster pace. As an example, prototypes of the grand vision of a digital personal assistant existed only as research projects starting around 2005 with the Cognitive Assistant that Learns and Organizes (CALO), funded by the Defense Advanced Research Projects Agency (DARPA) and developed jointly by many

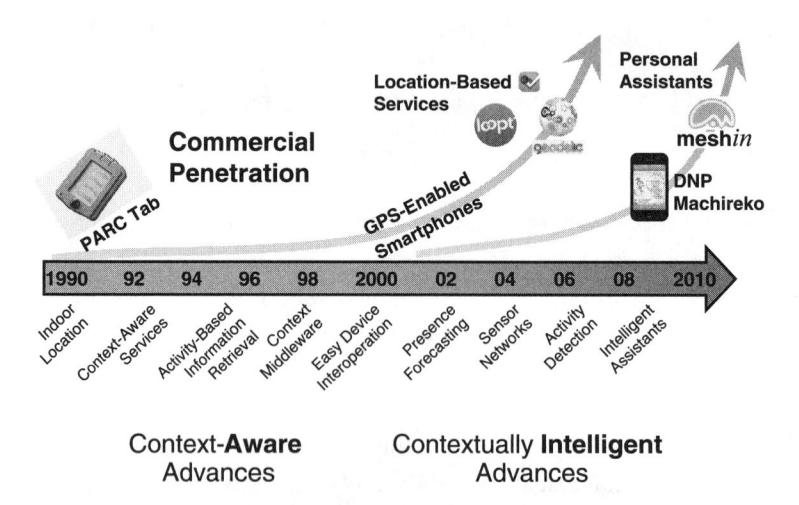

Figure 3-4 Timeline from research to commercial adoption of context-aware services. The adoption rate is accelerating now that critical mass of wireless networking, handheld computers, sensors, and networked information services exists.

academic and commercial research firms. Later advances included a mobile phone prototype codenamed Magitti for providing personalized recommendations of restaurants and stores (described in more detail in Chapter 8, "Breaking Out of the Supply Chain Gang"). It was developed by PARC and Dai Nippon Printing (DNP) in 2007[11] and commercially released for the iPhone in 2010.[12] A subsequent prototype system called Ubidocs combined content-analysis along with digital context to find and present the people, events, and pieces of information related to your email. It was prototyped at PARC between 2008 and 2009 and was commercially released as Meshin in 2010. These early digital personal assistants do not have the full power of a competent human assistant, and research and innovation are still needed to achieve that vision. The take-away message is that commercialization of research in context-aware services will be *much* faster-paced now than ever before.

What Are You Trying to Achieve?

The ultimate goal of context-aware systems is not simply to know the state of the environment, but to have insight into the intentions and goals of people acting in the environment. This is largely determined by a person's tasks and activities, which can be partially inferred by combining inputs from multiple sensor types, as well as content of electronic data that the person has generated or accessed. For example, if the system observes people entering a conference room, combined with the fact that a meeting is scheduled in that room, the system may infer that the activity of the people is a *meeting*. The system may even know the topic of the meeting and information related to the meeting, from information associated with this location and collection of people. This concept formed the premise of the Activity-based Information Retrieval (AIR) in the early 1990s. Since then, we have seen considerable advances in activity detection, to the point that systems are able to detect activities at multiple levels of granularity: from mechanical actions (walking, biking, brushing teeth, and so on) to longer-lasting and cognitive levels of activity (playing football, eating in a restaurant, compiling a report, planning an outing, socializing, preparing a meal, and more). Activity detection provides insight into a person's state of mind. As an example, researchers have demonstrated that people are less mentally receptive to an interruption when a system detects that they are actively involved in conversation or work tasks (explored in more depth in Chapter 10, "Coordination") .

Summary

In contrast to the early days of Ubicomp research, mobile wireless devices are common today in the form of smartphones, laptops, and embedded sensors. Ubicomp innovation is now centered on reducing some of the complexity in our pervasively connected lives: information overload, device management, social connectivity, and network bridging. The Ubicomp field today can be described as pursuing the use of *ubiquitous interoperation* of devices, networks, and services for the creation of *interactive and proactive services* that provide *personal assistance and knowledge.*

Ubicomp systems have several characteristic technologies:

- **Ubiquitous interoperation** is the exchange of information and commands among all systems to perform a task. Ubicomp systems must interoperate with a wide range of system types, including web services, sensors, digital media, phones, building control, medical equipment, games, transaction services, and social network services—any and all encodings of information across all types of technology.
- **Natural interaction** allows humans to use their anatomy and cultural history of interacting with people, objects, and information in the physical world.
- **Multimodal interaction** allows the use of multiple forms of input simultaneously: speech, text, vision, touch, and so on.
- **Physical and embodied interaction** (also called tangible user interface) allows people to directly manipulate physical objects to perform digital tasks.
- **Implicit interaction** occurs when systems automatically perform tasks without requiring directive commands. Automatic door openers are a simple example.

- **Context-aware systems** use the state of the physical and electronic environment (location, nearby objects, people, recently exchanged email, calendar appointments, and so on) as factors in performing an information service.
- **Activity detection** is the use of sensors to identify the physical or cognitive activities of people.
- **Proactive systems** anticipate the user's goals and suggest or perform actions to facilitate their accomplishment.

Although Ubicomp systems employ intelligence and personalization, they fundamentally differ from the notion of an intelligent agent that provides a single locus of control with the world, letting the user specify rules and policies that the agent performs. In a Ubicomp system, the user performs the work and engages with the world through the use of well-designed tools that extend the user's inherent personal abilities.

These capabilities create new classes of applications and services that will have increasing business relevance. The remainder of this book outlines some of the major classes of new services, illustrated with case studies of their applications in business.

Endnotes

[1] Philip K. Dick, *Ubik* (New York: Random House, Vintage Books, 1969).

[2] Mark Weiser may have been aware of this irony when he used the domain name ubiq.com for the initial website of PARC's Ubiquitous Computing research group (archived by PARC at www.ubiq.com/).

[3] A. Fox, S. D. Gribble, E. A. Brewer, and E. Amir, "Adapting to Network and Client Variability Via On-demand Dynamic Distillation," *SIGOPS Operating Systems Review* 30, no. 5 (December 1996): 160–170.

[4] M. Newman, S. Izadi, W. K. Edwards, J. Sedivy, and T. Smith, "User Interfaces When and Where They Are Needed: An Infrastructure for Recombinant Computing," *Proceedings of the 15th Annual ACM Symposium on User Interface Software and Technology* (UIST '02), Paris, 30 October 2002, 171–180.

[5] K. Edwards, K. Newman, and J. Sedivy, "The Case for Recombinant Computing," Xerox PARC Technical Report CSL 01-1, 2001.

[6] See also M. W. Newman, A. Elliott, and T. F. Smith, "Providing an Integrated User Experience of Networked Media, Devices, and Services Through End-User Composition," In *Proceedings of the 6th International Conference on Pervasive Computing (PERVASIVE '08)*, Sydney, Australia, 2008: 213–227.

[7] H. Ishii and B. Ullmer, "Tangible Bits: Towards Seamless Interfaces between People, Bits, and Atoms," *Proceedings of the ACM Conference on Human Factors in Computing Systems* (CHI '97), Atlanta, March 1997, 234–241.

[8] B. Piper, C. Ratti, and H. Ishii, "Illuminating Clay: A 3-D Tangible Interface for Landscape Analysis," *Proceedings of the ACM Conference on Human Factors in Computing Systems* (CHI '02), Minneapolis, Minn., April 2002.

[9] R. J. Jacob, A. Girouard, L. M. Hirshfield, M. S. Horn, O. Shaer, E. T. Solovey, and J. Zigelbaum, "Reality-Based Interaction: A Framework for Post-WIMP Interfaces," in *Proceedings of the ACM Conference on Human Factors in Computing Systems* (CHI '08), New York, 2008: 201–210.

[10] W. Zhang, M. Chu, and J. Begole, "Asynchronous Reflections: Theory and practice in the design of multimedia mirror systems." *ACM Multimedia Systems Journal*, 2010.

[11] DNP News Release, "DNP, PARC Jointly Develop Recommender System for Mobile Terminals," 26 September 2007, www.dnp.co.jp/eng/news/2007/070926.html.

[12] DNP News Release, "'Downtown,' an Information Distribution Service Machireko Guide, iPhone for Field Trials Starting in Ginza and Yurakucho" (in Japanese), 25 March 2010, www.dnp.co.jp/news/1213051_2482.html.

4

Still Stupid after All These Years

For me context is the key—from that comes the understanding of everything.
—Kenneth Noland, American abstract painter[1]

When I first heard the term *personal computing* in the 1980s, I thought, "Finally! I'll have a device and software tuned to my personal needs and ways of getting things done." And for a while, I believed it. The PC let me create small programs (batch files on DOS, scripts on UNIX) that customized and combined functionality in ways that I wanted them to work together on that individual machine. Of course, you had to be something of a programmer to make it happen, but that was pretty much true of all customers in the computer market at the time. Not too much later, though, the industry created operating systems that included the desktop metaphor and graphical user interfaces (such as X-Windows, MacOS, and MS Windows) that let you tailor the "look and feel" to your personal preferences—setting colors, fonts, placement, icons, and background images to your individual taste. You didn't have to be a programmer on these GUI-based systems, but you *did* have to manually specify each custom setting. I don't know how many hours I spent tailoring such settings, only to have redo it all every month or so: The operating system got wedged and needed to be reinstalled, or I upgraded the graphics card to provide more colors to choose from, or something else happened. (I've given up on all that customization and use a pretty vanilla configuration these days—must be middle age.)

This kind of personal computing was tolerable when you had to configure only your one personal computer. But computers turned out to be like bunnies. Pretty soon, I had two in my life: one at work and one at home. Then they started popping up at schools, libraries, hospitals, airports, and friends' houses and offices. The United Nations data on the number of computers per 100 people in the United States (see Figure 4-1) has grown at an average annual rate of roughly 10% since 1994; the country passed the one-computer-per-person mark in 2007, and projections estimate the number of computers in 2010 to be 120 for every 100 people.[2] Forrester estimates that the average number of computers in U.S. households ranges from 1.4 to 2.2, depending on household demographics.[3] In my own home, at one time we had eight PCs for two adults and three kids who were too young to read. My wife has since imposed a computing-reduction plan, so we have winnowed it down to seven.

Computers per 100 People in the U.S.

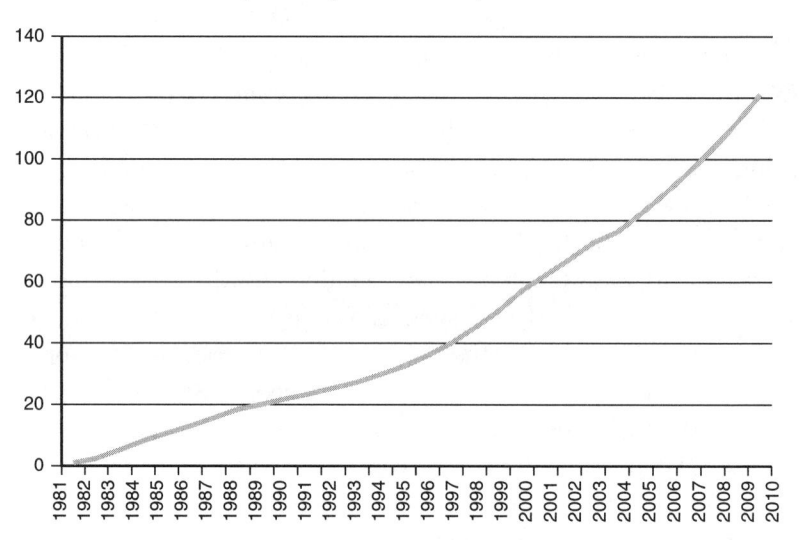

Figure 4-1 The number of computers per 100 people in the United States has grown at an average annual rate of 10% since 1994.

(Source: United Nations Statistics Division)

This number doesn't even factor in the number of other home information technologies (broadband and wireless routers, external storage, multifunction printer/copiers), handheld computers (smartphones and personal digital assistants), digital media devices (high-definition televisions, portable media players, video servers, music servers, Internet radio), vehicle electronics, digital cameras, game consoles, and other types of digital devices that we interact with daily. The Consumer Electronics Association[4] estimates that the average U.S. household contains 23 consumer electronics devices. Across all demographic segments (early, middle, and late adopters; male and female; income level; education level; and size of household), the average number ranges from no fewer than 17 to as many as 33 devices owned.

These devices increasingly use digital formats and provide interconnectivity with conventional computers and the Internet. The good news is that this leads to network effects in growth of value to the consumer. One of the inventors of Ethernet at PARC, Bob Metcalfe, characterizes the value of devices in a network as proportional to the square of the number of connected devices.[5] While the cost of n devices grows at a constant rate by price, the derived value grows exponentially at $n^2 - n$ because the devices can share media and functionality with each other. The bad news is that the average U.S. household has to customize, configure, and manage on the order of $23^2 - 23 = 506$ device interconnections. We are going to need IT support staffs for our homes (already a growing business).

Captain, the Engines Are Overloaded— She's Gonna Blow!

The rapid growth of information on the Internet and the World Wide Web has unleashed Pandora's box of information, resulting in *information overload*. The International Data Group (IDG) estimates that the "information universe" grew by almost 500 exabytes (500 billion gigabytes) of information fueled by the increasing conversion from analog to digital media of print, audio, image, and video information. At an annual growth rate of approximately 65%, IDG predicts a five-fold total increase in four years. Other sources report similarly alarming rates of growth in the amount of information that we confront. The implication of these reports is that we need more efficient technologies to store, transfer, and retrieve information.

Another implication of the explosive growth of information, which some reports only lightly cover, is the increasing amounts of time people spend organizing and finding what they need to get things done. In a different report from International Data Corporation (IDC is a subsidiary of IDG),[6] a survey found that people spend as much as 26% of their time trying to forestall information overload and that cutting information overload by 15% could save a company of 500 employees as much as $2 million per year. Whereas we used to pay money to get *more* information from newspapers, television, magazines, and analyst reports, most people today would gladly pay a service to find *less* information and only the items that are pertinent to what they need.

The problem of information overload resonates with many people, but it is a fairly amorphous term. How can there be an overload of information? Certainly, digital information and distribution are increasing exponentially, but there are widely used web services like search, personal portals, and filtering to help make sense of it all. Perhaps the information itself is not overloading us; maybe the problem lies in how we receive and process information. Perhaps the overload has more to do with our increasing number of communication channels, such as email, phone, social media, text messages, and others by which we share attachments, brainstorms, action items, FYIs, reminders, warnings, and meeting requests. The IDC survey points to communication media (email and voice calls) along with documents and forms (in paper or digital) as the leading contributors of information overload. Basex, an analyst firm specializing in information overload, estimates that knowledge workers spend as much as 25% of their day handling unnecessary interruptions from instant messaging, spam, telephone calls, email, and other distracters.[7] Cumulatively, this creates an estimated $900 billion drag on the U.S. economy. My personal pet peeve is waiting for a web page to load; if it takes more than half a second, I'm on to something else. As a consequence, I have left many half-finished emails sitting unsent on my desktop because of some distracter.

Research into the practices of communication and collaboration by Victor González and Gloria Mark at University of California, Irvine has shown that workers spend an average of three minutes of sustained time on a particular task before being interrupted.[8] They grouped tasks into projects (which the researchers refer to as "working spheres") and found that the average amount of time spent on a project is only about 10.5 minutes before switching, usually due to an interruption. Furthermore, of the interrupted projects, only 82% are resumed before the end of the work day, meaning that as much as 18% of interrupted work is not resumed (at least, not on the same day). In later studies, Mark and colleagues found that workers who are habitually interrupted work more quickly but more superficially, with lower-quality output.[9]

In the old days of analog media (television, radio, and paper), the recipient of information was mostly in control of how fast he or she read memos, watched reports on television, and listened to news. These days, our friends and coworkers send innumerable links and pointers to must-read items because they don't want us to miss a thing that we might somehow, someway, someday find useful. So maybe we're really suffering from "communication overload," as the Internet makes us all more interconnected.

Or maybe the problem is "task overload," as we all take on more activities to lead complete lives and increase productivity at work. Or perhaps it is "application overload," as we need to manage the interchange of information across separate silos of services and applications. Or perhaps the heart of the problem is simply "lifestyle overload," as we all cope with the multiple complex demands of personal health, work, family, and social lives. Regardless of whether the prime culprit is information, communication, tasks, or combinations of these, the old information filters of physical distribution and social filtering have been bypassed by the frictionless distribution of digital information on the Internet, leaving us searching for new ways to get personal control of the information fire hose.

Personal Services, Not Personal Computing

When the web came along, it offered far more personalization than personal computing ever did. Web portals allowed you to select your favorite set of information "widgets" to display: calendar, weather, and the obligatory stock ticker. Multiple vendors offered personalized services for banking and finance. As with the desktop PC, you had to manually specify your personal account settings, and now you had to do it across multiple vendors, each running a separate software service.[10] But at least from the web, this personal information stays the same regardless of which of your several "personal computers" you use to access it. You can log in to each web service from whatever device is at hand.

More important, the web has brought true "personalization" of some services, particularly in terms of personalized product, media, and news recommendations. Product pages include sections that show other products that shoppers who looked at this product also looked at, the percentage of people who considered this product and purchased it over similar products, and other statistically generated recommendations. Movie rental services (such as Netflix) show individually calculated scores for movies based on your prior ratings of movies and others who rated those movies similarly. Internet radio services such as Pandora provide personalized playlists of songs that suit your personal tastes.

Although we're only now seeing commercial viability of personalization, many of the techniques and applications have been demonstrated at technology research conferences, such as the Association for Computing Machinery's (ACM) Special Interest Group on Information Retrieval (SIGIR), held since 1971; User Modeling, Adaptation, and Personalization (UMAP), held since 1986; and ACM Multimedia, held since 1993. The algorithms are many and varied, but they generally fall into two classes:

1. Characteristic-based filtering, which identifies items similar to items you liked.
2. Collaborative filtering, which identifies items liked by people similar to you.

These techniques are described more fully in Chapter 7, "The Soft Sell: Personalized Marketing."

For super-popular items, such as blockbuster movies, you don't need to use any special algorithm; most people like them. But as Chris Anderson explains in his 2006 book *The Long Tail: Why the Future of Business Is Selling Less of More*,[11] full commercial value includes items that are less widely popular but are highly valued by those who *do* like them.

Making Sense

It seems that since the widespread adoption of Mac OS and Windows GUIs in the 1990s, not a lot has fundamentally changed in IT. It's all just gotten smaller, cheaper, faster, and more distributed, but you still can do basically the same things today as a decade ago: document editing, email, search, teleconferencing, chat, and database form entry (now all on the Internet, but same capability). Sure, grand challenges such as true artificial intelligence (however you define it) still have to be solved, so there's that to keep the scholars busy, but the ground-shaking revolution of information technologies for businesses and consumer applications seems all but complete. Is it all just a matter of IT service consolidation and integration now?

On the other hand, computers *theoretically* might answer questions that are currently beyond their abilities. What nearby restaurant would I like best? When will the project be done? Where is that slide I used in March? Why did we lose that sale? Who made that decision? How should we cut costs? Basically, what does it all *mean* to *me*? Such questions are not easily answered by conventional technologies because they involve combining multiple pieces of ambiguous information.

Let's look at the first example: What nearby restaurant would I like best? Hotel concierges worldwide adeptly handle this question several times a day, yet it is beyond the ability of IT services today. To answer it well, the concierge needs to combine several pieces of information: What restaurants are nearby? How far is "nearby" to you (by foot or by cab)? Are you in the mood for anything in particular? No? Then what do you *usually* like? How much variety do you like? What restaurants have you been to recently? What price range suits you? Are you with companions? What are *their* preferences? Some of the answers may conflict with each other, yet the concierge identifies the tradeoffs in the given context and makes useful recommendations.

The concierge's recommendation process is an illustration of one aspect of human intelligence called "contextual intelligence." We face similarly complex problems in many domains: business, healthcare, travel, communication, shopping, finance and more. Contextual intelligence technologies identify the important contextual elements that help answer the hard questions that normally require human intelligence today. In contrast to the grand challenge of artificial intelligence, which aims to emulate the breadth of human intelligence, contextual intelligence utilizes technologies that aggregate relationships among information, people, and places, and uses the resulting context in useful ways to provide insight and support information problems.

In psychology, the term *contextual intelligence* describes the kind of "street smarts" or practical common sense that people use to make sense of their environment and where they fit with respect to other elements in the environment. This is one of the three categories of intelligence in psychologist Robert Sternberg's Triarchic theory of intelligence,[12] which also includes analytical intelligence (problem solving) and creative intelligence (creativity, intuition, vision). Computers excel at analytic intelligence and are practically incapable of creative intelligence.[13] Contextual intelligence, on the other hand, is well within reach of information technologies but has not yet been well studied in computer science or exploited by the IT industry.

Sternberg describes cases in which people employ contextual intelligence to adapt to their environment. They do so by understanding the relationships between items and themselves. Computer systems, for the most part, understand only what they are told to do: type a word, enter a number, add a column, and so on. If a number is related to a word, a human being has to identify that relationship and preserve it in a database. But system developers know only about the information needs of their individual application, so they do not preserve relationship-defining information that can be seen when a contextually intelligent system looks across applications: When did this paragraph get changed, who was recently involved in conversations about some topic, where did that image originally come from, what is the sequence of operations used by highly productive people? Such information could be inferred if systems captured and organized the relationships. Currently, however, our systems do not record data beyond the specific needs of an application, so important contextual information is lost. That will likely change as we see increasing value in leveraging *how information is used* beyond just what it contains.

Contextual intelligence provides the following key benefits for users of information systems, allowing businesses to become more efficient and allowing individuals to enjoy their personal lives more richly.

- Show more of what you would not know to search for
  - Discover new information serendipitously
  - Show pertinent information you would not know to look for
  - Deliver pertinent information proactively
- Show less of what you do not want
  - Provide better filtering and sorting of information queries
  - Autoupdate processes without requiring explicit user action
  - Summarize large information sources
- Make hidden relationships visible
  - Identify unrecorded relationships between people, times, tasks, activities, events, places, and topics
  - Support multitasking by preserving state between task switches, enabling fast recovery

At Your Service

Context-aware services are ones that use information about the user's current physical situation (location, time, activity, presence of others) to adapt their behavior appropriately. The earliest example, at PARC, was an application that listed the closest printers to users of a wireless handheld computer. As part of the Ubiquitous Computing deployment, researchers at PARC created a wireless network using infrared as the transmission medium. At the time, infrared was more commonly used for wireless communication than radio frequency, which is in common use today. Because infrared requires line of sight for transmission, each room in a subsection of PARC was outfitted with an infrared network hub. A happy side effect of this was that a mobile device knew the identity of the hub it was connected to and, thus, the room where it was located. Recognizing the potential usefulness of this, the researchers devised a number of services that took advantage of the location, such as finding the nearest office printer, locating a colleague in the building, routing calls to the nearest telephone, and other "context-aware" applications.[14]

In addition, context awareness provides a new way of organizing and accessing information that leverages human associative memory.

Instead of having to recall the hierarchical folder structure in which you filed a presentation, you can remember where you were when you last showed the presentation. Or perhaps you remember a unique person you met at the presentation—you can use the record of that meeting to find the information. Organizing information by physical context enables you to use your spatial memory to quickly retrieve items.

In those early days of Ubiquitous Computing, just making a machine aware of its physical situation was a technical challenge; the term *context-aware* reflects the challenge of that time. Today providing awareness of context is no longer the difficult technical challenge: Many handheld devices are equipped with a variety of sensing technologies, such as GPS, microphones, cameras, accelerometers, digital compass, and other sensors. Today the challenge is not in making services that are *aware* of context, but in creating services that intelligently *use* that context. At this point, our technical notion of relevant "context" goes far beyond location, and context-aware services are even more complex and useful than finding the nearest printer (although I *still* can't do that on any commercial products).

Threads of Context

The word *context* is derived from Latin for "weave together." In common usage, it refers to the text that comes before and after a phrase that establishes the meaning of a phrase. Many words and phrases have multiple possible meanings that are clarified by the context of their use. For example, the word "break" has several meanings: fracture, time off, good fortune, interruption, escape, and others. Such ambiguity is rarely a problem in common practice because content makes the meaning clear: "let's take a break," "there's a break in the dam," "don't break her concentration."

Roughly, think of *context* as the associations between a central item of interest and surrounding items. The existence of the surrounding items clarifies the "meaning" of the central item. Typically, in information services, context is coded as metadata describing both the existence of a relationship between two items and the nature of the relationship. Just as the meaning of a word in a sentence is determined by its context, contextual metadata defines the "meaning" the items have with respect to each other. These relationships form a semantic network with which to clarify the meaning of items in the network. Ironically, *context* is itself ambiguous, referring to any of a broad range of different information types:

- **Physical context:** The physical attributes of people, devices, and objects in a physical environment: time, location, light, sound, weather, temperature, physiological state, and so on. These attributes may be detected with sensors carried on the body (such as in a smartphone), in the environment (such as with cameras), or in vehicles (such as in vehicle telematics).

- **Social context:** The relationship and roles of people with respect to each other and objects. Sources of information about the relationships include communication tools (such as email, phone, and social network services) and physical sensors. Social context includes the ratings and reviews that people apply to objects (such as product ratings) or to the amount of social attention that an object receives (as with web site popularity).

- **Behavioral context:** The patterns of people and objects over time, including patterns of interaction with devices and services. Such patterns detect and predict formalized procedures (such as workflows), recurring sequences of actions (such as routine tasks and typical locations), types of motion (such as walking, running, and standing), tasks (such as having dinner, washing clothes, and fixing the car), and goals (for example, socialize, hire, sell, be fit, or simply enjoy).

- **Content context:** Relationships between pieces of content (email, web pages, documents, and so on). These relationships can be detected by finding shared occurrences of names, places, organizations, dates, times, linguistic structures, layout, images, and more. Pieces of content that share such elements are related.

Your Personal Semantic Network

Humans adeptly use context, the associations among pieces of information, to determine the most likely intent of a word in a sentence or the implications of an action taken by another person. Computers, on the other hand, are traditionally poor at making such inferences. They perform best when *no ambiguity* is associated with the type and value of information: phone number, name, address, serial number, and so on. Such explicitly structured information is not needed for human consumption, however, because we readily recognize that a string of digits is a phone number, address, zip code, and so forth without having to look up a metadata tag. Information in a database poses no ambiguity to information systems because each item is stored according to a schema that defines the type and relationships among elements in the database. The grand vision driving the Semantic Web[15] technologies is to similarly tag every piece of electronically generated information with its type and relation to other elements, creating a web of semantic relationships.

The Semantic Web is certainly within the realm of technological feasibility—the main technical challenge is supporting the mass scale of potential relationships among elements on the web. The real difficulty, however, is in agreeing on a vocabulary to describe items and relationships. As part of the Semantic Web community, some standards are emerging that attempt to identify only the pertinent relationships and types for certain problem domains.[16] An unfortunate consequence is that any of the agreed-upon vocabularies are usable only within each problem domain, falling short of the ultimate vision of universally understandable information. Unfortunately, there is no way around this. "Meaning" is a social construct, something that requires agreement among a group of people. Because we cannot all participate in the negotiation of all meanings, it is inevitably left to a subset of people to create meaning, which is then unclear to the rest of us.

Another problem with the vision is that the creation of unstructured information is far outpacing the generation of structured data (data tagged with meaning). The unstructured information is largely created for human consumption in the form of slide presentations, email, documents, web pages, instant messages, wikis, audio, images, video, and other media. As mentioned, humans can generally differentiate a segment of information and can make sense of its relationship to other elements. Increasingly, technologies are sprouting that can detect the contextual associations among elements within unstructured formats. Linguistic analysis can identify names, organizations, phone numbers, addresses, and other entities that are shared among pieces of unstructured data. Similarly, image analysis can identify recurring segments of images, slides, company logos, products, photos, and other visual information. Context is also implicitly generated through the use of previously mentioned "context-aware" devices that are able to sense their environment: location, time, sound, other people, and so on. Location-based services, for example, are a fast-growing segment of applications that utilize just the location of a device, but these, too, miss the opportunity to combine other elements of context.

Contextual Intelligence

Collecting and re-creating context is just the first step. Contextual intelligence includes novel ways of aggregating the context to extract meaning from it. Context aggregation includes pattern-matching approaches such as workflow activity detection, hybrid recommender algorithms, knowledge representations of context, and automated reasoning around context. Stepping far beyond the early examples of simple *context*-aware applications, contextual intelligence enables several additional types of awareness:

- **Physical awareness:** Identifying where people and things are relative to each other
- **Preference awareness:** Characterizing the typical tastes and interests of a person or group
- **Rhythm awareness:** Predicting typical temporal patterns such as arrival and departure times of people and things, as well as times of events and durations of tasks
- **Activity awareness:** Knowing the sequence of actions that are related to accomplishing a larger individual or team activity
- **Receptivity awareness:** Detecting a person's mental receptivity to intrusion, interruption, and information
- **Goal awareness:** Inferring the overarching goal or purpose of an individual or group.
- **Relationship awareness:** Identifying how a set of facts, information sources, and people relate to each other

The underlying foundation of contextual intelligence comprises three layers on top of unstructured information, illustrated in Figure 4-2 and described in the following sections.

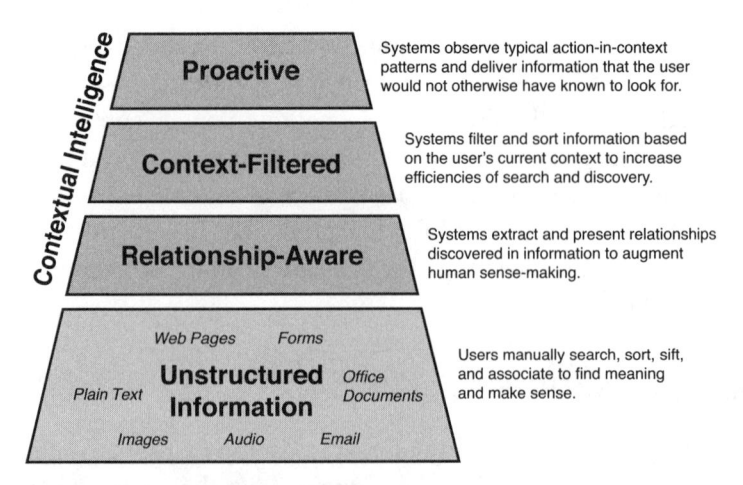

Figure 4-2 Contextual intelligence takes the vast ocean of unstructured data; identifies relationships among information, people, places, times, and locations; and enables the proactive delivery of information and services.

Unstructured Information

At the lowest level is simply information in a variety of unstructured and unassociated formats: text, image, audio, email, web pages, office documents, order forms, places, people, things, events, and so on. This system has no intelligence at this level, but human intelligence can make sense of the information and use it.

Relationship-Aware Systems

These systems represent the associations between pieces of information, people, locations, time, and so on. Relational databases, spreadsheets, and even web hyperlinks are examples of structured information in which relationships are explicitly represented. Relationships in unstructured information can be detected using content-analysis techniques to identify matching elements between two pieces of information. Such relationship networks can be used in these ways:

- Navigate information by association, allowing a person to retrieve information by switching among the most relevant attributes (time, topic, other people, location, and so on)
- Discover information that is most highly rated or used by humans and in what circumstances

- Assess the veracity of information by tracing its relationship to other items
- Summarize email and other communication by seeing the topics and related entities
- Synthesize the most relevant and up-to-date information on a topic using the collective web browsing behaviors of many people
- Capture organizational knowledge via services that find the latest or most relevant information on a topic using information about the documents, presentations, reports, and so on that employees are finding, reading, and writing
- Estimate progress on projects toward goals, based on communications and intermediate products of project team members

Context-Filtered Systems

These systems use associations between the user's current location, time, nearby people, and other aspects of a person's physical or digital environment to constrain the results of an information query. Consider these examples:

- Location-based search
- Local information
- Location-based advertising

The basic concepts of contextual intelligence are similar to other semantic technologies, such as those utilized by Semantic Web. By examining the nature of the entities and their relationships to each other, systems can extract and synthesize increasingly complex levels of information. Contextual intelligence and Semantic Web share the use of knowledge representations using semantic networks and a variety of reasoning techniques. However, the Semantic Web primarily focuses on providing the semantics that allow web services to understand other web services, whereas contextual intelligence focuses on providing understanding between human users and information services in general. In addition, the Semantic Web is largely based on structured information that is described with agreed-upon ontologies, whereas contextual intelligence technologies reconstruct associations and infer the salient associations among unstructured data.

Proactive Systems: Making Machine Intelligence Work for You!

The goal of an intelligence system is to provide "actionable" information. In most cases, the best action depends on a complex combination of constraints, best left to human judgment. In such cases, the analysis and presentation of context can help the human making a decision by providing information she is not otherwise aware of or by providing associations among information that she can navigate to find what she needs.

In some instances, systems can proactively anticipate a subset of alternative actions that are most likely to be selected in a given situation—perhaps a subset as small as one. When the cost of being wrong is low and outweighed by the benefit of automation, it may be appropriate for the system to proactively take action on the user's behalf, reducing the user's load.

Automatic door openers are proactive because it is assumed that someone approaching a door wants it to open, and the cost of a mistake is usually small. On the other hand, the grand vision for context awareness is the personal assistant who knows your personal tastes, can tell how you would react in any given situation, adjusts for social/political objectives, and behaves proactively only when you would want them to. Between the triviality of an automatic door opener and the ultimate executive assistant lies a broad range of proactive services that can be subdivided into the following tiers. Each tier uses different types of contextual meta-data and analysis that enable different classes of services.

Context-triggered systems have awareness of a person's current physical or digital environment and proximity to other items (information, people, places, events). Context-triggered systems enable applications that are triggered by a change in physical context and can take immediate action with little or no interaction from the user, because the action to take is agreed upon in advance. Such systems include these:

- Motion-sensing light switches
- Heating, ventilation, and air conditioning
- Storage of data indexed by context (such as geotagged photographs)

- Location-based services
- Asset tracking
- Reminder systems

Behavior-aware systems detect and use the patterns of an individual's actions in different contexts based on temporal characteristics (such as sequence, duration, frequency, recency, or recurrence). "Behavior" can be conscious or unconscious, overt or covert, and voluntary or involuntary, such as typing, walking, standing, holding, turning, clicking, and so on. Behavior-aware systems enable applications that infer, and potentially respond to, present behavior without necessarily understanding the user's conscious activity or intent. Consider these examples:

- Shopping behaviors (behavioral advertising)
- Presence patterns (call routing, HVAC and building-management systems)
- Security monitoring (anomalous use of credit card detected)
- Traffic patterns (Contextual reminders)
- Information-use behaviors (systems that collect data about what information people are using and what they are doing with it, to assist in future information activities)

Activity-aware systems model the person's activity from observations of context and behavior patterns. In contrast to "behavior," in which a person's actions are not necessarily consciously made, "activity" is a conscious, voluntary pursuit (for example, shopping for clothes, writing a report, searching for an answer, making tea, explaining a solution, and so on). Examples include these:

- **Intelligent communications:** Detecting priority of incoming messages and best times to interrupt
- **Elder care:** Detecting engagement in activities of daily living and alerting caregivers if problems arise
- **Activity-targeted advertising:** Understanding a lifestyle, preferred ad placement, and work role
- **Shopping support:** Identifying the stage of shopping and proactively providing useful information

- **Sales force automation:** Autopopulating the stages of the sales process with relevant info

Goal-aware systems have insight into what the person is aiming to accomplish, inferred from context, behavior, and activity models. Goal-aware systems not only detect the user's current situation, but also adequately predict future behaviors or actions that a person is likely to do to achieve the goal and suggest suitable alternatives for those steps. Examples include these:

- Proactive information delivery (a leisure activity planning tool to find shops, a restaurant, and a movie that you would like)
- Planning systems (travel routes, service routes, task plans, and so on)

Each layer builds on the information gleaned by the lower levels, as Figure 4-3 illustrates. As we go up the layers, the accuracy of the inferred information is lower but is still useful for applications, as we explore next.

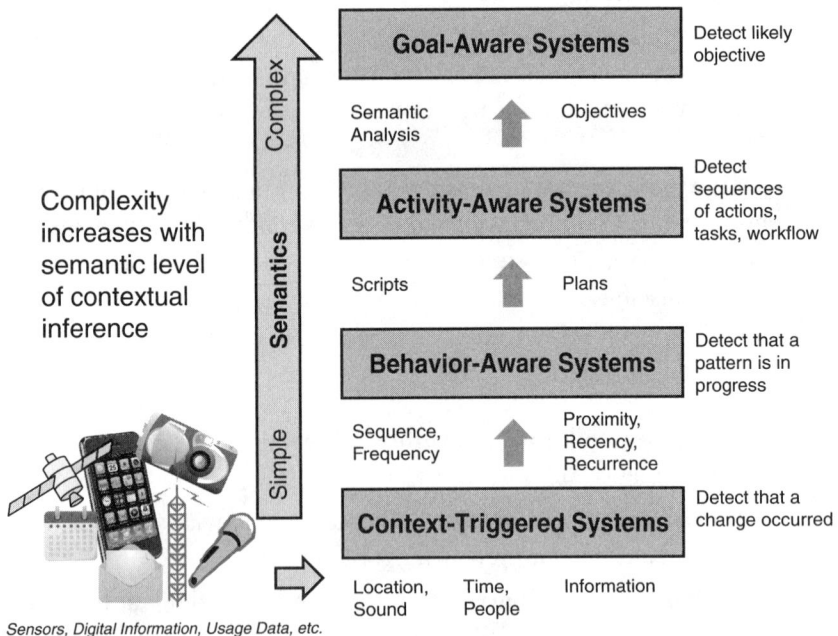

Figure 4-3 The layers of proactive intelligence build on each other, starting with simple sensor triggers and moving to more complex levels of inference.

Actionable Information

We use information technologies for a variety of purposes, from pure entertainment to actionable insights that provide a competitive edge. Frankly, it is not always clear which purpose information technologies serve. People consume news reports as much for the gossip, entertainment, and drama as for anything that will cause them to act differently. Businesses waste inordinate time creating reports and presentations that contain as much fluff as figures, many of which end up forgotten, unread, or unheeded.

When businesses invest money in information technologies, it is under the expectation that the technologies will provide a positive return on investment by making the operations of information exchange more efficient. Unfortunately, reducing costs of information exchange does not address the underlying question of the value of that information—what proportion of it is actually useful. The problem is that identifying useful from fluff is nearly impossible to do correctly, and businesses have to rely on human judgment to make the determination ... leading us ultimately back to the problem of information overload.

Large businesses are beginning to get a handle on the value of their information, however, through large-scale business intelligence (BI) systems. These systems use business process theories and metrics to spot trends and important variations in business outcomes, such as productivity per dollar across various business divisions, costs and reliability metrics across suppliers, projections of product lifespan in various markets, and other fine-grain analyses of business metrics. BI systems consist of advanced technologies for accurate reporting and dissemination, along with a variety of technologies for data mining, text mining, and predictive analytics. By analyzing trends and notifying the right people about important business indicators, BI systems help business people make better decisions.

For the most part, the results of a BI system are consistent with human intuitions, perhaps because they are constructed by human understanding of business models. Business people who see the same data going into BI will perhaps more quickly notice any *dramatic* anomalies than the system will. On the other hand, BI systems have validated their investments by identifying small anomalies that human analysts miss. At the global scales of many businesses today, shaving even a few cents off the costs of operations can add tremendously to the bottom line.

BI works because it is explicitly not entertainment. It is an impassionate examination of the costs and tradeoffs of various options, leaving out all considerations to the social and political pressures within a workplace. The information that comes out of BI is actionable—providing an assessment of various options that confront a decision maker. But note that a human or a group of humans still makes the decisions; the right place for computers in this process is doing the mundane work of analyzing reams of data and sorting the various outcomes by likely usefulness, but leaving the ultimate decision to humans. The aim of BI is to describe a set of options that the human decision maker can visualize and comprehend to serve as a *supplement* to a group of people's own knowledge. Advanced BI systems enhance the cognitive capacity of people by synthesizing data into a computationally derived prediction along with the underlying data. These can expose information that would otherwise fall below the threshold of human awareness. People can assess the veracity of the calculations against their own internal mental models of the situation and, augmented with their own understanding of the patterns and knowledge not available to the computational model, adjust the calculations mentally before deciding on an action.

Personal Actionability

The main objective of business intelligence is to provide "actionable information" for globally scaled business processes. It works because of the large amounts of data that such businesses generate and ingest in their day-to-day operations. The data sets are of such massive scale that sporadic anomalies (noise) are washed out. What makes this interesting to the rest of us is that we, too, are generating similarly massive data sets as we interact with Ubiquitous Computing in our day-to-day lives.

Individually, we create enormous amounts of data about ourselves through our interaction with computing devices, electronic services, media, and home electronics—not to mention the various sensors we carry in our phones and computers and via public surveillance. We probably create as much data as any large corporation does—but we don't use it for introspection as a business does. For many reasons, we haven't been leveraging our information output: computation cost, inaccuracy of inferences, and invasion of personal privacy. I explore these and ways to mitigate their impact in more depth in Chapter 5, "Missing Ingredients."

Actionable information is different for an individual than for a business. Information is "actionable" when it potentially causes you to act differently than you would have *without* the information. For an organization, that can mean high-level decisions such as budgeting and spending that may not show an impact on the business until a subsequent quarter. For an individual, though, *actionable* means something that causes you to operate differently *in the moment* of your actions (whether the activity is business or pleasure).

For example, if you get an email stating a new company policy when preparing proposals, but you are not preparing a proposal and do not anticipate doing so in the foreseeable future, that policy is not actionable and will be forgotten quickly (if read at all). On the other hand, suppose that you unexpectedly are involved in preparing a proposal and the new policy comes up on your screen. *Then* it is actionable. Companies already know that they prefer to get information out when it is actionable, but there is no way for them today to determine such moments. With contextual intelligence, a system can detect the sequence of actions that typically precede proposal preparation (for example, receiving email from colleagues talking about a new proposal, opening an old proposal to copy text from, searching for corporate proposal templates, and so on) and trigger the just-in-time delivery of the pertinent policy.

It's all about timing. As another example, suppose you are in a sales meeting pitching the glories of your new product line when one of the customers in the room says, "Actually, we've had a sample of your new product for two weeks and have complained to your customer service several times." Oops, you didn't know that. It would have been nice if someone in customer service had told you about that before this meeting. But how were they to know you were going on a sales call to this customer today? Finding out about the problems during the meeting is actionable to some extent (you now need to change your pitch to address the concerns), but it would have been more actionable *before* the meeting. A contextually intelligent system would have seen that you had that customer visit planned in your calendar and identified that there had been several trouble calls related to the new equipment. It would connect the dots between the problem reports and your objectives. Salespeople are usually selling the newest products, and the contextually intelligent system would have identified the correlation between salespeople and recently launched products, along with their need to be aware of problems with new products and the context of those facts with respect to the sales meeting on their calendar. By identifying these contextual relationships, a system can proactively deliver pertinent information.

Determining "Actionability"

The process of converting raw data and information to actionable information involves several stages, illustrated in Figure 4-4. This process begins with data collection and moves up to the presentation of the alternative courses of action to a human who makes the decision of which course to take.

After the human selects the course of action, the process continues by assessing the outcome of the execution of the action and feeding those results back into the predictive components of the system, illustrated in Figure 4-5. The feedback allows these components to improve from real-world experience. Such feedback provides a new stream of data from which the system learns to recognize patterns. The feedback may also be used to adjust the confidence of recommendations for different courses of action in the future.

There's really no magic here. The loop in Figure 4-5 is essentially no different than the classic feedback loop in control theory: measure, decide, act, and repeat. Of course, not all feedback loops are well behaved, but robust, stable models can be derived using careful design methods. I describe a concrete example of such a system in Chapter 8, "Breaking Out of the Supply Chain Gang," and how feedback improves the accuracy of the system over time.

4 • STILL STUPID AFTER ALL THESE YEARS

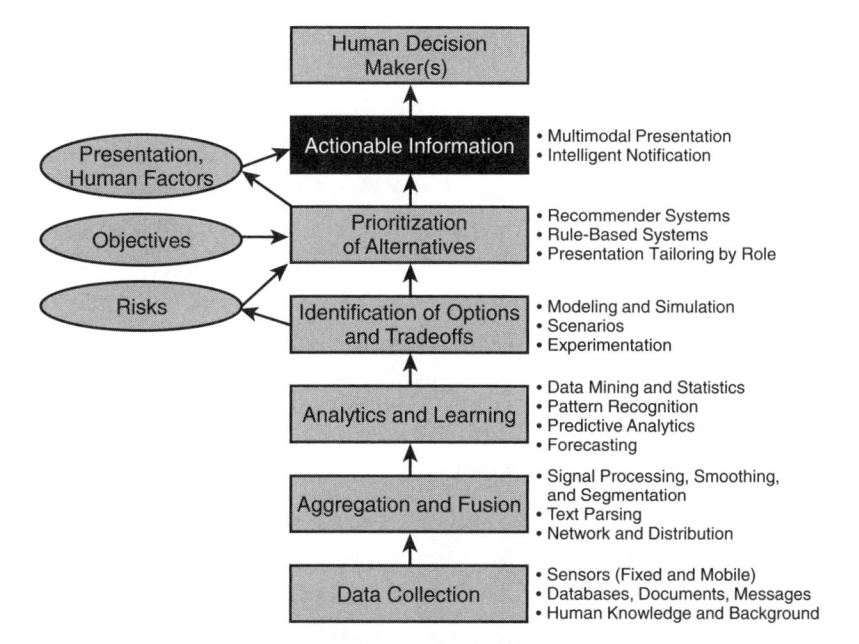

Figure 4-4 Identifying "actionable" information involves several stages of processing. The ovals represent sources of information that influence the processing within a related rectangle.

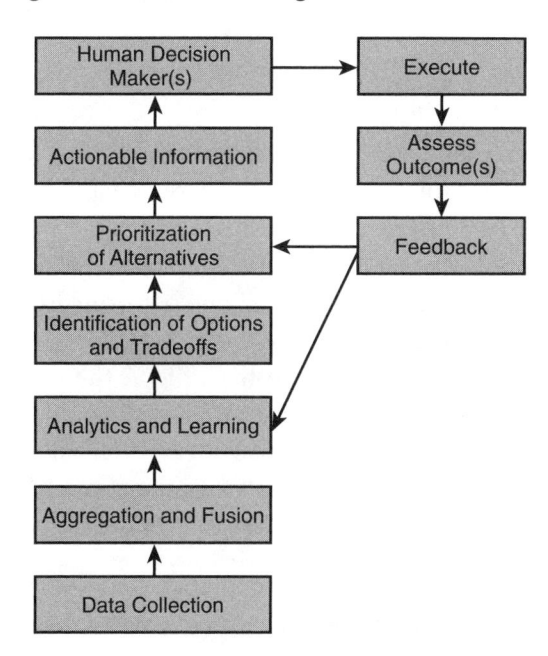

Figure 4-5 The process continues by feeding the results of the selected actions back to the system.

The Brains: User Models

In addition to the two types of contextual information (physical context and electronic context), contextual intelligence requires two components that make sense of the contextually related elements with respect to the individual user: an interest model and a behavior model of the user (or a class of users), collectively referred to as user models.

The interest model contains a description of topics and their relative importance. The topic list can cover different aspects of the person's interests, including these:

- Expertise in various topics
- Preferences for various characteristics of products, media, and food
- Activities at work, home, school, and other places
- Side interests in hobbies and extracurricular activities

The interest model helps prioritize the likely relevance of objects that a system would present, such as the results of a keyword search; recommendations for restaurants or stores; news items for work, school, and other places; business events related to their expertise or work activities; and more.

The behavior model contains a description of the typical actions that the individual (or people *like* the individual) has taken when placed in a similar context in the past. That is, when this person was previously in a similar physical situation and received similar types of information in the past, what action did he perform? For example, to describe behavior such as "typically this person does not answer the phone when talking to someone in her office," the behavior model would contain some formulation such as `when talking and in_office, phone_answer_likelihood=13.2%`. The behavior model can be rules, statistical descriptions, or combinations of both, and is generally indexed according to contextual dimensions such as the following:

- Geographic location (in one region of a city, for example, the individual usually goes to restaurants and not to stores)

- Time (for example, the individual usually does grocery shopping at a particular time on a particular day of the week)
- Event sequence (for example, the individual usually opens a spreadsheet after receiving an email containing the term *quarterly budget*)
- Physical activity (such as talking, running, sitting, reading, and so on)
- Environmental condition (such as weather, noise level, lighting, and so on)

Behavior models can be programmed manually and learned automatically. When programmed, they usually take the form of a trigger-action pair. When the specified set of conditions is detected, the specified action is triggered. The early forms of context-aware systems used such rule-based trigger-action pairs. Many forms of electromechanical automation are founded on this approach, including automatic door openers, grocery store conveyor belts, and vehicle antilock brake systems. However, the appropriate action for a set of conditions is not always universally agreed upon. A funny example is the scenario of a couple watching television when the phone rings: One person may want the television volume to go down so they can talk on the phone, while the other person may want the volume to go up so they can hear the television over the phone conversation. Impasse! (Of course, this has never happened in my household.)

Learned behavior models are derived by observing actions and situations over time and constructing statistical descriptions of the frequency of behaviors within situations. The technologies for learning models are commonly employed today: machine learning, statistical modeling, and probabilistic reasoning. The basic idea for predicting future activities is to match recently observed events against prior observed sequences of events in a repository, as illustrated in Figure 4-6. If there is a "close" match, there is some likelihood that some portion of the previously observed future sequence will be repeated—perhaps not precisely, but with some probability. The probability would be low if the pattern had been observed only a few times and would increase with the frequency and recency of the pattern.

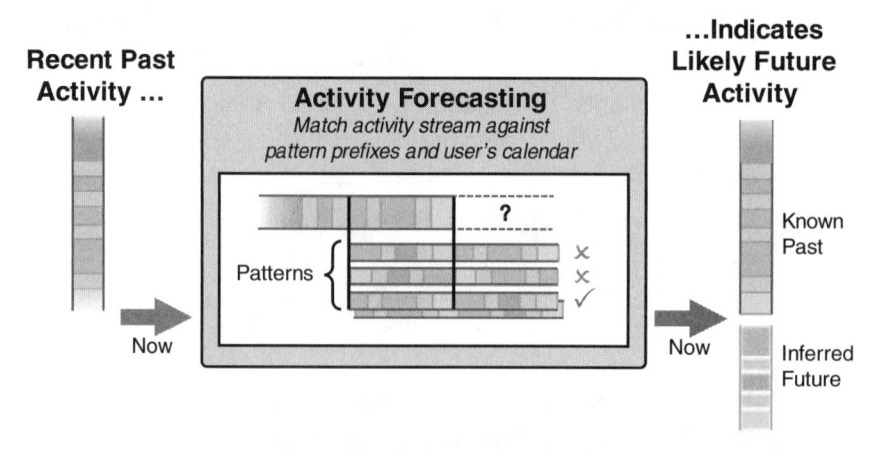

Figure 4-6 If recent activity "matches" some set of prior observations, there is some probability that future activities can be forecast. (Figure credit: Kurt Partridge)

The major technical difficulty with activity detection is that no two situations and no two actions are *exactly* alike. Some metric for *similarity* must be devised that allows the system to group similar situations and actions. In some cases, similar conditions are fairly straightforward to determine, such as whether it is raining. Unfortunately, for many human-level problems, similar conditions are ambiguous and *depend on the context,* such as whether two people with the same job description and performance rating will do the job just as well (it depends on their motivation for the project objectives and interpersonal working relationships—motivation is not solely about compensation and benefits, after all).

The ultimate goal of a contextually intelligent system is to infer the user's state of mind. Despite some predictions to the contrary, we're still a long way from computer mind reading, but a contextually intelligent system can provide an approximation of the topics of interest or actions that are likely to come next. Figure 4-7 shows conceptually how the comparison of the current situation against previously observed patterns can indicate what people are doing, what they are trying to accomplish, what their plans are for accomplishing it, and what they already know (or have done).[17] With this estimate, the system can set up services in anticipation of their need.

4 • Still Stupid after All These Years

Current Situation
- Physical Context: Location, Time, Nearby People
- Electronic Context: Calendar, Calls, Email, Documents

Previous Patterns
- Interest Model: Tastes, Interests, Expertise
- Behavior Model: Past Actions
- Social Model: Others' Interests and Behaviors

↓

Activities and Interests

↓

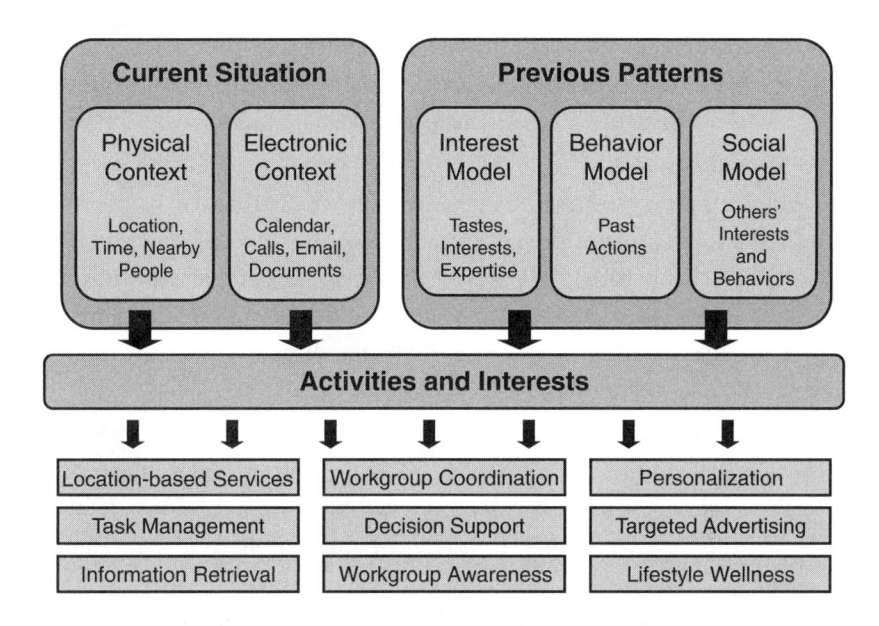

- Location-based Services
- Task Management
- Information Retrieval
- Workgroup Coordination
- Decision Support
- Workgroup Awareness
- Personalization
- Targeted Advertising
- Lifestyle Wellness

Figure 4-7 Contextually intelligent systems detect the current physical and electronic situation, combined with models of the individual's interests and behaviors in similar situations to estimate the person's activities, goals, plans, and knowledge. The social model provides information about how other people who are socially connected or similar would act in the situation. A variety of services are enabled by these estimates, from information retrieval to lifestyle and wellness.

By comparing the cost of an incorrect estimate against the benefit of a proactive service, the system can determine whether it is worth the downside risk. If the benefit of the prospective service or information is estimated as low, it may not be worth the cost of being wrong (including the cost that can arise simply by disrupting the user's attention). When the estimated benefit outweighs the estimated cost of being wrong, it is probably worth at least suggesting the service or information to the user, though perhaps not taking action directly. When the cost of being wrong is minimal, the action may be taken directly.

Summary

In psychology, contextual intelligence is a type of practical "street smarts" that people have but information systems today lack. Achieving contextual intelligence involves identifying the relationships among pieces of information, people, organizations, events, times, and places, and using these to establish the meaning of ambiguous information.

Computing systems are traditionally incapable of contextual intelligence because information needs to be explicitly described to be processed. Fortunately, content analysis and contextual inferencing technologies are emerging that make it possible to extract or construct a network of the contextual relationships across one's digital and physical interactions.

Contextual intelligence helps filter and prioritize information, increasing the precision of search. Contextually intelligent systems are also able to proactively detect situations when you need some information but would not have known to search for it. Proactive delivery increases the unanticipated discovery of information (or services) that a person might not otherwise learn of, augmenting that person's knowledge and abilities to accomplish tasks. CI systems retrieve "actionable information"—that is, information that may cause one to act differently than without it, accomplishing goals more quickly and making better decisions.

The core intelligence of these systems consists of two key modules: an estimate of the current situation (both physical and digital) and a set of instructions for how to act in the situation. The instructions may be specified manually in the form of "rules" or may be learned by the machine by observing actions in situations over time.

Endnotes

[1] Kenneth Noland, "CONTEXT," speech delivered at University of Hartford, March 1988. Available at www.sharecom.ca/noland/nolandtalk.html (accessed 20 August 2010).

[2] United Nations Statistics Division, http://data.un.org/Data.aspx?d=CDB&f=srID%3a29971#CDB (accessed 3 February 2010).

[3] Forrester Research, "The State of Consumers and Technology: Benchmark 2009, US," September 2009.

[4] "Consumer Electronics Association Market Research Report: 11th Annual Household CE Ownership and Market Potential" (May 2009).

[5] Carl Shapiro and Hal R. Varian, *Information Rules: A Strategic Guide to the Network Economy* (Boston: Harvard Business Press, 1998).

[6] John Gantz, Angéle Boyd, and Seana Dowling, "Cutting the Clutter: Tackling Information Overload at the Source," IDC whitepaper, March 2009.

[7] Jonathan Spira and David Goldes, "Information Overload: We Have Met the Enemy and He Is Us," March 2007, http://bsx.stores.yahoo.net/inovwehamete.html.

[8] V.M. González and G. Mark, "Constant, Constant, Multi-tasking Craziness: Managing Multiple Working Spheres," in *Proceedings of the SIGCHI Conference on Human Factors in Computing Systems*, New York, April 2004, 113–120. http://doi.acm.org/10.1145/985692.985707.

[9] G. Mark, D. Gudith, and U. Klocke, "The Cost of Interrupted Work: More Speed and Stress," in *Proceeding of the Twenty-Sixth Annual SIGCHI Conference on Human Factors in Computing Systems*, New York, April 2008, 107–110. http://doi.acm.org/10.1145/1357054.1357072.

[10] Thankfully, personal account manager services offer "single sign-on," including PayPal, Yahoo!, Google Account, Liberty Alliance, OpenID, and others that allow multiple vendors to use your settings. Ironically, vendors' support of the varying schemes is fragmented, and there are so many single sign-on account managers that you end up having to manage a *multitude* of *single* sign-on account managers.

[11] Chris Anderson, *The Long Tail: Why the Future of Business Is Selling Less of More* (New York: Hyperion, 2006).

[12] R. J. Sternberg, *Beyond IQ: A Triarchic Theory of Intelligence* (Cambridge: Cambridge University Press, 1985).

[13] There are systems that "create" artifacts according to programmed formulations with random perturbations that satisfy an aesthetic metric, including visual arts, music, poetry, jokes, and more. For the most part, however, these are special-purpose programs that *synthesize* creativity within one class of artifact; the computers are not independently creating novel artifacts.

[14] B. Schilit, N. Adams, and R. Want, "Context-Aware Computing Applications," 1st International Workshop on Mobile Computing Systems and Applications, Santa Cruz, California, 1994: 85–90.

[15] T.B. Lee, J. Hendler, O. Lassila, "The Semantic Web," *Scientific American*, (17 May 2001), 34–43.

[16] See http://semanticweb.org/wiki/Ontology for examples.

[17] These three pieces of information roughly correspond to the beliefs, desires, and intentions theory of intelligent agents, as described in A.S. Rao and M.P. Georgeff, "Modeling Rational Agents within a BDI-Architecture," in *Readings in Agents*, San Francisco: Morgan Kaufmann, 1998: 317–328.

5

Missing Ingredients

Later, I realized that the mission had to end in a let-down because the real barrier wasn't in the sky, but in our knowledge and experience of supersonic flight.
—Chuck Yeager, test pilot[1]

The research community has demonstrated the technical feasibility of personalized context-aware services. From a business perspective, the next question we should ask is, how much needs to be invested to commercialize these concepts? A completely accurate answer isn't possible because it hasn't been entirely done before, but we can at least characterize the difficulty of the problem and get a sense of the rough boundaries.

Inaccuracy: When Does "Almost" Count, Outside of Horseshoes and Hand Grenades?

Despite the amazing growth in the number of people tweeting their every clever thought, we should not expect people to take the time to tell systems what they are doing all the time. The first challenge to address is the complexity of the artificial intelligence needed to distill meaningful descriptions of activity from raw data. This involves combining low-level electronic information sources and weighting them appropriately to infer higher-level meaning.

One complication is that the inherent inaccuracy of sensors and ambiguity of the information leads to increased error when inferring higher levels of meaning. Let's examine the example in Figure 5-1, which assumes the existence of location-detection technologies that can be combined with the time of day, information from an individual's calendar, and detection of the devices the person interacts with. The location-detection technology will tell us roughly where the person is located but carries some amount of inaccuracy (10–30m is currently typical of Global Positioning System, or GPS). Nevertheless, by looking at a series of location readings, it should be possible to detect whether the person is walking, running, or driving, although not with 100% accuracy. Appointments in an online calendar may be cryptically worded in terms that make sense only to the owner of the calendar, though when combined with the location traces, it may be evident that the person is en route to the scheduled item in the calendar (again, however, the system cannot be certain). Stepping up the levels, as the system gathers more information, the inaccuracies are compounded. However, occasional points of detail may clarify ambiguities. The user's driving route could indicate a likely destination at a ski resort, resolving the cryptic entry in their calendar that read "Think snow."

How much inaccuracy can be tolerated? It depends on the type of service that would be provided. Taking marketing as an example (we explore this in more depth in Chapter 7, "The Soft Sell: Personalized Marketing"), providing ads that are more personally relevant and useful benefits both marketers and consumers. Because of the inherent uncertainty, though, mismatches will inevitably happen. The objective is not to avoid all possible mismatches, but to reduce the number of mismatches compared to conventional targeting and segmentation of advertising.

It is safe to say that artificial intelligence will never be 100% correct, any more than human intelligence is. Such systems are making an estimate based on the evidence they see, but information may be missing. Fortunately, they don't have to be correct all the time any more than people have to be correct all the time; they just need to be designed such that the cost of being wrong does not outweigh the value of being right. That was the mistake of the infamous Microsoft Clippy, which was very accurate in detecting "It looks like you're writing a letter. Would you like help?" Well, sure, if you could write the letter for me, Clippy, that would be great. But if all you're going to do is show me how to use the word processor, no thanks—I've got that covered. In many cases, Clippy was correct but wasn't offering anything valuable, while at the same time incurring a cost by distracting the user's attention.[2]

To summarize, the uncertainty of an inference rises along with its semantic interpretation and usefulness. The best way to mitigate the inherent uncertainty is to design systems in which the cost of false inferences is outweighed by the benefits from accurate inferences. In the case of an advertisement, the cost of a falsely targeted advertisement is fairly low, as an uninterested recipient can simply ignore it; on the other hand, the benefit of accurate targeting is valuable to both the advertiser and the customer. Applications beyond advertising have similar net positive value to users, such as recommendation systems for stores, restaurants, movies, and so on. Applications also can benefit knowledge workers, such as serendipitous information discovery (finding information that is valuable but that you wouldn't have searched for).

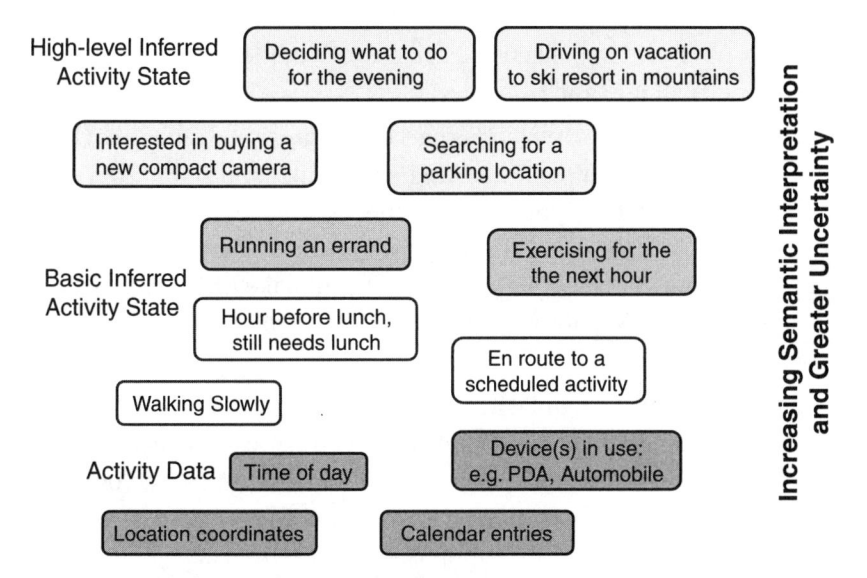

Figure 5-1 Higher levels of meaning come with higher levels of ambiguity and uncertainty. (Figure credit: Dan Greene)

Incorrigible Computers: "How Many Times Do I Have to Tell You ...?"

We're seeing exponential growth in the amount of information available for machine learning and other probability-based computation. However, the amount of data needed to detect statistical patterns robustly is quite large. Web services that receive hundreds of thousands of user interactions per second are collecting more than enough data in 1 second to robustly detect patterns of population behaviors and preferences (such as whether a 2-pixel border leads to more click-throughs than a 1-pixel border). Building a model based on data from one individual's behavior, however, takes longer. The number of data samples is not necessarily the limiting factor; rather, it is the granularity of the pattern that the system is trying to detect. For example, a sample rate of one per second produces roughly 86,400 samples over 24 hours, which would seem to be more than enough samples to test for statistical significance. However, when the patterns we are trying to detect are those that reoccur over multiple days and weeks, one full day's worth of data is really only one sample. For example, if you check email once an hour at work, collecting samples on any particular work day should pick up the pattern in one day. However, if you buy groceries every Tuesday, collecting a full day of samples on any other day of the week will miss the pattern.

Systems can use many techniques to minimize the amount of data needed to detect a pattern (boosting, clustering, and so on), but fundamentally, more than one sample is needed, which could take days to observe. Some delay will always exist between when a person starts to use a personalized service and when it can make useful predictions of the individual's pattern, which we refer to as *personalization latency*.

A similar delay occurs when a person *changes* his or her pattern, which we refer to as *change latency*. A pattern can change for any number of reasons: change in lifestyle, school calendar, road damage or improvement, and so on. A system cannot immediately discern whether an anomalous observation is just a one-time exception or the adoption of a new pattern. As a general rule of thumb, change latency is about half the amount of time of personalization latency, because determining that a pattern is no longer robust requires about half the number of observations that it took to ascertain that the pattern was robust in the first place. One way to reduce the change latency is to ask the user whether the pattern has changed every time the system detects an anomaly from the pattern, but the whole point of personalization is to reduce the burden on users, not pester them with questions.

Another form of latency in these systems is the amount of time it takes between when a person becomes engaged in some pattern and when the system has enough confidence to act on it, which we call *detection latency*. For example, consider a system that tries to detect when people are in a "conversation" (a lengthy interchange of dialogue) without being able to recognize the content of their speech (detecting sounds that indicate humans are speaking is a simpler problem than recognizing the words being spoken). At the onset of detecting speech, it is not clear whether the people are just exchanging greetings or are engaging in a conversation. The system needs to detect *sustained* speech over some minimum amount of time, which is its detection latency. In at least two cases, colleagues and I,[3] as well as researchers at IBM Research,[4] found that such conversation detection required at least three minutes before systems reached enough accuracy to be reliable. Shorter times resulted in too many "false positive" detections of conversation. A human observer, on the other hand, would have *immediately* known whether people were engaging in conversation or merely saying "hi."

Accuracy and latency are purely technical problems, but personalized services must contend with some additional challenges that are not simply technical, but also social and cultural, such as privacy.

Privacy: Getting to Know You, Getting to Know All about You

What about privacy? Behavioral targeting depends on recording and reviewing an individual's actions. Releasing such data carries a risk that someone might use the detailed information for undesirable purposes. In the dotcom era, a number of "spyware" companies popped up that bundled monitoring software into desirable applications that then recorded the web pages you visited—even portions of credit card numbers. The software then analyzed the electronic routes you took and retrieved and displayed personalized advertisements, sometimes overwriting ads placed by the content provider of a web page. Today most antivirus programs detect and remove spyware, and several of the early spyware companies have shut down, in part due to the negative backlash they faced from consumer privacy and civil liberties groups.

The precedent of spyware gives us all cause to question whether the benefit of behavioral targeting is worth the cost. The benefit is potentially receiving information of higher relevance and usefulness than we encounter in advertising today. How much risk is that worth? What *are* the risks? Let's unpack this issue of privacy a bit to understand the root concerns. Multiple layers of risk are at play, each with differing costs.

Economic Risk

Some concern arises that marketers could use data analytics for profiteering, perhaps exploiting vulnerable customer segments. Many of us have heard some version of the apocryphal story of how a data mining system detected that when men bought diapers at a drug store in the afternoons, they also often bought a six-pack of beer. Although it is clever, it is also disturbing to think that a retailer might use this insight to increase beer sales to new fathers. The actual correlation of beer and diapers is disputed, but the tale gives rise to the concern of using personalization technologies that might encourage undesired behavior for profit. Although this tension is one that consumers deal with daily in a market-driven economy, many people are reluctant to give marketers even more power.

Although it is possible to combat economic costs by developing stronger sales resistance, consumers are also concerned about personal economic risks in areas in which they have limited choices, such as insurance. Insurance actuarial calculations are already partitioning the population into buckets of varying risk and insurance premiums. Why give insurance companies more ammunition with context-sensing and tracking technologies? Sure, if we could identify individuals who habitually engage in risky driving, it would seem to make sense to charge them a higher insurance premium—it might even encourage people to drive more safely. Indeed, some insurance companies are already offering discounts for safe driving, verified by in-vehicle sensors. Driving style is something you can control; but what if an insurance company calculated that your commute route has more traffic accidents than average and charged you a higher premium on your auto insurance? At a macroeconomic level, this kind of precision would be a benefit by increasing the efficiencies in insurance markets. However, although a bad driver can certainly improve his or her habits and reach the lower premium, an individual has only limited control over how to get between home and work in an efficient amount of time. We may never see insurance companies charging a premium based on commute route patterns, but people fear that personal contextual data could identify aspects of their life over which they have only limited influence and for which they would not want to be charged a premium.

Security from Crime

A more serious concern is the security risk that someone might use such information for criminal activity: financial account theft, harassment, and stalking. Certainly, laws already protect us, to some extent, but there's no reason to make it any easier for criminals to do harm.

Preventing criminal activity is more of a *security* concern rather than a privacy concern. Account numbers and addresses certainly should be held private, but when we talk about privacy, we more generally are talking about less critical information. Most behavioral targeting systems do not capture personally identifying information; they use identity codes that are not coupled to financial account information, street address, or place of work.

On the other hand, security researchers have shown that it is possible to identify individuals or small sets of people by combining behavior-tracking data with publicly available information, such as medical studies, voting lists, school and police records, or census statistics. In one famous example, Latanya Sweeney demonstrated that by combining a public record of Massachusetts state employee health claims, which carefully did not include the names of employees or other personally identifiable information, along with voter registration records, which did include name and address but not health record number, she was able to learn that the then-governor of Massachusetts had cancer.[5] Sweeney's analysis of U.S. census data showed that 87% of the U.S. population is uniquely identifiable, given their full date of birth (year, month, and day), sex, and the zip code where they live.

Sweeney's work resulted in a metric that describes the identifiability of personal information, called k-anonymity, which is the number of people who share the same attribute (data of birth, sex, zip code, and so on). A larger k-anonymity number means that there is a larger group of people who share those attributes, making it harder to identify a unique individual within the group. If you live in an urban zip code region with a population over one million, it is probably safe to share your birthday (day and month) because about 2,740 others in the same zip code have the same birthday. But if you live in a rural zip code of 1,000, only about 2 or 3 people will have the same birthday.

Larger k-anonymity is more secure, but it is difficult to predict just how identifiable some pieces of information will turn out to be. For example, what about the postal code of where you live or work? Zip code regions are fairly large—you certainly wouldn't be able to find a friend's home if all he did was give you the zip code where he lived. In fact, in a recent analysis at PARC,[6] Philippe Golle and Kurt Partridge showed that, for 90% of the people in the United States, the postal code where they live *or* work results in a k-anonymity of more than 1,000 other people. Pretty safe. However, keep in mind that postal code information is fairly easy to determine. In many cases, it is possible to identify the zip code where a computer is located from its Internet address. Many smartphones and in-car navigation systems can track a person's location via GPS technology, from which it is fairly straightforward to identify the rough coordinates of an individual's home and workplace.[7]

If you have the zip code of where a person both lives *and* works, Golle and Partridge showed that 50% of the U.S. population would have k-anonymity of 21 or less. That is, for a person who lives in one postal code and commutes to another postal code for work, for half of the U.S. population, only 21 or fewer other people live and work in that same combination of postal codes. Someone with malicious intent would have to go through only 21 people to identify the 1 being targeted. This is not saying that we're all at risk; the other half of the U.S.

population has k-anonymity from 22 and up to 100,000 when you combine the postal codes of where they live and work. But note that, for 7% of the U.S. population, the combination of home and work postal code results in a k-anonymity of 1. That means that, out of 100 million U.S. workers, 7 million are unique in the combination of where they live and work at the level of a postal code. Sounds like cause for concern.

It's not that simple, of course. First, a criminal mind would need to get the combination of home and work postal codes for a large number of people—say, a hundred. He could theoretically identify seven unique people in that set. Then he would need to combine the identity with some valuable piece of information about the seven people, such as a list of credit card accounts. It's not easy to do, but the risk to security *does* exist. People are right to be concerned, and this concern hinders the adoption of contextual intelligence technologies.

Public Relations

We already take care to protect most of the types of information I've described so far: home address, health records, financial accounts, and so on. In addition to the potential for real damage from exposing such private data are psychological factors that simply make people uncomfortable about sharing personal data electronically, even when the same information is publicly displayed. Collecting and distributing data electronically heightens concerns of being susceptible to undesirable uses. Why would people be more concerned about public information when it is in electronic form?

In the early 2000s at Sun Microsystems, colleagues and I ran an experiment to test this. We were developing tools for distributed workgroups to coordinate their activities effectively and were particularly focusing on ways to increase spontaneous conversation among remote coworkers—the kinds of conversations that co-located employees have as they encounter each other in hallways, meeting rooms, and common areas. Among the variety of technologies we created, one used a motion sensor to detect when a person was physically present in an individual office. It also had a microphone that could detect when there was a conversation in that office, but not who it was or what was said. The system, called Lilsys ("little sister," as opposed to "big brother"), was intended to provide the same cues to remote coworkers that co-located coworkers use to determine whether any particular time is good for an interruption. Chapter 10, "Coordination," has more details about Lilsys and related systems.

Before we built the system, people expressed some discomfort with having sensors on all the time. To mitigate this concern, we added a timer switch to the sensors that let a person turn them off for a period of time, as well as an on-off toggle switch that let them turn it off entirely. We deployed four of the systems for three months (and more) in offices in California, Massachusetts, and France. Over the entire time of the trial, no one used either switch. Ever. Nevertheless, users were reassured by the ability to opt out at any time they wanted.

Opting out is an effective strategy, but why was there any concern to begin with about sharing this information with remote coworkers? Co-located people can physically see when others are in the office and can physically see whether others are in a conversation and usually with whom. So why would there be more concern when such information is captured electronically and sent to remote coworkers? Why do people seem to want control and awareness of information about them?

One explanation can be found in the work of Erving Goffman, a renowned sociologist who studied the fine-grained mechanics of human interaction. In the 1950s,[8] Goffman studied the ways in which people take pains to influence how others will perceive them. In what he referred to as "face work," people try to control the information that others see about them and how the information is interpreted. People pre-empt, detect, and repair negative impressions if they perceive that some cue they have given off might be perceived negatively. For example, when someone physically sees you in the office, you can see them back and know who it is. It would not bother most people if a coworker noticed that they were staring out the window in the office. If the boss happened to notice, though ... well, it might have been better to have looked busier. We all engage in some kind of personalized public relations campaign with friends, family, and coworkers to varying degrees and using varying methods.

Face work is made much more difficult when personal information is recorded electronically. First, in contrast to the vagaries of human memory, the persistence and precision of digital records leaves less room for reinterpretation of facts. Ambiguity gives people the ability to influence others' memory and manage the way in which something is perceived. When precise records of activity are made digitally available, it is more difficult to adjust how it is interpreted by others. Second, electronic information is trivial to copy and distribute, resulting in copies spreading far beyond where users can keep track and know how it is being used. Our ability to detect and repair negative interpretations of information is decreased because we don't know who is seeing what; maybe there's not a problem, but we don't know, and that uncertainty can be disconcerting.

One way around this is to let people find out what interpretation others are making from their personal information, such as credit scores. U.S. law now specifies that individuals can request details of their credit rating from the rating agencies once a year free of charge. Similarly, Google has made the inferred profiles of people it tracks available to them and allowed them to choose to opt out of the profiling. However, tracking these interpretations takes time and effort, in contrast to the face work that is typically performed subconsciously and in the moment. Furthermore, although it is straightforward to determine that a low credit rating will leave a negative impression on creditors, it is not as easy to detect what attributes of a profile might give off an unwanted impression to others. (Do the fast food restaurants I visit leave a bad impression with some of my friends?) It's not simply a matter of designing technologies that avoid making "negative" interpretations, because the definition of "negative" varies with time, context, and relationships. A widely circulated article from *The Wall Street Journal* in 2002[9] reported that the TiVo recommendation system was pigeonholing some viewers into inaccurate stereotypes and that their attempts to correct the machine's impression swung too far into opposite poles.

Another prominent sociologist, Irwin Altman,[10] examined the tension between people's desire to publish and to maintain privacy. He identified three dimensions along which people choose how to balance their desires to be simultaneously public and private. The first and most obvious dimension is the binary choice of whether to disclose information at all. Today systems are increasingly providing access controls to restrict who can see what. For example, Facebook recently introduced a new set of controls that provides a number of levels of restrictions and access. Users can create groups of friends and control their access to photos, activities, news, and other items. By the time this book is released, we should have a better idea how much effort Facebook users are willing to put into managing this kind of access control. My suspicion is that the vast majority of people will leave the settings unchanged from the default values. Research in the field of computer-supported cooperative work (CSCW)[11] since the 1990s has found that approximately 80% of users do not change their sharing settings from the default.

But face work involves more than just fine-grained access controls. Altman's second dimension is identity. When people do disclose personal information, they shape the information so that it reinforces and does not undermine the individual and group identities with which they associate. That's where the problem with the TiVo recommendations came in—they weren't consistent with the identities those people affiliated with. Similarly, suppose that the preference profile accurately infers that you like to buy junk foods, animal furs, and high-watt light bulbs. Even if that's true (which I'm sure it is not), if those tastes are not consistent with the kind of identity you *want* for yourself, it may cause discomfort in you to be confronted with the reality.

Third, Altman identified a temporal dimension to what one would be willing to disclose. Things that are suitable for disclosure at one time (those college party photos) could become embarrassing in the future. Traditionally, people expected that certain information would be ephemeral: the clothes they wore, the times they arrived at work, the music they listened to in the 1980s and so on. Electronic infrastructures today provide no means for information to expire or to rescind access to information that you've previously disclosed. You may be able to block future disclosures, but if it has been recorded somewhere, you can't control someone else from releasing it.

These and other issues regarding privacy are changing rapidly. Technologies are beginning to support varying degrees of disclosure. At the same time, social expectations for persistence of data are increasing and the acceptability of exposing personal information is growing. We are all adjusting to the reality of changes in personal and group identity over time. Nevertheless, personalization will probably always irritate deeply ingrained sensitivities surrounding impression management.

Best Practices to Mitigate Privacy Concerns

I want to recap the techniques we have seen as most effective in mitigating the concerns people have about security and privacy of their personal information. Many of these are obvious, but they bear repeating to prevent negative backlash against personalization.

- Disclose fully, honestly, and simply what information is being collected and for what purpose.
- Accept only users who *opt in* to the service.
- Allow people to *opt out* at any time, and guarantee destruction of their personal information.
- Allow people to see (and edit) the personal information.
- Keep personally identifying information separate from other pieces of information.
- Keep k-anonymity of combined information high.

Summary

Contextually intelligent systems cannot avoid several purely technical limitations. The first is that the accuracy of such systems is limited and that they can have false positives and false negatives. The accuracies are nevertheless adequate for many applications. The best way to ensure a net positive benefit is to design services so that the negative cost when it is incorrect is far outweighed by the beneficial value when it is correct.

Such systems can have three kinds of delays. *Personalization latency* is the amount of time (or the number of sample observations) that a system requires before it can build a robust model of an individual's pattern. *Change latency* is the amount of time before a system can be confident that a series of anomalous observations is not just a string of one-time exceptions, but an indication of a persistent change in the pattern. *Detection latency* is the amount of time needed for the system to observe a sustained behavior before it reaches enough confidence that the user is likely engaged in a pattern.

The most imposing barrier to widespread adoption of such systems is the concerns they raise about invasions of privacy. The key underlying reasons that these concerns exist include personal economic costs, criminal activity, and impression management. These very real concerns cannot be entirely avoided, because of the inherent need for contextual data to personalize information and services. However, well-designed systems can employ several practices to inform and mitigate the risks to individuals.

Endnotes

[1] Chuck Yeager and Leo Janos, *Yeager: An Autobiography* (New York: Bantam, 1986).

[2] Colleagues at Microsoft Research have said that the original design of the system did include a cost-benefit analysis, but evidently it did not make it into the released product.

See also Eric Horvitz, Jack Breese, David Heckerman, David Hovel, and Koos Rommelse, "The Lumiere Project: Bayesian User Modeling for Inferring the Goals and Needs of Software Users," in *Proceedings of the Fourteenth Conference on Uncertainty in Artificial Intelligence,* San Francisco, Calif., July 1998, 256–265.

[3] J.B. Begole, N.E. Matsakis, and J.C. Tang, "Lilsys: Sensing Unavailability," in *Proceedings of the ACM Conference on Computer Supported Cooperative Work* 2004, 511–514.

See also J. Begole, "Implications of Rhythm Awareness and Availability Inferencing in an 'Always On' World," Workshop on Awareness Systems at the *ACM Conference on Human Factors in Computing Systems 2005.*

[4] J. Fogarty, S.E. Hudson, and J. Lai, "Examining the Robustness of Sensor-Based Statistical Models of Human Interruptibility," in *Proceedings of the ACM Conference on Human Factors in Computing Systems* 2004, 207–214.

[5] Latanya Sweeney, "k-Anonymity: A Model for Protecting Privacy," *International Journal of Uncertainty, Fuzziness and Knowledge-Based Systems* 10, no. 5 (2002): 557–570.

[6] P. Golle and K. Partridge, "On the Anonymity of Home, Work Location Pairs," in *Proceedings of the 7th International Conference on Pervasive Computing.* Berlin: Springer, 11–14 May 2009. 390–397.

[7] J. Krumm, "Inference Attacks on Location Tracks," in *Proceedings of the fifth International Conference on Pervasive Computing (Pervasive 2007),* Berlin: Springer, 2007.127–143.

[8] Goffman, *The Presentation of Self in Everyday Life* (Garden City, N.Y.: Doubleday Anchor, 1959).

[9] Jeffrey Zaslow, "If TiVo Thinks You Are Gay, Here's How to Set It Straight," *The Wall Street Journal,* 26 November 2002, sect. A, p. 1.

[10] I. Altman, *The Environment and Social Behavior: Privacy, Personal Space, Territory and Crowding* (Monterey, Calif.: Brooks/Cole Pub. Co.).

[11] L. Palen, "Social, Individual, and Technological Issues for Groupware Calendar Systems," in *Proceedings of the SIGCHI Conference on Human Factors in Computing Systems: The CHI Is the Limit,* Pittsburgh, Penn. 15–20 May 1999. http://doi.acm.org/10.1145/302979.302982.

Part II

Business Opportunities

6

Making Choices

Strategy is about making choices, tradeoffs; it's about deliberately choosing to be different.
—Michael Porter, Harvard Business School[1]

Throughout this book, you've been introduced to a number of Ubiquitous Computing technologies and examples of their business applications. After almost 20 years of exploring these techniques and applications at PARC, we've identified a number of patterns regarding the strategic implications of these technologies on business.

First, let's look at how technology research contributes to creating business. Technology research is not about developing business strategy; it's about invention. As Alan Kay of PARC once quipped, the best way to predict the future is to *invent* it. Usually, this means that technology innovators are left to devise new technologies and validate their inventions to the scientific community, not offer business advice.

I don't buy that. Unlike government-funded research, businesses invest in research solely to gain strategic advantage, creating prospects for future business.[2] Fortunately, I work in a commercial innovation center whose impact on the world comes from *breakthrough* inventions that make their way through the vagaries of business processes to become products and services. PARC has a long track record creating technologies that have transformed the computing industry: laser printing, graphical user interfaces (GUIs), personal computing, Ethernet, WYSIWYG (what you see is what you get) word processing, multiplayer games, object-oriented programming, Ubiquitous Computing, and much more.[3] We know the realities of what it takes to work with commercial partners in multiple ways to make our research have commercial relevance.

A conventional model of the inventor's place in the value chain looks something like Figure 6-1.

Invention → Business Need → Product → Revenue

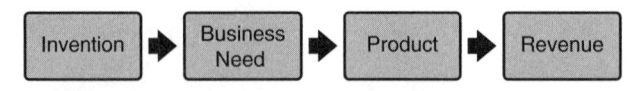

Figure 6-1 Conventional view of the innovation-to-product pipeline.

At an abstract level, this holds true, but it is only slightly more sophisticated than the business plan of South Park's Underpants Gnomes. There's an invention, business needs and value are identified, and the invention is integrated into a revenue-generating product or service that hopefully garners revenue. But in practice, it doesn't work this way at all. First of all, invention doesn't start the chain—*problems* start the chain: *Necessity* is the mother of invention.

Notice that the arrows in the invention pipeline (sometimes drawn as a funnel) imply a flow from left to right, suggesting that the invention flows into business needs. The sad truth is that inventors are notoriously bad at identifying business needs. First of all, necessity really is the mother of invention, and inventors solve the needs they see. Technologists spend so much time trying to understand the complexities of technologies that they rarely have the capacity to identify business problems. Furthermore, even when an innovation does have potential business value, inventors rarely understand the difficulties in monetizing that value. Solving a problem does not necessarily mean that someone is willing to pay much for it, so we see that successful new technology companies arise as much from innovative business models as from novel technologies. Examples include advertising that supports so much web-based content and services, the virtual currency of virtual worlds, and notorious software "maintenance" subscriptions that provide a more consistent revenue stream than the conventional model of product purchase.

Google's transition from a search company to an advertising company is a great example. Better search results solved a real problem—indexing large sets of web pages or documents—but there was no obvious way to monetize it. Google's first business model was to create a whole new product category that needed time and testing for the market to understand the monetary value: enterprise search appliances (still only a niche market segment today). Advertising, on the other hand, was an *established* industry with known business processes that tackled the eternally acute problem of informing consumers of prospective products. That's where Google's value lies—better search has real value but is more difficult to monetize than tapping into an existing value chain that had real problems to solve in the new domain of online advertising.

The most common strategy for creating business value from innovation is referred to as *technology transfer*, in which innovations are gestated in a research organization and then transferred to people with better business sense. That rarely works, because the technologies rarely fit directly into an existing business opportunity. Continuing the Google example, making the connection between search and advertising required another round of invention to fuse keyword search results to advertising content.

The upshot is that invention and business value is not a pipeline in which handoffs occur between different people at different stages. It requires continual interconnection and learning among all the components, something more akin to Figure 6-2.

Not only is *revenue* at the center of this process, but revenue is also caged in by the other components. You're not going to see revenue unless successful interaction takes place among *all* the components. No one component comes first, and no component can be eliminated.

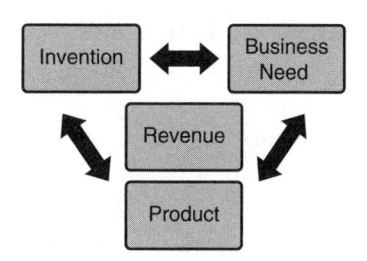

Figure 6-2 Realizing revenue requires interaction among all elements of commercial innovation.

I'm writing this book for two reasons: to strengthen the interconnection among all of these components by sharing my understanding of the technologies of Ubiquitous Computing, and to demonstrate some models for commercialization based on businesses we have created at PARC and elsewhere. My aim is that you, the reader, with even deeper business insights in your field, will hear about inventions from the Ubiquitous Computing research field and see other more direct channels for monetization. At the same time, I hope to engage with you to learn about new problems that need inventions of the sort that colleagues in the field of Ubiquitous Computing can tackle.

Who Wins, Who Loses?

Ubicomp technologies come into play at the points where digital and physical worlds connect, which occurs to some extent in all industries because, ultimately, real people are involved. However, Ubicomp technologies will have more impact on industries that are more closely connected to physical elements, such as construction, rather than others that are almost entirely oriented toward the manipulation of information, such as finance. The latter have already been revolutionized by information technologies and global networking. All enterprises have information processes in their operations: finance, accounting, human resources, payroll, and more. Most industries consist of a mix of information-based value that either already is or will be digitized and connections to the physical world to create, identify, assess, or deliver goods or services. Let's look at the potential of Ubicomp's impact on the prominent industry segments in a little more detail.

- **Finance (investment, loans, and banking):** Finance is fundamentally about manipulating information: prices, exchange rates, interest rates, projections, transactions. At some point, the information is related to some physical resource, but the industry operates largely independent of the physicality of those resources. On the other hand, the very nature of this kind of work allows it to be performed from almost any location; the spread of ubiquitous networks and wireless computers will affect the workforce of this industry, if not the work itself. We look at how Ubicomp technologies will affect the communication and collaboration inherent in any enterprise in Chapter 10, "Coordination."

- **Insurance (life, medical, and property):** Insurance is similar to finance, in that it is largely based on setting prices, projecting risks, and paying out claims. Payouts go toward physical services performed by other industries (healthcare, automotive, construction). Unlike finance, however, the insurance industry does have some critical points of connection to the physical world: estimating risk and assessing damage claims. Some amount of physical validation needs to get done to make sure the information matches reality. In fact, there is a growing trend in automotive insurance to install in-vehicle telematics that can report driver behavior and provide a discount to safe drivers.

- **Media publishing (books, movies, music, and news):** Publishing is a bit of an odd duck and one that digital technologies have quickly overtaken. Regarding the publishing industry, we have the perception that we are paying for the information content, but the way the industry monetizes that value is through charging for the distribution that media companies provide for home or retail delivery. This industry is quickly becoming undermined as the manufacturing and delivery of media that once was consumed in physical form (magazine, newspapers, records and books) is being supplanted by increasingly ubiquitous digital displays and networks. We look more at the publishing industry in Chapter 8, "Breaking Out of the Supply Chain Gang."

- **Advertising/marketing:** The trends in this industry are a close parallel to media publishing. The content is increasingly distributed and presented electronically. By observing online clickstreams, web-based advertising has introduced behaviorally targeted ads that receive higher response rates than nontargeted ads. Online advertising has also revolutionized the field of ad metrics, which track and estimate the effectiveness of advertising. Ubiquitous computing technologies introduce even richer information sources for personalized targeting through sensors on mobile phones and embedded in stores, shopping malls, and other physical environments. This industry segment is the focus of Chapter 7, "The Soft Sell: Personalized Marketing."

- **Manufacturing:** Whether it is constructing buildings or creating consumer or industrial goods, manufacturing processes have similar information problems that Ubicomp technologies address. First is the physical state of machinery used in the process—where they are located, their status, and their predicted availability. The locations of supplies and components need to be tracked to anticipate arrival and optimize the processing line. The quality of pieces throughout the process needs to be verified and repaired when problems arise. Beyond reducing the cost of production, there is tremendous opportunity in potentially increasing the value of products by expanding their interoperation with other products. We look at examples of novel ways of interoperation among devices in Chapter 9, "Discontinuous Connections."
- **Energy and utilities:** These industries deal with the continual distribution of environmental resources to consumers. To operate optimally, they need as much information as possible to project the demand and consumption of the resources at the end point. The "smart grid" will allow utility companies to monitor power generation and consumption at different times in different locations, setting prices to optimize the efficiency of the distribution network.
- **Hotels and restaurants:** This segment deals with physical assets of fixed capacity. They use physical information to project demand, set prices, and allocate space for customers. Customers in this industry also face information problems in understanding the physicality of what a remote hotel or restaurant offers.
- **Airlines and transportation:** Similar to hotels and restaurants, this segment deals with the allocation of assets that have fixed capacity. The problem is complicated, though, in that the assets are not in static locations and may be en route or stopped at remote terminals. They can optimize the allocations using real-time information about asset location and estimations of future locations.
- **Telecommunications:** Whether wired or wireless, the objective of this segment is to provide portions of a limited

resource to consumers on an as-needed basis. The more information about the point of need they can get, the better they are able to plan and construct the necessary infrastructure.

- **Retail:** The fundamental that service retail stores provide is the end distribution of relatively unlimited resources: commercial products. Retailers act as a storage buffer, ideally never running out of product but also not carrying more than will be sold. Retail efficiencies are optimized by having as much information as possible about physical inventories and sales projections. For some product categories, the projections may shift depending on physical conditions such as weather and time. Shoppers also encounter interesting information problems as they explore and select products. We explore these in more depth in Chapter 11, "Clear Sailing."

- **Healthcare:** This is a large segment with a variety of subindustries whose characteristics are covered by previously described segments. The pharmaceuticals subcategory has similar characteristics to the manufacturing of goods. Hospital facilities and managed care are similar to the hotel and restaurant categories. A unique aspect of healthcare, though, is at the point of direct care, where medical staff examine and treat patients. Testing and examination requires probing and recording physical characteristics of the patient. Ubiquitous networks and devices make it possible to do some testing and monitoring at home and elsewhere, rather than at a medical facility.

Deliberate Transformation

I've seen the following kinds of business strategies work well in the past for commercialization of Ubiquitous Computing technologies. Other strategies may also succeed, but these are the ones that have demonstrated success:

- Capture new value by changing position in your industry's value chain
- Increase the value of your product with digital interfaces to its services
- Increase value by personalizing content

- Decrease operating costs and increase productivity through enhanced internal operating efficiencies
- Create new markets via blue-ocean opportunities

These kinds of successes can be realized through means other than Ubiquitous Computing technologies, but those technologies do provide some unique and novel capabilities that make it easier to succeed by investing in Ubiquitous Computing; you'll see this in the case studies included for each approach. These broad directions do not necessarily apply to all businesses, so those of you with deeper knowledge of the processes and technologies in your own industry must decide whether and how to apply these patterns to your industry.

In this book, I primarily focus on identifying technology solutions that can be incorporated into a product or service, or that can be spun into whole new business opportunities. A successful business needs more than just a technology, however; success involves interweaving many capabilities, including marketing, distribution, and customer service. Because most of those elements are not needed until there is a product (or service) to offer, we start by looking primarily at ways to identify and develop the offerings within each of these strategies. The following chapters describe case studies of problems in particular industries and the application of Ubiquitous Computing paradigms to create new business opportunities.

Summary

Creating a strategy means making choices about what you will and will not do to be different. A strategic choice to innovate in Ubiquitous Computing requires investing in technology invention. The conventional model of a pipeline of invention leading to business is flawed because it is largely based on the idea of creating an invention first and then finding the business. This approach has yielded an occasional success, but success is more common when invention is coupled with business need, and product is coupled with revenue as a central aim.

This chapter described the current and projected impact of the new wave of Ubicomp technologies and services on major industries, including finance, insurance, media publishing, manufacturing, energy and utilities, hotels and restaurants, airlines and transportation, telecommunications, retail, and healthcare. Almost all major industries are affected in some aspect of their operation, whether in how they acquire material, operate internally, or interact with customers. The impact is greater for industries that connect to physical elements in one or more aspect than for those that mainly manipulate information.

Endnotes

[1] Keith H. Hammonds, "Michael Porter's Big Ideas," *Fast Company* 44 (28 February 2001): 150–156.

[2] In fact, some governments fund research to foster new business as well.

[3] See www.parc.com/about/milestones.html.

7

The Soft Sell: Personalized Marketing

> *Because the purpose of business is to create a customer, the business enterprise has two—and only two—basic functions: marketing and innovation. Marketing and innovation produce results; all the rest are costs.*
> —Peter Drucker, *Management: Tasks, Responsibilities, Practices*[1]

In my teens, my family drove on the Blue Ridge Highway in the Appalachian Mountains to visit my grandparents in North Carolina. The repetition of curves in the winding roads and the vivid fall colors of the trees would put me in a trance ... only to be shattered by the sight of a billboard reminding me that good eats could be found off exit 81 just 3.2 miles ahead! Curse those who would despoil nature! For centuries, marketers have deliberately found times to crassly grab our attention for profit. Why would anyone want to encourage the increasing pervasiveness of such disruptions?

Some marketing campaigns, however, are more subtle, fitting the messages into the environment, into the rhythm of life. On those grand road trips, the incremental display of signs for Burma-Shave shaving cream on the side of the road delighted travelers: A peach / Looks good / With lots of fuzz / But man's no peach / And never wuz / Burma-Shave.[2] The sequential presentation of the slogans fit the rhythmic monotony of the roads instead of jolting the mind with information. The amusing wordplay tickled the mind instead of triggering a jarring disruption. The brand successfully raised awareness without raising consumer resistance. Since then, we've seen more sophisticated means of associating a product with a lifestyle and integrating marketing seamlessly into items that draw our attention.

In some ways, advertisements are providing information that can actually benefit consumers: They make consumers aware of product options, show solutions to major and minor problems and inconveniences, describe evaluation criteria, compare the features of their products against others, point out when competitors are misleading consumers, and are *sometimes* entertaining.

Yet advertising is widely despised. A *New York Times* article in April 2004[3] reported the results of a survey by market research firm Yankelovich, in which 65% of respondents stated that they "are constantly bombarded with too much" advertising and 69% said they "are interested in products and services that would help them *skip* or *block* marketing" (emphasis added).

If advertising is a form of communication, providing at least *some* beneficial information to consumers, why does the majority of the population hold it in contempt? The Yankelovich survey sheds some light. Fifty-four percent of respondents stated they "avoid buying products that overwhelm them with advertising and marketing;" 61% agreed that the amount of advertising and marketing to which they are exposed "is out of control." These answers suggest a diagnosis of information overload.

In spite of the examples of advertising done well, the very mention of *advertising* makes most people cringe as they recall the many times it is done poorly. In fact, most ads seem to miss the mark so widely that it makes you wonder why more than $125 billion dollars was spent on advertising in 2009.[4]

Why Do Advertisers Keep Pestering Us?

Given such negative impressions, why do advertisers continuously subject us to "overwhelming" and "out-of-control" advertising? In 2006, Jim Morris, then Dean of Carnegie Mellon's campus in Silicon Valley, gave a talk at PARC called "Advertising is Flirtation"[5] that clarified some of the mystery. Even when ads are irritating, there can be positive economic results. Look at it from an economist's perspective. Economists are neutral on whether any particular individual person or company comes out ahead, as long as the aggregate value to society increases. Some categories can show losses, but as long as the net gains outweigh the losses, we're increasing the economic value of our society.

Think of advertising at the economic level, which is counting the aggregation of business transactions. The sender of an advertisement gains value if more products are sold. The receiver gains value if he or she learns about something that would be useful and relevant, perhaps learning about products that are cheaper or higher quality than what he or she already knows. That's a win-win scenario!

But the win-win scenario is oh-so-rare. More often, ads inform us of things we already know of or are not interested in. By the cold calculus of economics, however, even when many individuals are irritated, if a few more are informed of benefits that lead to an increase in the aggregate number of product purchases, the net value of the advertising campaign is positive. That's the case for those jarring roadside billboards—they are irritating to most people who see them, but some number of drivers wouldn't otherwise know of the existence of some of those gas stations, restaurants, and outlet stores. Despite having annoyed a large number of people, the economic value is a net positive, indicated by the shaded regions of Figure 7-1. Based on the nearly universal dislike of advertising among consumers, I would surmise that the large majority of advertising falls into this net positive category. There's little negative *economic* impact to being irritating, and even negative publicity is good publicity from the marketer's perspective.

Despite evidence to the contrary, marketers are humans, too. For the most part, they'd all prefer to be developing win-win material. They want to send information that is both highly *relevant* and highly *useful* to people. Relevance is the degree to which information is *related* to the receiver's interests, needs, or objectives. Usefulness is the degree to which such information *satisfies* a desire or need. Of course, these definitions are vague and imprecise, but we generally acknowledge a sense that things can be relatively *more* or *less* relevant and useful. Marketers would like to make ads better, but until recently, they've had little information to help determine relevance or usefulness to a particular individual at a particular time, so they resort to scattershot methods and hope enough eyes land on something they like to offset the cost of irritating others.

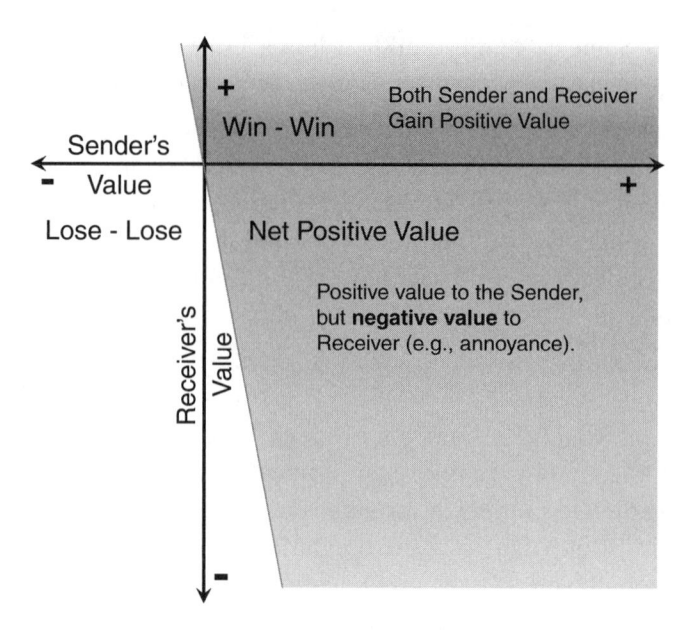

Figure 7-1 Advertising has net positive value, but largely at the cost of irritating prospective customers.

Scattershot methods are not entirely aimless. Ads can be bundled alongside content on the same topic, as done in magazines. We can assume that the topic of the content is at least *relevant* to someone who takes the time to read it and that ads on the topic that a person reads will be more relevant to that person than ads on other topics. We still don't know how *useful* the ads are to the person in the moment. Is there any utility in learning about a hair care product while reading a magazine? It's hard to tell.

Then there's search-based advertising, which bundles ads on the same topic as the results of a *keyword query* entered into the search engine. We can assume that providing information on the topic would be more useful in this moment than at moments when the person is *not* searching for information. Search-based advertising is really a panacea—people are not only *explicitly* stating the topic they want information about, but they are also telling the system that they want to receive the information at that moment. Search-based advertising has increased relevance and usefulness over conventional content-bundled advertising. That's the secret to online search advertising's success.

Similarly, annoying billboards are effective because *some* of those people passing by on road trips *do* need to refuel their vehicles and their bodies. Not everyone looking out the car window is a passenger merely looking at the trees—some of those people are looking for a good place for a pit stop.

Getting to Win-Win

In addition to search query targeting, Internet users provide additional information about things that are relevant to them simply by following links on the web. Each time a person clicks a link in a web page, that person is indicating at least mild interest in the topic of that page. By tracking these streams of clicks, demographic and psychographic algorithms can classify the categories that matter to groups or individuals. Google, Yahoo!, and several other services offer these kinds of analytics to advertisers by tracking "cookies" placed on web pages that display advertisements brokered by them.[6] These techniques push more of the economic value of advertising into the win-win quadrant, as seen in Figure 7-2.

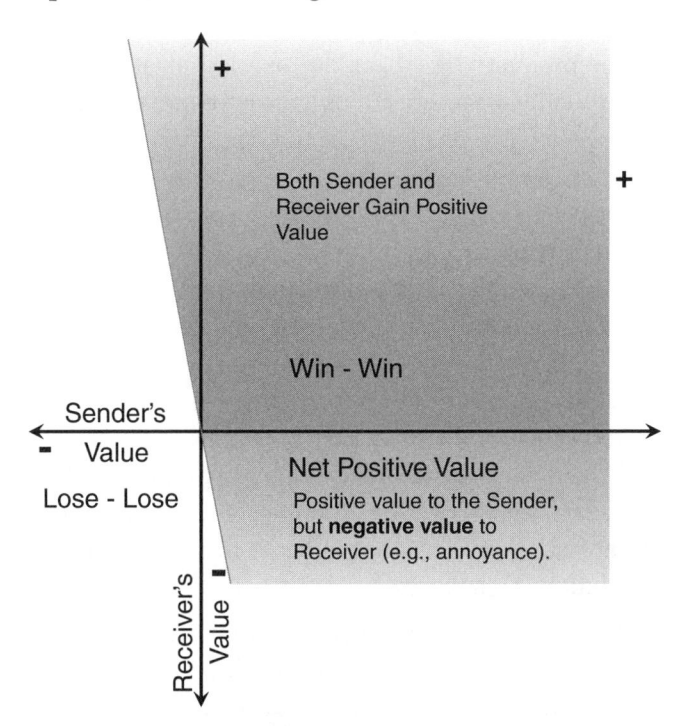

Figure 7-2 If targeting is effective, the number of ads that are of positive value to the receiver increases.

Personalized targeting not only reduces irritation to consumers, but it also increases the effectiveness of advertisement to businesses. In a survey conducted for the Search Engine Marketing Professional Organization and released in February 2009,[7] 75% of advertisers reported that they would be willing to spend 13% more, on average, for behaviorally targeted advertisements. Another agency, eMarketer, projects near-exponential growth in behaviorally targeted online advertising, from $775 million in 2008 to $4.4 billion by 2012. Personally, I'll be surprised if the revenue is not higher than that by 2012.

How does it work? The approach has many variations, but most boil down to two fundamental techniques by detecting either similarity between the characteristics of the *items* that a person likes (called characteristic-based filtering) or similarity between people (called collaborative filtering).

Characteristic-based Filtering

Characteristic-based recommendation systems use the scores you have provided to products and calculate the likely score you would give to other products based on the overlap of attributes such as price, color, functional specifications, genre, year of creation, artist(s), and other aspects. The challenge in this approach is identifying the aspects that *matter* to customers (do people care more about coffeemakers' capacities or programmability?) and how to calculate the differences in aspects among products (for example, red is closer on the color wheel to orange but is also similar to blue, in that red and blue are both "primary" colors). As you can imagine, these assessments are *very* subjective and idiosyncratic—theoretically, there may be a rationale for each customer's subjective opinion, but it is difficult to discern. Another problem is that many products are purchased infrequently, and their attributes do not correspond to attributes in another product category (for example, my preference for coffeemaker capacity (low) does not indicate my preference for digital camera resolution (high)).

In characteristic-based filtering, each item is described by a set of attributes (referred to as "features" to the algorithmically inclined) or metadata about the item. The characteristics included in the feature set vary depending on the type of item and how it is typically evaluated. Movies, music, and books typically use features such as price, genre, artist, author, director, date, and so on. For digital cameras, the feature set includes price, resolution, zoom range, light sensitivity, size, and so on. You can even use these techniques to help filter electronic documents, news, or web pages using features such as title, date, author, topics, length, frequency, recency of access, and more. These kinds of features can be specified as the item is entered into a database, or they can sometimes be extracted by analyzing the item (for example, topics of a web page can be extracted using linguistic analysis).

Another feature can be the ratings others have given to the item, which users of a service such as Netflix and Yelp can explicitly specify, or the rating can be inferred through implicit indicators of popularity, such as frequency of clicks on a link or number of in-links to a web site (for example, Google page rank).

The next step in characteristic-based filtering is to measure how close each feature is to the optimal value of that feature to the user. That's the hard part—knowing what will matter to an individual. Characteristic-based filtering is fairly effective when most people generally agree on the features that matter most (for example, in electronics, this is usually cheaper price, smaller size, faster speed, and more features), when an item is generally popular (for example, Harry Potter books, the *Titanic* movie), or when there are a small number of items whose features are far "higher" than those of most items in that class (for instance, currently Wikipedia entries have higher page ranks for reference material than other reference sites).

Collaborative Filtering

Collaborative filtering takes a slightly indirect approach that avoids having to understand the rationale for customers' subjective opinions. Marketers know that people who have liked the same things in the past will probably have similar likes in the future. Marketers categorize groups of customers with similar preferences into market segments. The collaborative filtering technique was invented at PARC in the early 1990s[8] to automatically identify groups of people with similar preferences, without necessarily understanding the cause of those preferences. The original algorithm was designed to reduce the explosion of emails that the researchers were having to read (even in 1992, email was overwhelming people), and it turned out to have other commercial applications. The basic idea is to identify groups of people who have rated items similarly. In essence, this is what market demographics is all about. Instead of using just coarse indicators such as gender, zip code or age, however, collaborative filtering uses people's actual selections to identify the groups with similar tastes. Then for each group, it sees what items some members have rated highly but that others in the group might not have seen, and recommends those items.

Characteristic-based filtering is less effective when a person's overall satisfaction is derived from an ambiguous combination of perceptual factors, such as artistic quality, richness of color, depth of analysis, style, or social appropriateness. Such things strike people differently. Demographic attributes such as age, gender, cultural ethnicity, and others provide some coarse-grained segmentation. However, demographics provide only a *superficial* description of a person's interests; age, race, and gender are factors over which we have no personal choice. Savvy marketers have long ago switched from simple demographic segmentation to more *psychographic* segments based on lifestyle (including access to financial resources), political preferences, religious affiliation, and other personal choices. The Nielsen Company has created a list of 66 distinct market "segments" that group people of similar likes, lifestyles, and purchase behaviors. Introduced in 1976 and updated periodically, Nielsen's PRIZM list contains groupings with descriptive names such as "Young Digerati," "Kids & Cul-de-Sacs," "Traditional Times," and "Crossroads Villagers" that categorize the breadth of lifestyles in the United States. These categories are compared against purchase data to help marketers identify which segments will have greater or lesser affinity for their products. For the most part, membership in a PRIZM segment is determined by six demographic and geographic features: age, income, presence of children, marital status, homeownership, and urbanicity. Nielsen maps these segments to regions at least as small as zip code—sometimes smaller.

This kind of lifestyle-based segmentation can help target products with ambiguous, intangible characteristics such as style, artistic quality, and perhaps even political tendencies. Direct-mail marketers have been using PRIZM and other data sets like it for decades; however, because they are constructed largely by demographic characteristics over which people have little direct choice, the magnitude of preferences within the segments is slight—leading most direct mail to go directly into the waste bin. Although people living in a neighborhood may share generally similar leanings, their specific tastes can differ widely when selecting specific movies, books, music, or clothing. They may have individual health characteristics that influence their choices, along with many other idiosyncratic traits that are not easily categorized by demographic characteristics or geographic segments.

Geographic segmentation served well in the era of print newspapers and direct mailings, but our access to information is no longer constrained by our postal codes. More sophisticated techniques are called for. The main idea behind collaborative filtering is that people who have purchased the same items in the past (or read the same email messages in a similar order) will make similar purchases (or selections) in the future. (The name *collaborative filtering* comes from the idea that the people are working together unknowingly to identify the importance of items.) Groups are formed by identifying people who have purchased the same item (made the same rating) and may be supplemented with other factors, such as recency and frequency. When people in a group are observed to buy an item, the system can recommend that item to others in the group who have not yet purchased it (or who have not yet read the article). Other than the identity of each item, the system doesn't necessarily need to examine any attribute of the items. Catalina Marketing and other companies use this technique to manage customer loyalty programs.

Collaborative filtering techniques offer many advantages over traditional demographic clustering methods. First, members of a group can reside in widely separated geographies. Second, people can belong to different groups for independent product categories (books, cars, electronics, and clothing). Third, groups can be of any size, from two to thousands or more. Finally, the descriptive name of each group is immaterial. It doesn't matter whether you can determine the characteristics that drive members of a group to have a certain preference; all that matters is that the preference is robust and repeated. This allows dynamic and flexible identification of buyer segments.

As you might expect, combining collaborative and characteristic-based filtering techniques is common and leverages the strengths of each one. When the system does have metadata describing characteristics of the items, a characteristic-based filter can suggest items that are "close" to items purchased by members of a group. Similarly, groups can be created from observing purchase patterns of items that have overlapping characteristics.

Both techniques require examining a record of prior selections by people. E-commerce makes this easy because merchants can examine the purchase records of individual customers. In theory, physical merchants could record such information to better serve their customers—we hear anecdotes of *haute couture* designers, high-end suit tailors and hoteliers who do indeed maintain awareness of their individual customers' tastes. However, physical merchants have a more difficult time tracking individual purchase behaviors because a customer in a retail store doesn't have to create a user account and can pay in anonymous cash to check out.

Sizing Up with Sensors

Top salespeople have long known that the key to success is knowing your customer. From the moment a prospective customer appears in a store, a good salesperson tries to identify likely preferences and spending. Some explicitly ask questions, perhaps reading between the lines of the customer's response to gather deeper insight. Even before they interact, though, a salesperson does his or her best to "size up" a customer based simply on how the person looks and behaves.

Some physical characteristics are obviously useful filters for some product categories, such as gender for clothes, whereas others are less telling. No single clue tells the whole story, and putting these clues together to form a reliable picture requires long experience in connecting dots. A wise salesperson also knows that appearances can be deceiving and seeks more information to avoid mishandling a prospective customer. There is a risk of jumping to the wrong conclusion when you judge a book *solely* by its cover, but you have no choice other than to *start* with the cover and then probe more deeply.

Customer-profiling practices are common for high-end products and services such as *haute couture* fashion and high-end hotels.[9] These are businesses with high margins and "high-touch" personalized sales processes that help preserve the margins. Currently, this kind of personalization can be provided only by humans, who can perceive and combine subtle clues and who can quickly adjust as they learn new details about the customer's needs. Computers are notoriously inept at handling these kinds of ambiguous interactions—but they are getting better, and as they improve, the labor cost needed to infer and provide personalized sales is coming down.

Computer vision technologies already exist for recognizing anatomical demographics of shoppers, such as age range, gender, and even race. A research group at the National University of Singapore recently demonstrated an advertising system that adjusted its content in real time depending on the age and gender demographics in the audience.[10] Actually, this cat was let out of the research bag several years ago and there are now several products available on the market that can detect audience demographics and adjust media content in real-time such as Samsung's PROM[11] and NEC's Eye Flavor.[12]

A person's anatomical attributes are only a superficial indication of preferences because physical demographics are beyond our personal control. I can't do anything to change my age, gender, or race (well, not much anyway). More telling of people's internal preferences are the clothes they wear and the behaviors they exhibit. These are visible attributes that people have direct control over and use to express internal characteristics. Even when we intend our clothing to be innocuous and unexpressive, the colors, fabrics, accessories, and how we wear garments (for example, tucked in or out) can tell a lot about our personal standards of "normal."

Recent advances in computer vision indicate that even amorphous problems such as categorizing clothing styles are within reach of technologies over the next few years. For example, in a project at PARC, we designed vision algorithms that could differentiate among four types of men's shirts: T-shirt, polo shirt, casual shirt and business shirt. To characterize men's shirts, we used the following attributes: color, pattern complexity, collar shape (crew, v-neck, pointed collar), emblem presence and placement (large design across the shirt versus small design over one breast), sleeve length, and button placket length (full, half, or none). Combining these, we saw correct classification across all four classes of 72.7%, nearly three times better than chance (25%), and between T-shirts and business shirts with 95.7% accuracy.[13]

Recognizing men's shirt categories is simple compared to the variety of women's tops. Women's fashions are far more varied and will require several years of research to detect the factors that indicate general preferences and that can adjust for cultural changes in tastes over time. The shirt you wear doesn't tell much of your story, though, and a complete solution that adjusts as it learns more about you is further off. Recognizing clothes is just barely scratching the surface of what computers might eventually perceive. Yet even this relatively simple recognition can give merchants an initial indication of how much a customer might be willing to spend, depending on the product and other contextual factors. For example, will the customer wearing a business shirt spend as much in a skateboard store as the one wearing the T-shirt? What about for a sports coat? The point to take away is that reading and assessing such subtle cues is no longer solely a human capability: It is within the reach of computer vision today and will increase in the near future.

Visual Recognition Techniques

Recognition problems can be approached in a number of ways, generally falling into two categories: structured recognition and statistically learned classification. In the first approach, the system parses the structure of a scene and uses the elements to identify the meaning. For example, if you wanted to recognize windows on houses, the system could search for straight lines forming parallelograms as candidates for "window" and then use further differentiating details to improve the accuracy. Structured recognition works well for consistently formed objects such as a window and extends to some fairly complex structures such as insects.[14] On the other hand, some objects, such as people and animals, are highly deformable which makes it difficult to identify distinct elements (other than faces—despite the wide range of expressions, a face is fairly easy to detect because of the relative consistency of the placement of eyes, nose, and mouth).

For some cases, a statistically learned recognition technique is used, in which many samples are fed to a computer that extracts the statistical correlation between features of the images (colors, shapes) and the classes to recognize. This kind of technique has achieved accuracies as high as 83% to distinguish between images of cats and dogs, which is much harder for a simple-minded computer than it is for humans because of the differences between breeds within each species (for example, Siamese versus Persian cats, and Bulldogs versus Collie) and the similarity of some features across species (for instance, fur colors are similar across cats and dogs, and some dogs' ears are shaped like cats').

In both structured recognition and statistically learned classification, it is possible to calculate a "similarity" distance between items. However, in structured recognition, the attributes of similarity are generally easier for human comprehension than the attributes of similarity in statistically learned classifiers. For example, a structured recognizer might score a Chihuahua dog as similar to a cat because a Chihuahua's ears have a similar shape to cats' ears—an understandable mistake (do an image search right now for "Skippyjon Jones" to see what I mean). On the other hand, a statistically learned classifier might have "learned" that images of cats are most often sitting, whereas dogs are more often standing on all fours, which would lead to images of cats that happen to be standing on all fours being considered more similar to dogs. While the shape of a Chihuahua's ears is an easy mistake to understand, the computer's rationale of rating standing cats as dogs may not be easily understood.

Which technique is best? Statistically learned classifiers are easier to construct *if* you have a large set of sample images to learn from. If not, you need to spend resources to gather and manually identify a sample set. Structured recognition also requires resources to construct and test the scene-parsing techniques and is viable only if the images are of relatively nondeformed objects or when the deformations are well understood (for example, an eye may be opened or closed). In general practice, combinations of both techniques are employed. However, if you want to be able to have humans interact with the recognition algorithm, the attributes of the recognition must be understandable. For applications that browse similar products, parsed recognition is more useful. For applications that detect the presence of flawed parts coming off a manufacturing line, a statistically learned classifier suffices.

Pervasive Advertising

Ubiquitous computing technologies allow us to take things to an even deeper level of relevance and usefulness by gaining insight into more aspects of a person's preferences and appropriate timing of information. Mobile phones contain location-tracking technologies, images from cameras can be analyzed to interpret behavior information, and a wide array of other sensors (motion sensors, audio, pressure, and so on) can be employed to detect fine-grained details of a person's lifestyle and preferences.

An article by John Krumm suggests, with some lament, that advertising may well be "the killer app" of Ubiquitous Computing.[15] He describes four ways that combinations of context-awareness, indoor location sensing, and privacy-controlling technologies can help advertisers: targeting, feedback, knowing the customer, and privacy. Let's look at the state of digital advertising today and its likely future, supplemented by Ubicomp technologies.

Pervasive Advertising Today

Mobile advertising is a relatively recent subcategory in the advertising industry and is growing fast. In June 2009, Gartner Research[16] projected spending in mobile advertising to go from less than $1 billion in 2009 to more than $13 billion by the end of 2013. This is largely driven by the increasing adoption of smartphone platforms, which have power and displays that enable rich presentation of media, along with sensors (GPS, sound, light, and so on) that can determine the location and situation of the person using the phone. That latter set of capabilities is enabling revolutionary changes in advertising presentations. Mobile advertising is expected to heat up big in 2011 as advertisers adopt broad-based digital advertising strategies.

That broad-based digital advertising strategy will go far beyond mobile devices. Digital out-of-home (OOH) advertising is another subcategory whose growth is outpacing the overall growth in the advertising industry. This category includes video advertising networks, digital billboards, and other forms of "ambient" digital advertisement. Industry analysts[17] project between 9% and 20% compound annual growth rate (CAGR), compared to 1% to 2%

CAGR for nondigital OOH advertisement. Digital OOH is still a small portion of advertising spending, projected to reach roughly $4.6 billion in the United States by 2013, but digital OOH will likely capture a larger share of spending than conventional OOH.

Pervasive Advertising in the Future

In May 2009, colleagues and I organized the first research workshop on pervasive advertising,[18] which we held in Nara, Japan (lovely place, do go), in conjunction with the 2009 conference on Pervasive Computing. This workshop brought together only a handful of the highly inventive minds developing new ways of understanding needs, timing, and relevance of product information, along with novel techniques of presentation. This research field is mostly led by European academic and industry laboratories, with only a few representatives from U.S. industry labs and no U.S. academic institutions. As I've mentioned previously, the European Union fosters Ubiquitous Computing as a field of research and invention more than the United States does.

Since that initial meeting, our pervasive advertising community has held two more workshops and published a collection of research and visions in a book.[19] Our aim each time is to envision advertising 25 years in the future and identify the technological and social challenges that need to be addressed to achieve the visions. Researchers present prototypes of a number of novel advertising technologies, including: interactive dynamic displays that modify information based on the emotional reactions, cognitive state, and body movements of individuals and groups looking at the display; community bulletin boards that allow people to post messages as easily as stapling a flyer today; computationally generated aesthetic designs; user-generated advertising; use of scents in the environment; results of various layout algorithms for mobile displays; novel ways to "blend" advertisements with media consumption; new techniques to infer personal preferences while ensuring privacy of personal information; coupon distribution and automated redemption; new mobile billing schemes; sensor infrastructures; new technologies for audience metrics; electronic advertisements worn on clothing; results of eye-tracking studies; and our own work at PARC on inferring the activities of people to identify personal interests and optimal times to present information. We all presented early prototypes of the technologies, but even these unrefined systems demonstrate the coming age of personalized and nondisruptive advertising in the environment.

A recurring discussion among the researchers was the idea that individuals may become walking advertisements for the products they wear or use. We're talking far more than just showing the designer logo on your handbag, though. The following scenario illustrates the concept.

Imagine the year 2035:

> After work, Sabine and Monica walk out to their personal vehicles.
>
> Monica shows Sabine that she just downloaded the Danica Patrick street performance tuning package for her GTO Nouveau, and it sounds *much* cooler than the high-pitched *whoosh* these gravity-powered vehicles normally emit! Sabine also loves the "retro" sound of a combustion engine, and she gets a copy of the tuning package for her roadster.
>
> As a registered broker of the Personal Transport Vendors of Northern Hemisphere, Monica's e-money account gets credited with a portion of the proceeds from Sabine's purchase. Monica can use the funds in this account only for vehicle-related products from members of the PTVNH brokerage. Monica has to manage a multitude of brokering accounts in various product categories to get everything she needs. Fortunately, her digital accountant manages the complexity and advises Monica on how to maintain a healthy portfolio.
>
> On the weekend, Sabine goes out with her family for a bike ride. At a rest stop, Sabine's bicycle suggests she look at the bike she's parked next to because it has tires that would fit Sabine's riding style better than her current tires (Sabine has an off-road bicycle but actually rides most often on trails and roads, so street tires would be better). Sabine looks at the other tires and her system adds them to her online "wish list." Later, when Sabine buys those tires, the owner of the other bicycle gets a cut of the profit as a member of that tire company's broker consortium.

What's So Hard? Is There Really Anything to Invent?

The brokering system is a complex but already feasible account-tracking system, so not much is needed to invent technologies for that part of the scenario. In addition, the underlying system keeps a record of Sabine's activities and the items that she encounters during the day, which allows her to look back in the record of a day to see items she encountered that might be of value to her. Again, this may have scalability issues, but it doesn't require fundamental new inventions.

More invention is needed to create the *user preference model,* however. The hypothetical system does the following:

- Continually updates the model of Sabine's preferences based on the items Sabine actually expresses interest in
- Understands that Sabine sometimes shops for other people (for her kids and for friends and family)
- Detects when it has been more or less successful in timing the presentation of information, determining whether to tell Sabine about products at times when she is likely to be more interested in the information (such as *after* the tennis game, not *during* a serve)
- Detects Sabine's points of decision—that is, the moments in time when she is considering whether she will make a purchase

When the preference model does not already have information that a seller would want to know about, the advertisers can submit queries to her model that process the information without exposing Sabine's personal information to unwanted scrutiny. For example, suppose that the system was not monitoring Sabine's bicycle riding style, but it does have records of all her prior rides. An advertiser could submit a query to her model that would execute a function to classify her riding style without exposing all the location details of her prior rides. This kind of secure query is not yet practical, but some theoretical progress has been made in the field of private information retrieval.

Activity-Targeted Advertising

Few of the workshop attendees actually believe it will take 25 years to realize the technologies in the previous scenario—with the exception of gravity-powered vehicles. User profile modeling and activity detection are already well established in web-based marketing, so it's just a matter of applying similar techniques with physical activity collected by Ubicomp technologies and sensors. Since 2000, researchers in the field of Ubiquitous Computing have been inventing algorithms that combine information from a variety of sensors to determine modes of transportation (walking, biking, running, traveling by train, driving, and so on), mechanical actions (hammering, using a screwdriver, and so on), activities of daily living (making meals, using the bathroom, and so on), office-work activities, and temporal patterns (presence and availability at different times of day). None of these techniques are as accurate as humans at sensing activities, but they could theoretically determine at least a subset of the activities that matter to a person. Before we dive too deeply into inventing technologies that detect activities and couple advertisements to that, we need to determine whether there is any value in doing it.

Intuitively, there should be value in marketing according to the activities people engage in. Just as content-bundled ads are effective because people are interested in things that they read, activity-based ads would be valuable because people are interested in the work they do, the sports they play, the types of places they frequent, and the hobbies they enjoy. Furthermore, just as part of search-based ads' effectiveness is due to a searcher being in a mode to receive information, activity detection can infer times when people are more receptive to receiving information or when they are too busy to be bothered. In addition, location-based behavior tracking could even anticipate future opportunities for acting on a received advertisement and optimize the timing of the presentation before you go to the store.

From such intuitions, we can imagine that activity-based advertising *might* enhance the results of search-based advertising by adding personal activity to the customer profile, but search-based advertising already performs far better than previous advertising models (such as bundling ads with content), so why add even more complexity to advertising systems? Here's why: You can reach customers even *before* they are aware that they have an interest in a product and *before* they go to a search service. That is, advertisers can reach people who have a latent, unexpressed need for a product or service category, reaching them *before they've already made a decision* of what to purchase. This is an unreached market today, with "blue ocean" opportunities for growth.

"Effective Advertising": An Oxymoron

Let's look a little more deeply into the effectiveness of advertising. Two kinds of advertising exist: awareness raising and transactional advertising. Before the web, most advertising was to raise customer awareness of the existence of a product, in hopes that when customers were later in need of that product category, the advertised brand would come to their mind and they would seek it out. This kind of advertising is commonly referred to as brand awareness. The second type attempts to drive the consumer to make a purchase, send for more information, or take some other action, which is referred to as transactional advertising. Coupons fall into this bucket, as do television advertisements for products that you call a number to buy (self-sharpening knives and the like).

Merchants have long known that advertising is inexact and immeasurable. John Wanamaker, the early department store merchant of the late 1800s and early 1900s, is famously quoted for saying, "Half the money I spend on advertising is wasted; the trouble is, I don't know which half." Until recently, it was nearly impossible to actually measure the effectiveness of brand awareness advertisements directly because there was no way to track which, when, and how many times brand advertisements were seen prior to purchases. The effectiveness of transactional ads is more tractable because merchants can track the number of "conversions" (sales or actions) that occur immediately after the ad campaign. Even that is not straightforward, however, as multiple campaigns may be ongoing and it's not clear whether a coupon actually compelled the shopper to make the purchase or whether that person might have made that purchase even without the coupon.

Web-based advertising has changed that and turned the advertising industry on its head. With web metrics, merchants can tell *exactly* how effective a specific ad was by how many users "click through" for more information and, of those, how many result in a "conversion" to take an action. From this, advertisers now know that the vast majority of advertisements, far more than Wanamaker's "half," are wasted. Finding hard numbers for the click-through rate of search advertisements is difficult, in part because it varies according to industry and keywords. The estimates I've seen on the web range from 1% to 25%, with an average of 3–4%.[20] The click-through rates for Internet "banner ads" are as low as 0.28%, in one report.[21]

Those are the hard numbers for the effectiveness of transaction-based advertising, but brand advertising has yet to be measured because too much time passes between seeing brand advertisements and getting to the point of purchase. Brand advertising is *thought* to be effective because established brands continue to be popular even in product categories where switching is easy, such as soaps, sodas, or search engines. One theory for this is the idea that by reminding people of a brand with enough frequency, it will stay on their mind until their next purchase of that product category.[22] Because it is impossible for merchants to detect when you will next make a purchase, they have to flood the environment with reminders.

Theoretical Effectiveness of Activity-Based Advertising

The goal of the marketer is to find customers "in the market" for a product or service and trigger them to take action. Two key elements affect the effectiveness of advertising.

Open demand exists when a consumer is "in the market" *and* is "open" to suggestions of which products and services to buy. That is, the consumer doesn't already know everything about a product and won't be as irritated by an advertisement.

Consumers with open demand are the valuable targets for an advertiser.

Actionable receptivity is the state of mind when the consumer is *both* willing to receive an offer *and* able to take action upon receiving the offer.

Receiving an offer when the consumer is actionably receptive means that the offer has more potential to influence the consumer's buying decision and compel him or her to act.

Three specific aspects of online search-based advertising are critical to its success:

- Users *tell* the system what they are interested in by entering keywords. Thirty to forty percent of instances of search are to find product alternatives, in which case users are even telling the system that they have not yet made up their mind about what to buy. This is a clear indication of open demand.
- Users express the desire to be given information by virtue of using a search tool. Consumers searching for information have gone past receptive and are actively *seeking* product information.
- The information is *actionable* at that moment. In contrast to ads in traditional media (paper, magazines, billboards, radio, television), online commerce makes it possible for the person to take an action (make a purchase) right then and there.

Activity-based advertising utilizing Ubicomp technologies can also provide these three characteristics:

- People are interested in products related to the things they do. In some cases, the system can detect that a person is undecided about a product, such as when prospective home buyers visit open houses or newcomers to a city need to find restaurants they like.
- Systems can detect circumstances in which a person is more *receptive* to information (such as when waiting in line, leaving work, going out for lunch, and so on) and also circumstances in which a person is probably *not* receptive to information (such as being in a conversation, driving, running late, and so on).
- Systems can hold information until it is most *actionable*, such as when the person is near a store that carries the product. Systems can also filter the advertised product categories to fit the estimated amount of time the person has available. Buying a drink would be quick, but if there is enough time, higher-involvement product categories, such as birthday gifts, can be suggested.

Testing Technology before It Exists

Activity-targeted advertising *should* be effective theoretically, but we don't know for sure. Targeting marketing information to personal activity has no precedent in the advertising industry, so it bears validation before investing too much research and development.

How can we test the value of an intelligent system that has not yet been fully realized? For inspiration, we can borrow the magic used by the Wizard of Oz: Fake it. Instead of investing a great deal of technical resources to prototype an activity-detection system, colleagues at PARC installed software on a smartphone that periodically *asked* the user, "What are you doing now?" You can't expect people to answer such a question in real use, but for purposes of experimentation, we found coworkers who were willing to live with this PEST (Proactive Experience Sampling Tool) for three days. We saw answers such as "catching up on some school work," "talking to Mom," and "waiting in line." We sent each of these responses to Amazon's Mechanical Turk, where online "turkers" do small pieces of work for small amounts of money. This service provides a way to *simulate* artificial intelligence before it has been developed (*artificial* artificial intelligence, as Amazon puts it). The turkers proposed products or services that would be used along with the stated activity. The PEST user was then presented with either a randomly selected ad or an ad matched to the activity-based product recommended by the turkers. We asked the PEST users to rate the usefulness and relevance of the ad on a scale and compared the user ratings for activity-based ads against randomly selected ads. Figure 7-3 shows the results. Activity-targeted advertisements were significantly *more relevant* than random advertisements over all types of activity that PEST users reported. However, they were not necessarily more useful, indicating that the information did not necessarily arrive at actionable moments.

When we segmented the activities into different types (see Figure 7-4), activity-targeted advertisements were considered *more useful* in activities other than work-related or communication-related activities. This may be because the user was engaged in work or communication when interrupted by PEST. Users' cognitive and sensory availability affects their perception of how well they can make use of an advertisement. For context-aware advertisements to be effectively

7 • The Soft Sell: Personalized Marketing

relevant and useful, collecting contextual data is not enough—the data must be synthesized into an activity and used to determine both advertising relevance (what) and user receptivity (when).

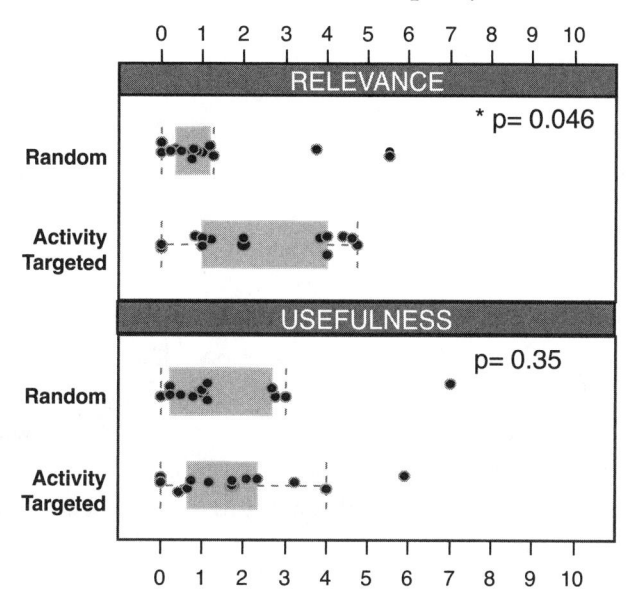

Figure 7-3 Activity-targeted ads were significantly more relevant than randomly targeted ads over all activity types, but not necessarily more useful. (Figure credit: Kurt Partridge)

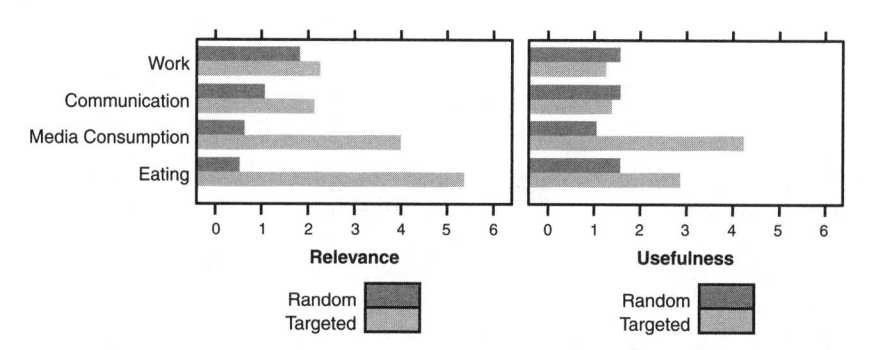

Figure 7-4 Activity-targeted ads are more useful than random ads for activities except when the user is engaged in work or communication. (Figure credit: Kurt Partridge)

Summary

An obvious application of personalization is in helping marketers connect to customers. We explored futuristic visions of activity-based marketing based on wide-spread Ubiquitous Computing technologies.

We also explored more near-term applications of activity-based advertising based on smartphone technologies. Activity detection provides capabilities that make it potentially as effective as search-based advertising. The first key to search-based advertising is that users enter information into the system about what they want. With activity detection, the system can detect a person's latent need for some product or service category based on what that person does. The second fundamental advantage of search-based advertising is that the user is receptive to information. With activity detection, the system can detect times when a person is more or less receptive to information and can do so in advance of the person sitting down to search for a product.

Experiments at PARC have found that activity detection is more useful for certain product categories (food and media) than for others and that the timing of the presentation is as important as the content.

Endnotes

[1] Peter Drucker, *Management: Tasks, Responsibilities, Practices* (New York: Harper & Row, 1973).

[2] See http://en.wikipedia.org/wiki/Burma-Shave.

[3] Stuart Elliott, "The Media Business: Advertising; A Survey of Consumer Attitudes Reveals the Depth of the Challenge That the Agencies Face," *The New York Times*, 14 April 2004, edition, Section C, Column 3, Business/Financial Desk, p. 8. www.nytimes.com/2004/04/14/business/media-business-advertising-survey-consumer-attitudes-reveals-depth-challenge.html.

[4] Bradley Johnson, "Top 100 Outlays Plunge 10% but Defying Spend Trend Can Pay Off," *Advertising Age* (21 June 2010), v. 81, no. 25. http://adage.com/article?article_id=144555.

[5] Jim Morris, "Advertising is Flirtation," PARC Forum, 2 Feb 2006, http://www.parc.com/event/439/advertising-is-flirtation.html.

[6] Miguel Helft, "Google to Offer Ads Based on Interests," *The New York Times*, 11 March 2009, B3.

7 • THE SOFT SELL: PERSONALIZED MARKETING 135

[7]"The SEMPO Annual State of Search Survey 2008, Summary Results," February 2009.

[8]D. Goldberg, D. Nichols, B. M. Oki, and D. Terry, "Using Collaborative Filtering to Weave an Information Tapestry," *Communications of the ACM* 35, no. 12 (December 1992): 61–70. http://doi.acm.org/10.1145/138859.138867.

[9]Christina Binkley, "The Gatekeeper: How Posh Hotel Sizes Up Guests," *The Wall Street Journal*, 10 May 2007, p. D1.

[10]B. Ni, S. Yan, G. Zhu, Z. Song, Y. Lu, D. Guo, and J. Yan, "A Vision-Based Demographic Advertisement System," In *Proceedings of the International Conference on Computer Vision* (demo), 2009.

[11]Samsung PROM: www.samsunglfd.com/solution/feature.do?modelCd=Samsung%20PROM.

[12]"NEC Launches Eye Flavor, Japan's First All-in-One Digital Signage Board with Face Recognition Technology," NEC Corporation, 28 January 2009.

[13]W. Zhang, J. Begole, M. Chu, J.J. Liu, N. Yee, "Real-Time Clothes Comparison Based on Multi-view Vision," Second ACM/IEEE International Conference on Distributed Smart Cameras (ICDSC 2008), Stanford University, 7–11 September 2008.

[14]N. Larios, H. Deng, W. Zhang, M. Sarpola, J. Yuen, R. Paasch, A. Moldenke, D. A. Lytle, S. R. Correa, E. N. Mortensen, L. G. Shapiro, and T. G. Dietterich, "Automated Insect Identification Through Concatenated Histograms of Local Appearance Features: Feature Vector Generation and Region Detection for Deformable Objects," *Machine Vision and Applications* 19, no. 2 (January 2008): 105–123. http://dx.doi.org/10.1007/s00138-007-0086-y.

[15]John Krumm, "Ubiquitous Advertising: The Killer Application for the 21st Century," *IEEE Pervasive Computing* 18 (January 2010). IEEE Computer Society Digital Library, http://doi.ieeecomputersociety.org/10.1109/MPRV.2010.21.

[16]Gartner, "Dataquest Insight: Consumer Location-Based Services, Subscribers and Revenue Forecast, 2007–2013," 23 June 2009.

[17]"Forecasts Show Digital Out-of-Home Still on Track for Growth," quoting PQ Media's "Global Digital Out-of-Home Media Forecast 2009–2014" and BIA Kelsey's "Digital Out of Home: Hyperlocal and Hyper Growth?"

[18]Pervasive Advertising website. www.pervasiveadvertising.org/

[19]J. Müller, F. Alt, D. Michelis, Pervasive Advertising, Springer-Verlag London Limited, 2011.

[20]Webmaster World.com discussion forum, www.webmasterworld.com/forum81/1772.htm (accessed 5 March 2010).

[21]"Examining the Effectiveness of Internet Advertising Formats" in *Internet Advertising: Theory and Research*, D. Schumann and E. Thorson (eds). 2nd edition. London: Psychology Press, Routledge. 2007.

[22]Erik Du Plessis, *The Advertised Mind: Groundbreaking Insights into How Our Brains Respond to Advertising* (London and Sterling Virginia: Kogan Page, 2008).

8

Breaking Out of the Supply Chain Gang

It is difficult to free fools from the chains they revere.
—Voltaire

If your product or service is becoming a commodity such that margins are shrinking and market share is hard to maintain, shift to another point in the value chain of your industry. It's common business advice to move to a higher position in the food chain. The business ecosystem consists of many entities adding value to resources acquired from a supplier and selling the added value to customers, hopefully for a profit. As each takes a portion of profit, those closest to the customer dollar reap the largest share.

Skipping Links

A large proportion of the world's economy consists of businesses selling products or services to other businesses, creating a chain of businesses from raw material to consumer with each adding value on the way. The classic supply chain concept looks something like Figure 8-1: Businesses act as both a customer and a supplier to other businesses, up to the final consumer.

Typically, an industry's supply chain consists not of a single stream, but of a network of suppliers and customers. If your company is one of those links selling to another business, you probably try to shape your offerings to match what your customers base their buying decisions on. If you've studied supply chains, you may even shape your offerings to match what your customers' customers want so that you can help your customers successfully repackage your output to sell to *their* customers. If your customers are smart, they will tell you what you need to know to meet *their* customers' criteria, making their business more efficient.

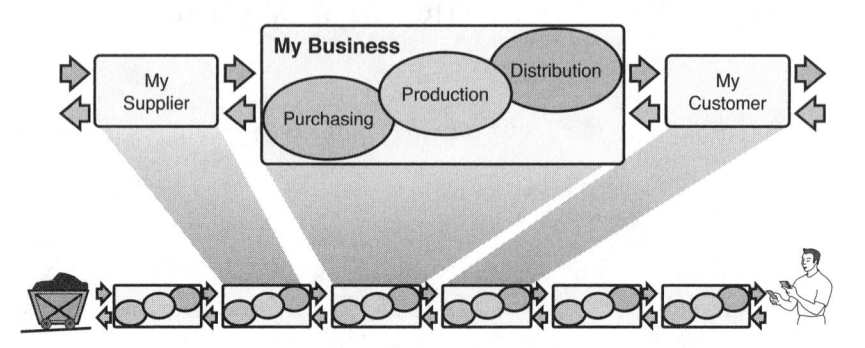

Figure 8-1 Supply chain concept. Businesses in the chain are both customers and suppliers of other businesses.

The risk to your customers is that they might tell you so much that you turn around and sell directly to *their* customer. This is an acceptable risk, for two reasons. First, for supply-chain optimization to succeed, the participants must have enough trust in their partners and faith in their own value-add that they can afford to supply information to improve the overall efficiency of the supply chain. Second, because of globalization, the primary source of competition is not that of businesses versus other businesses, but of supply chains versus other supply chains in an industry, such as the car makers in different parts of the globe. Therefore, the success of the each business in a supply chain depends on the overall efficiency of the supply chain relative to competing supply chains. Theoretically, to improve the efficiency of your supply chain, each participant must streamline and enhance the overall process, even at the cost of supplanting each other.

Theory aside, if your customer gets wind of you stealing his customers, your relationship will become strained, at best. An alternative is to look backward in the chain and see if you can reduce your supplier's role, perhaps buying directly from his supplier.

Fused Links in Media Publishing

Information technologies are undercutting some of the businesses that previously added value in the chain. Obvious examples are media companies that once provided tremendous value by connecting the output of writers and artists to customers through their physical distribution channels. Now the Internet makes distributing content simple, and media companies are losing their ability to capture money from their market.

In the past, most of our media was distributed in some physical form (paper, vinyl, magnetic tape) that required physical distribution, providing a natural point for media companies to tap into the monetization of entertainment and news information. The success of newspapers required efficient and reliable local distribution as much as it depended on the quality of its reporting. Similarly for entertainment media, distribution efficiencies were at least as important as the quality of the content, explaining the long-running success of big-studio movie productions over higher quality independent media productions.

But media companies have also provided value beyond just distribution of content: They generate interest in the product, provide a way to categorize artists (such as record labels that specialize in sets of artists of certain music genres), and provide productization services to artists. The music industry, for example, gets too little credit for the value created by its well-tuned hype machines. Just as the universe is held together by the unseen forces of "dark matter," the media industry is driven by unseen forces of promotion and emotion. As individuals, we may regard the hype fostered by the industry as crass manipulation, but from an economic standpoint, it is generating demand in the market for a product that consumers might otherwise not know of.

News media, however, is suffering even more than entertainment media. So many sources of news and information exist that it has become more difficult for a consumer to discriminate news based on quality than to discriminate entertainment media based on personal tastes (although it seems that many of our news selections today are based as much on personal taste as on veracity of information).

When we think of media companies, we typically think of the large content owners, the broadcast networks, video networks, movie studios, newspapers, magazines, and music recording labels. Many other entities are involved in the production and distribution of physical media. The production of magazines and newspapers requires suppliers of the core materials (papers, inks, coatings, bindings) and printers to produce the physical material. Then, of course, supply-chain companies bring the materials to the producers, and distribution companies take the product to retailers and consumers. All these links add value and provide points at which to monetize that value. The Internet makes all that physical production and distribution superfluous.

Yes, paper will be around forever, because it provides many conveniences: It's lightweight and portable, readable in natural light, has no reflective glare, can be spread out onto the space available, can be easily manipulated with fingers, and so on.[1] Electronic devices cannot (yet) fully meet some of these, but the widespread success of e-readers and smartphones point to a time in the very near future when the predominant way of displaying text will be digital, not physical.

I do not predict that the entire media industry is doomed—simply that the parts of it that specialize in the *physical* media itself are being commoditized and displaced. Tremendous value still lies in the creation, selection, collation, formatting, and presentation of the content. Ubiquitous computing technologies provide new opportunities beyond what we've come to expect of multimedia presentations on the web.

- **Personalization:** A new generation of mobile technologies can more accurately target the delivery of content based on its usefulness to individuals.
- **Multidevice presentation:** Presentation of personal information can be coupled across multiple devices (computer, television, mobile phone, outdoor display).
- **Ubiquitous access:** Near-universal wireless connectivity has already created an expectation of being able to acquire and select information at home, at work, in vehicles, on the street, at transit stations, in restaurants, in stores, at school, in hotels, and just about anywhere.

Amazon has shown us examples of skipping links in the supply chain in both directions. Figure 8-2 shows the supply chain of the media publishing industry prior to the web and illustrates the bridging of links since the web through to our current period of e-readers. Web technologies in the 1990s allowed Amazon to use the basic infrastructure of a wholesale book distributor that normally supplied retail outlets to directly sell to end consumers. Other large-scale retailers, such as Barnes & Noble, had a conflict with their retail outlets and were slower to adopt a large-scale web presence. More recently, Amazon started selling the Kindle e-book reader, which contains a direct connection to electronic content on its store. In this way, the value that manufacturers of printed books would have previously supplied to distributors such as Amazon is effectively reduced. Looking back over the last five years, Amazon's share price has risen 300%, while Barnes & Noble's has declined approximately 30%.

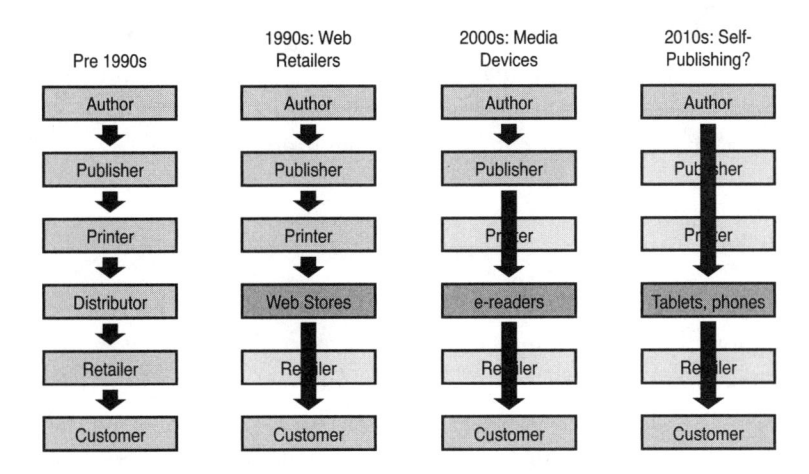

Pre 1990s	1990s: Web Retailers	2000s: Media Devices	2010s: Self-Publishing?
Author	Author	Author	Author
Publisher	Publisher	Publisher	Publisher
Printer	Printer	Printer	Printer
Distributor	Web Stores	e-readers	Tablets, phones
Retailer	Retailer	Retailer	Retailer
Customer	Customer	Customer	Customer

Figure 8-2 Example of supply chain disruption (media selling).

On the other hand, publishing houses, which own the controlling rights of how the content is packaged and copied, still control a major segment of the value chain—the interface to content authors. Will that link be disrupted in the 2010s with self-publishing as suggested on the right of Figure 8-2, just as other links in the supply chain have been skipped in prior decades? We are already seeing direct publishing between authors of web logs (blogs) and their audience. How much further can the chain be reduced, and to where will the bulk of the value shift in the 2010s? Digital technologies have been driving "disintermediation" for more than a decade now, but information and content must always be presented and consumed on some kind of medium, whether paper, LCD, e-ink, or something else. Someone also needs to play the role of broker to match readers to content that they will enjoy. Amazon seems to be in the position to play that role better than any publishing house. On the other hand, with access to new content and controlling rights to existing content, publishers control access to what people can buy.[2]

Methods to Remove Links

Seeing opportunities that one company captured and another one missed is easy in hindsight, but your goal as a strategist for your company is to *foresee* opportunities and position your company to take advantage of them. It's also easy to look at a block diagram and see that a link in a supply chain *could* be bridged, but the hard part is identifying a new way to make that bridge in a way that protects your current business interest. None of this is easy, but let me describe some of the techniques colleagues I have used in the past.

Ask Yourself

If you want to identify new opportunities, it isn't enough to simply know that a customer exists. You have to identify what motivates that customer and then offer a *better* solution that addresses that core motivation. But you have to go deep if you want to offer something that provides *radical* improvement over existing solutions—enough to motivate someone to break out of the default solution and give yours a try.

A time-tested technique for identifying root causes is the "5 Whys" method, introduced by Sakichi Toyoda and used in the Toyota Production System[3] (TPS, called Lean Manufacturing in the United States) to identify faults and inefficiencies in manufacturing processes. The process involves recursively asking "why" an effect is observed at least five times. Five is an arbitrary number of iterations—there isn't really an ultimate "root cause," other than the laws of physics, so 5 is just a general guideline to prevent us from applying the method *ad infinitum*. The following example[4] demonstrates the basic process:

My car will not start. (The problem)

- *Why?* The battery is dead.
- *Why?* The alternator is not functioning.
- *Why?* The alternator belt has broken.
- *Why?* The alternator belt was well beyond its useful service life.
- *Why?* The car service manual did not specify that the belt should be checked.

That is just one possible path of explanations. Another could probe why the battery doesn't recharge itself somehow. At the end, alternate solutions to the fifth *why* can be evaluated. Any successful solution to the fifth *why* can help prevent the problem in the future (and perhaps prevent other problems as well).

In its original use, the "5 Whys" method was designed as a troubleshooting tool, to go deeper than just the observed symptom in understanding what conditions had led to the observed effect. You can also use it as a general method for understanding the motivations behind observed actions regardless of whether there is a problem, which can identify business opportunities. Let's continue with the example of the book industry before the 1990s e-commerce revolution:

People purchase books at physical retail stores. (The pre-1990s situation)

- *Why?* They want to sample the books.
- *Why?* A bookstore has a variety of books on any topic.
- *Why?* It is cost-efficient to collect several books in one place.
- *Why?* It would take too long and be too expensive to send samples of books directly to prospective customers.
- *Why?* The order has to physically travel to and from the reseller through postal mail (remember back to pre-1990).

We could continue the examination, but let's stop here. The final *why* gives clues for *two ways* that information technologies changed the book market. First, web resellers re-created the mechanisms that catalog-based resellers used to describe content and made it easy to submit an order immediately that would be shipped the next day. Second, electronic books and e-readers made it easy and immediate to fulfill an order by downloading it directly, right away.

Ask Prospective Customers

Of course, instead of speculating five times about what caused a customer to make a decision, you could just ask. This is not quite as easy as it sounds. First of all, people don't always know why they think or do things, but they can easily rationalize their actions if asked. The rationalization may or may not be the real reason—if it isn't the real reason, creating a solution to address it will be a waste. Fortunately, sometimes it *is* the real reason. The trick is to know when.

Surveys

You can use survey methods and questionnaires.[5] Web sites such as SurveyMonkey make it easy to create surveys, send them to large numbers of people, and accumulate the responses for analysis. The field of administering and analyzing surveys has many pitfalls, but the one that matters most for our purpose is that you cannot always tell how a respondent is interpreting the question, and there is no way to ask for clarification. For example, consider a survey statement like this one:

- I buy books to read when I travel. [True/False]

  I intend this to be interpreted as buying books in advance to be read while traveling, and I hope most people read it that way. However, it could be interpreted as buying books during the course of traveling, and some portion of survey respondents *will* interpret it that way, skewing the results. Carefully designing the question to reduce ambiguity helps, but, except for very simple questions, ambiguity is difficult to eradicate fully.

- I buy books to read in advance of traveling. [True/False]

  No good. Do I just buy the books in advance of traveling, or do I read the books in advance of traveling? Make no mistake, if a statement can be interpreted multiple ways, it *will* be. You just won't know by how many of the respondents.

- In advance of traveling, I buy books to take with me that I will read during the trip. [True/False]

This is more precise but requires a respondent to remember and use their elementary school sentence-parsing skills. Survey respondents have very little patience for precisely worded questions.

Many, many other pitfalls arise in conducting surveys, but this one of interpretation is the most critical for our purposes. If respondents interpret questions differently than you intended or differently from other respondents, you may get a set of numeric scores that have *statistical significance,* suggesting that some effect is "important." But unless you talk to the respondents, perhaps clarifying the meaning, you may not know exactly what they had on their minds when answering the question. (The simplest, most reliable way to avoid misinterpretations is to pilot your survey with three to five people who aren't involved in your investigation and see if they understood your meaning; each time you change the phrasing of questions, try it again on three to five different people.)

Being a Customer

Ethnography is a method within the field of anthropology for studying ethnic cultures. Traditionally, ethnography uses participant-observation methods: The observer is not an objective bystander, but is involved in the activity. This is based on the premise that, to understand the motivations within a culture and why people behave the way they do, you have to be involved in the behaviors of the culture itself. Without being involved, an observer cannot have experienced the physical and social constraints that those in the culture feel; the observer might ascribe some interpretation from his or her own culture that completely misses the point of the behavior in the observed culture.

Although ethnography is specifically tailored for uncovering the subtleties of foreign cultures, the methods can also be used to understand the reasons people in our modern culture act as they do. PARC pioneered the use of ethnographic methods in the 1970s to identify workplace problems and to design systems to fit the goals of the people who will use them. The key to ethnographic research is sustained involvement with the participants of an activity: interviewing participants, participating in the activity yourself, shadowing participants and asking them why they are performing an action, and asking again when you see that action later. A successful, highly trained ethnographer manages to capture insights from this kind of intrusive involvement while simultaneously fading into the background.

A special breed of ethnographer is needed to identify needs and opportunities for new technologies—not just anyone can do it. An engineer might practice participant observation and other ethnographic methods and come up with more efficient ways the people could be accomplishing their goals, but the observation may completely miss the necessity behind the existing practices and fail. At the same time, some purely trained anthropologists may be able to explain why people behave a certain way but may not be able to envision how they could be doing it differently with a new technology. Practical, new concepts come out of only especially skilled ethnographers who combine deep insight and a strong ability to envision change.

Case Study: Dai Nippon Printing—Magitti

Dai Nippon Printing (DNP) is one of the world's leading commercial printing companies, with $16 billion annual revenue in 2009 and more than 40,000 employees. DNP prints a variety of products (catalogs, books, magazines, holograms, packaging) on any medium: paper, metal, glass, and tree bark—anything but air. DNP's businesses utilize a wide range of digital technologies, including the production of shadow masks for digital displays and light scattering for display backlights. One of the growth areas in which DNP is leveraging its business and technologies is "rich media" services—the combination of text, graphics, animation, video, and audio in interactive information systems.

DNP and PARC began collaborating in 2005. The overall future of print media was in obvious decline, and the growth of electronic media was already clear from the growth of web-based media. A few mixed signals emerged, though, about whether handheld computing would make much of a dent in print media. Small, dim screens and awkward interfaces made them difficult to use for any but the most hard-core road warriors. Touchscreens were not thought to solve the issues—if anything, the utility of touchscreens was in doubt, as the handheld PDAs that sported stylus-based touchscreens had largely been supplanted by feature phones with 10-key pads for text input using techniques such as T9. The digital services (email, news, web, and so on) on feature phones were impoverished by limited digital bandwidth and were poor cousins of comparable services on wireless laptops.

Nevertheless, everyone could see that the phones were getting more powerful and more capable of handling many of the commonly used applications of computers, particularly email. In Japan, the adoption of mobile phones, called *keitai denwa,* was growing rapidly even before the emergence of the Apple iPhone or the Amazon Kindle in North America. Even if signals were slightly mixed as to what would ultimately supplant print media (and the jury is still out), it was evident that smartphones would capture a significant portion of rich media consumption.

The more important consideration is not what medium will ultimately consume all others, but what content or services will be valuable on the emerging medium. This goal raises a bit of a problem for a printing company that does not own content. Printing is a form of manufacturing, and with print manufacturing being supplanted by electronic methods, shifting position in the value chain seemed crucial. However, DNP's business was largely based on printing content owned by publishing houses; these publishers contracted DNP to do the printing. If DNP attempted to emulate a conventional publishing company, it could be perceived as competing with its customers, who might take their business elsewhere. Some *new* value needed to be found that didn't compete with DNP's customers and that complemented DNP's competencies as a manufacturer of printed content.

Our goals for the project were the same as in many strategic business objectives:

- Identify one or more customer groups who would adopt a new media technology
- Identify one or more problems that those groups have and would pay money to solve
- Create a solution to those problems that provided a unique market position and did not compete with existing business customers

- Identify a business model that monetized the value of the solution

These were both broad yet confining constraints that could be satisfied in any number of ways but that must *all* be satisfied together. The order isn't strictly important; you can have a technology first and then search to find a group with a problem that it alleviates. Google didn't start off with the idea of doing search-based advertising as the problem that needed to be solved. However, if you start with a technology looking for a problem, you have to convince customers that they actually *have* that problem. On the other hand, if you start with an unaddressed problem, your innovations will have a ready market from the start. After all, Google had a profitable business in search technologies even before its explosive growth in advertising.

Identifying an Opportunity

Creating a unique solution may be the essence of innovation, but equally hard work lies in identifying unmet problems. As we age, we become accustomed to life's complexities and our work-around processes become second nature, making it difficult to even realize that some things *could* be done more easily.

In this particular case, we were looking for a group of users who would adopt new media technologies. Teenagers (13–18) and young adults (19–25) are typically more open to testing new technologies than older cohorts, and they generally consume more media as well. Of these two, which would be more likely to have a need for new rich media content and the time to consume it? In the United States, teenagers are thought to be particularly voracious consumers of movies and music, while many young adults are too busy as they start college, careers, or family. In Japan, however, the relative amount of leisure time between these two age groups is reversed: Most teenagers are too busy taking extracurricular college-preparatory courses and otherwise cramming to get into a good college, while young adults who have entered college have more spare time and have not yet entered the high-pressure workforce.[6] In our investigations, people in the range of 19–25 have an average of 40 minutes per day for leisure, while teenagers and older adults have an average of only 26 minutes per day, until retirement.

Having zeroed in on that prospective customer segment, the next stage was to understand how they like to spend their leisure time. Our ethnographers engaged in a number of exercises to uncover hidden problems, including interviews, storyboarding, and role-playing, sometimes with physical mockups of prospective devices. Interviews were conducted not only in static places, but also on the street, in sections of the city where many of the target customer groups get together.

What do young adults like to do with their leisure time? It's no surprise: They like to socialize. The only thing tricky about socializing in Tokyo is that friends may live on opposite sides of the very large, densely populated city. So they often get together by picking a metro station that is convenient to both parties and then meet up to "do something" together. It doesn't really matter what they do: going to shows, shopping, playing games, watching movies, eating out, and other things. In a 2006 survey,[7] the Japan Statistics Bureau found that people in their 20s showed the highest rate for "sightseeing with a friend" (30% for males, 45% for females), more than twice the rate for younger and older age groups other than retirement age (over 65).

Meeting up at a station is easy but there's a problem. They want to do *something* together, but in many cases, neither of the two knows much about what's possible to do in the local area. Usually, the rendezvous point is distant from both homes. PARC's ethnographers discovered this problem through on-street interviews of young people in a variety of popular Tokyo neighborhoods. Figure 8-3 shows the responses when people on the street were asked to rate "how well I know this neighborhood": Almost a third gave a rating of 1 ("not at all"), and less than 20% rated their knowledge between 5 and 7 ("extremely well"). Furthermore, younger people are often more open to suggestion than older groups. They haven't necessarily made up their minds about their likes and dislikes and are still exploring options.

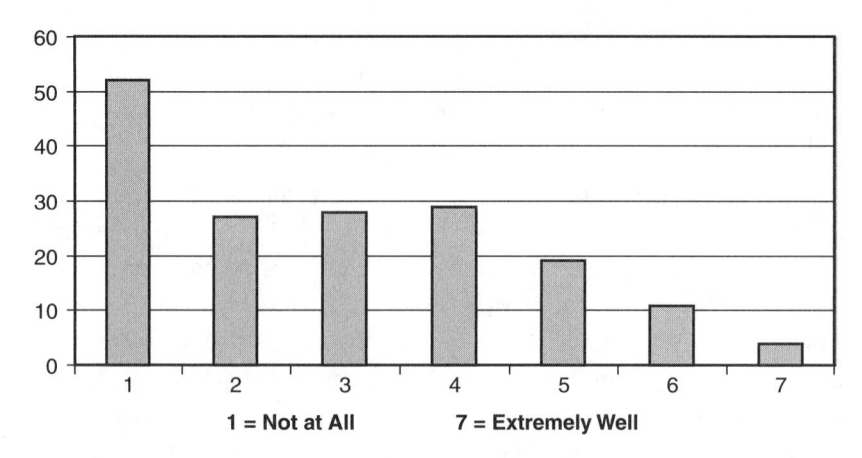

Figure 8-3 Ratings of "How well I know this neighborhood" given by 170 young people stopped on the streets in diverse neighborhoods in Tokyo. (Figure credit: Victoria Bellotti)

The upshot is that there is an information need that could be filled with a new rich media service. Tokyo is particularly dense with stores, restaurants, and game centers that are tucked away in hidden corners, basements, or upper floors that are not visible from the street. At the time (2005), location-based search and navigation on smartphones was beginning to emerge. Social networks were catching on as a way to communicate and coordinate with friends. Augmented reality was another capability that could be relevant to this problem as a way to see information about what people could not physically see, such as what stores were on upper floors of buildings. A number of other ideas came out of the ethnography-led brainstorm activities, and we conducted interviews to get feedback and prioritization.

Interviewees showed some excitement for all these new high-tech concepts, but they also identified a problem that none of these solve: information overload. In fact, concepts such as augmented reality actually make information overload more of a problem by laying electronic information atop the already cluttered signage of Tokyo. The young adults we interviewed pointed out that there are already several sources of information about what is available in different regions, such as regional shopping guides and leisure activity publications, including magazines printed by DNP such as *Tokyo Walker* (a periodical describing events, fashion, and activity trends). All the proposed technologies just increased the presentation of already available information, but none of them solved the underlying problem of sifting through alternative options and selecting one that fits the individual preferences.

- *Why?* There are too many options to choose from.
- *Why?* There is substantial diversity in things people like and not enough time to consider every possible option.
- *Why?* It takes a certain minimal time to learn enough about each option to form an opinion.
- *Why?* An individual's preferences consist of complex cost-benefit tradeoffs that depend on many factors that only humans can assess.
- *Why?* Computers are incapable of combining multiple aspects of an individual's life experiences, demographics, physiology, and patterns of behavior that shape people's preferences.

That final stage suggests a limitation of computing systems that theoretically could be bridged, if enough information were available and human-like reasoning could be applied.

The focus of our innovation became avoiding information overload while at the same time helping people serendipitously discover things they would like. Subobjectives also came out of the on-street ethnographic studies, such as the following:

- The mobile device must be operable with one hand, because the other hand is carrying something or holding a train-car handle.
- The system should learn user preferences without requiring users to explicitly enter the information, because they are busy and want to enjoy their outings, not enter data into a computer.
- The operations of the device should be easy to remember.

Personalized Leisure Activity Guide

In Chapter 4, "Still Stupid after All These Years," we explored the general capability and technical approach to personalization. The ethnographic work in Tokyo identified a specific example of a type of information that needs to be personalized: outdoor leisure activities such as shopping, eating, doing sports or exercise, seeing sights or movies or performances, and reading about such things. Plenty of related information is available online, including store descriptions, restaurant reviews, and information about gyms, theaters, parks, museums, sports facilities, and more; much of this is aggregated in online city guides and customer review sites such as Yelp, Yahoo! Local, Zagat, and UrbanSpoon. These days, most of these are available from smartphones as well, and if your phone is GPS enabled, it filters results according to what's close to you now.

The basic information exists, as it has in paper formats for decades, but it isn't easy to use or find things that matter to you based on your individual tastes. If you've ever used a city guide book, like a Michelin Guide, you'll remember how difficult it can be to find the nugget of gold among the chaff. Online tools make it a little easier to find things if you know what keywords to search for, but the point of sightseeing or going out with friends is to discover unknown delights—places that wouldn't have occurred to you to search for. At least two problems exist that mobile and online city guides don't solve:

- Too much information
- Manual browsing to find places that appeal to you personally

Think about how much easier it is to consult a hotel concierge for advice than it is to use a city guide. Or you might talk to a friend who knows the area you'll be visiting and also knows the kinds of things you like. Your friend knows you well and can tailor her suggestions to what she knows about you. The concierge doesn't know you intimately, but knows the area deeply and asks the right questions to match your tastes. How can a computer re-create the depth of knowledge and tradeoffs that humans use when making recommendations to each other?

The system we devised, codenamed Magitti (a contraction of "Magic Scope" and "Digital Graffiti," which were the candidate concepts that triggered the concerns about information overload), provides personalized recommendations of local leisure activity sites based on your current situation and what it has seen you do in the past in similar situations. The goal of Magitti, represented in Figure 8-4, was to present the user with a list of recommended stores, restaurants, theaters, museums, parks, sport facilities, and other items related to outdoor leisure according to what is most likely to be useful—all while also eliminating the need to enter data or search terms that people would otherwise have to input manually.

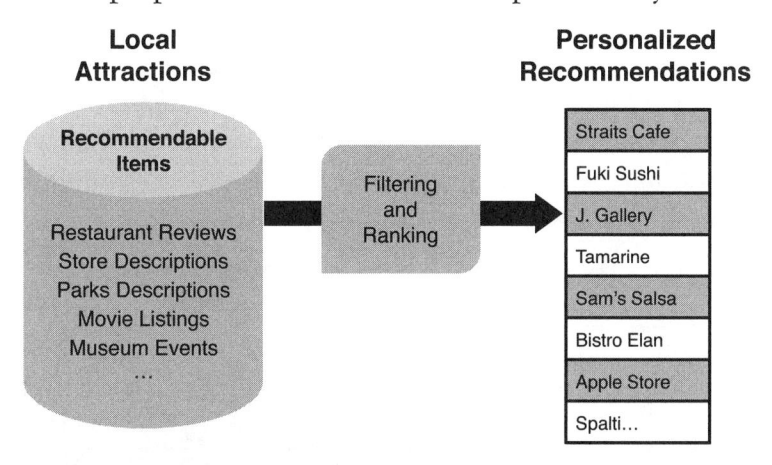

Figure 8-4 Magitti's objective was to recommend information about outdoor leisure activities to an individual, filtering the information into leisure activity categories and ranking them according to usefulness to the individual. (Figure credit: Kurt Partridge)

The Magic behind Magitti

Magitti's goal was to provide its users with the most relevant information to their current needs. It did this by observing their current situation, matching that to observations of what actions people generally take in that situation, and then using those observations to predict the likelihood of taking one of those actions in the current situation. We explored the progression of context-aware services in Chapter 3, "Harmless if Used as Directed," which use sensors to detect the state of the physical environment. In addition to the physical environment, a person's "situation" today includes the state of his or her electronic environment: what email was recently read, what section of a budget spreadsheet is being edited, and who the person talked to in the last few minutes. This kind of information is as useful to determining what is on someone's mind as his or her current location is.

In contrast to location-based search, Magitti's magic was to combine multiple cues of a person's context to filter and rank information. The system's process involves two key steps: to predict the likelihood of each type of leisure activity and, within each type, to rank the information by the user's personal tastes and the information's usefulness in the current time, location, and other factors. It constructed this "contextual intelligence" by recording the behaviors and contexts of users over time to build models of activities and preferences. After making a set of venue recommendations, Magitti could see which of those had been selected in the list and also which had been visited physically. This feedback loop, illustrated in Figure 8-5, is used to adjust the models and improve their accuracy over time.

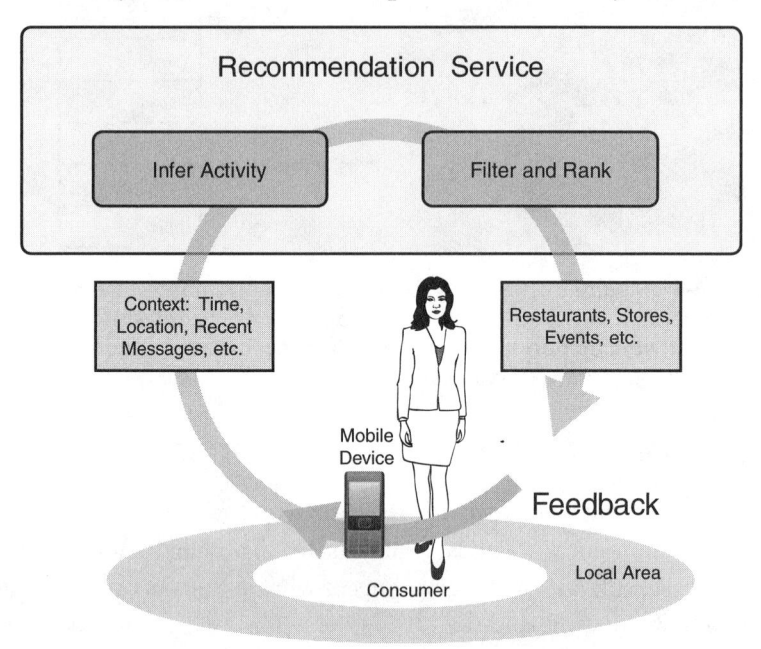

Figure 8-5 Magitti uses the current context to infer likelihood of interest in various leisure activities to filter content and then uses a model of personal preferences to rank and recommend relevant content. The system improves performance over time by observing which recommendations are followed. (Figure credit: Magitti team)

What Are You Doing?

The Magitti system was founded on the premise that an individual's behaviors are generally consistent over time. For the most part, an individual wakes up around the same time each day, eats meals around the same time, goes to similar places on particular days of the week or dates in the year, and generally follows sets of routine patterns in their life. This isn't a popular premise—most people like to think of themselves as spontaneous, idiosyncratic, and free-willed, and they are. Just as no two snowflakes are exactly the same, no two people behave the same, and no one person does the same thing *exactly* the same way twice. Nevertheless, individuals *do* exhibit general tendencies that are characteristic and predictable. A recent study at Northeastern University[8] of mobile phone location traces found that 93% of an individual users' mobility is predictable.

Still, it's not easy to predict exactly what an individual will do. In our ultimate tests of Magitti's performance, it exhibited an average accuracy of 82%[9] in predicting a person's most likely leisure activity (within the categories of Eat, Buy, See, Do, Read). That's by no means perfect, but it's greater than four times higher than random probability (20%) and almost twice as high as the baseline metric of always predicting people's most common outdoor activity, which is eating (43%), according to data collected by the Japan Statistics Bureau.[10]

Such an accuracy level requires balancing a number of different factors. Our system combined predictions made by the following seven different computational models, each of which uses a different method to arrive at its prediction. Each model made its best guess about the probability across the activity categories, and then all the predictions were combined into a final tally.

- **Population patterns:** This model consisted of a description of the general patterns of leisure activities at different times of day, on different days of the week, and in different weather conditions, derived from the Japan Statistics Bureau data of the entire Japanese population.
- **Place-time tendency:** This model identified the probability of activities in particular regions of the city at different times of day. For example, certain areas of the city have more restaurants than stores, and vice versa.
- **User calendar:** If the user already entered leisure activity plans into their electronic calendar, this model attempts to use that information. For example, an appointment such as "dinner with Taro" set for 7:00 would be evidence that dining information would be more useful around that time, regardless of whether that time is typical for eating.
- **Learned from visits:** As the user moves around in the city, the system observes what kinds of stores, restaurants, and so on

the person visits at different times and creates an individualized model. This allows the system to detect even wildly idiosyncratic patterns that can override the population prior model. For example, if the user works an odd shift and visits restaurants near 2:00 PM and not around noon, the system will predict that the user is interested in information about restaurants around 2:00 PM, even though the population prior model would have suggested noon.

- **Learned from interactions:** This model is built up when the user overrides the prediction and explicitly enters his or her own activity.
- **Future plans:** The people we interviewed in the ethnographic fieldwork said they often use SMS and email to make plans with friends, so this model watches for messages describing plans. (See the sidebar for an example of an SMS message containing plans.)
- **Document topic analysis:** In this model, the system uses common text-analytic techniques to detect topics of web pages, articles, or other documents that the user views on the phone. If the topics are related to leisure activity, any time or location information in the document is used to build a model of potential activity plans.

The outputs of these models are combined to estimate the likelihood that the user is now or soon will be engaged in one of the activity categories, as illustrated in Figure 8-6. The activity prediction provides a first-stage filter of the information space, determining the useful proportion of each type of information. That is, when users are more engaged in eating, they are more interested in restaurant reviews; when they more interested in shopping, they will find store descriptions more useful; and the same goes for seeing sights and doing other activities. For example, using the estimates shown in Figure 8-6, the final list should contain roughly 57% restaurant reviews; 11% store descriptions; 13% museum, gallery, movie, or play listings; 11% parks or fitness facilities listings; and 6% articles to read. In our example, the final list has room for about eight items per page and shows five slots for restaurants, one for sights, one for physical activity, and one for a store.

8 • BREAKING OUT OF THE SUPPLY CHAIN GANG 157

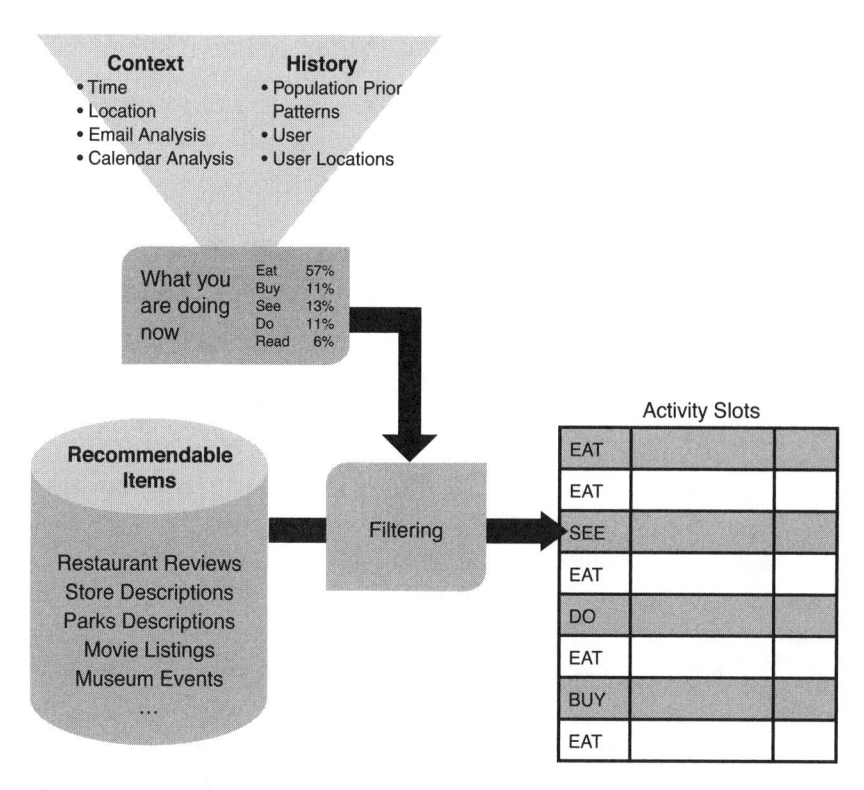

Figure 8-6 Combining information from multiple sources, the user's likelihood of being engaged in each of the five activity categories is estimated, to determine the number of slots to reserve for each type of information. (Figure credit: Kurt Partridge)

The system learns to improve its predictions in two ways. First, each module itself adjusts its parameters by observing what offerings the user selected for more information and where the user ultimately went. For example, if the user specified that she was interested in "Shopping" information at 10:15 AM, then the learned interaction model and the place-time model would increase their settings for shopping around 10:15 on that day of the week. Second, at the point where all the models' predictions were aggregated, the influence of each model was weighed according to how successful it had been in past predictions. When a model was correct, its weight increases; when it was incorrect, its weight decreases.

Bootstrapping the System: How People Spend Time

Before the Magitti system has been used by an individual, it bases its predictions of likely activity on the general patterns of activity in the population. But where does one get that kind of information? It turns out that governments are very interested in how populations spend their time, for a number of economic and policy reasons. In 2008, PARC researchers Kurt Partridge and Philippe Golle analyzed a number of such data sets to determine whether and how they can be used to bootstrap predictive systems.[11] Many of these datasets are publicly available for free and are indexed by the Centre for Time Use Research.[12]

In the United States, the Bureau of Labor Statistics conducted the American Time-Use Survey (ATUS) to estimate work not included in other statistics, such as home childcare. The survey was conducted by interviewers who called 12,943 participating households at the end of each day and recorded the day's activities at 10-minute intervals. The data set includes 263,286 activity episodes that contain the participant identifier, time, activity code, location, personal demographics, family demographics, employment, simultaneous childcare, and copresent individuals. Figure 8-7 shows the proportion of the population spending time in each of the 18 top-level categories, which can be broken out into two additional sublevels of finer-grained categories. The top-level categories serve as a coarse-grain approximation of the probabilities of a typical person being engaged in these activity categories.

Because the data sets contain the location of each activity, they are also useful to seed the model of what activities are common in a location (the place-time tendency model). Partridge and Golle's research showed that location alone is one of the primary predictors for many, but not all, types of activity. Combining location, time, and the previous activity can predict almost half of the top-level activity categories from the ATUS data set. Table 8-1 lists the activity categories that can and cannot be reliably predicted using location, time, and prior activity. The predictability can be increased by adding other factors into the calculation, such as age group, gender, employment status, and other demographics. Note that location is at the granularity of a building address, which approximates the accuracy of Global Positioning Service (GPS) of 10–30m. Location within a building would further differentiate some of the household and workplace activities, but ATUS does not capture that level of granularity.

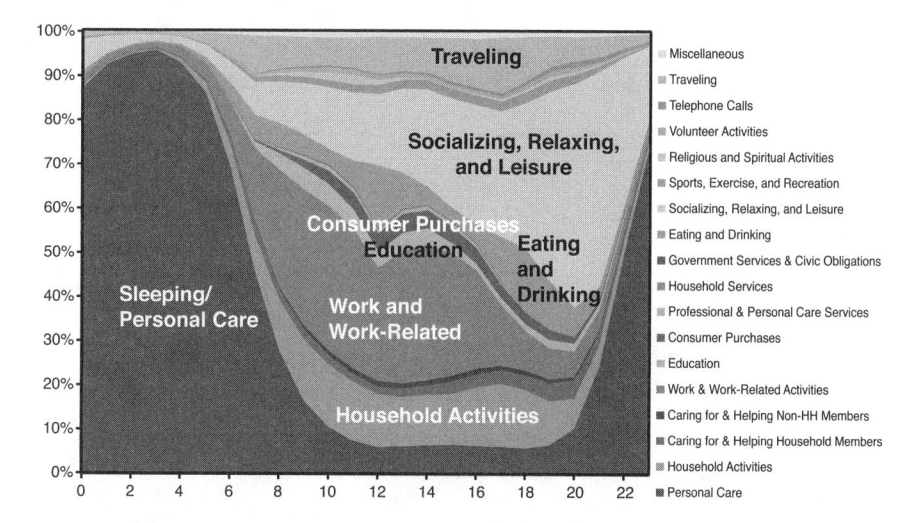

Figure 8-7 Proportion of population engaged in each of the 18 top-level activity categories throughout a typical day, recorded by the American Time Use Survey. (Figure credit: Kurt Partridge)

TABLE 8-1 Predictability of Activity Classes by Combining Location, Time, and Prior Activity

Predictable with F-measure in Top 25%	Unpredictable
Personal care (including sleeping)	Household activities (other than personal care)
Socializing, relaxing, leisure	Telephone calls
Work and work-related activities	Caring for others (household or nonhousehold members)
Eating and drinking	Sports, exercise, and recreation
Education	Volunteer activities
Consumer purchases	Professional and personal care services
Traveling	Household services
Religious/spiritual activities	Government and civic services

For the Magitti project, we based the population patterns on data collected by the Japan Statistics Bureau in a leisure-time activity survey. This data set contains the proportions of the activities performed by about 10,000 people during any 15-minute period on October 20, 2001. Figure 8-8 shows the proportion of the population engaged in each of four leisure activity categories (reading activity was not collected in the JSTAT survey) on a weekday.[13]

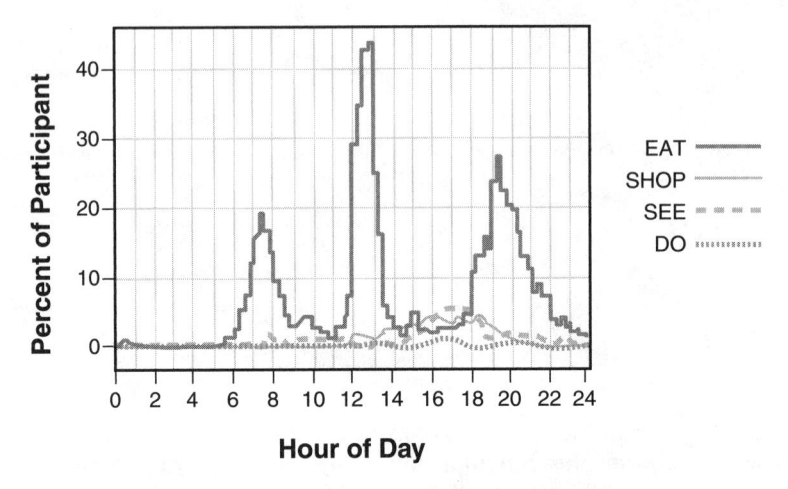

Figure 8-8   Percentage of population engaged in each of four leisure activity categories on weekdays in Japan. (Source: Japan Statistics Bureau, Leisure-Time Activity Survey, 2006. Figure credit: Kurt Partridge)

People's activity patterns vary with the day of the week. The data shown in Figure 8-9 was collected from a study of 21 Japanese college students over a one-week period who reported their activity by email from their mobile phone once an hour. The diagrams show the proportion of the respondents engaged in four outdoor leisure activity categories from 06:00 to 22:30 for different days of the week. In the morning and afternoon hours of Monday through Friday, people engaged in similar proportions of leisure activity. Saturday and Sunday have different patterns from each other and from weekdays. For evening hours, Sunday through Thursday is roughly equivalent, while Friday and Saturday evenings also show similar proportions.

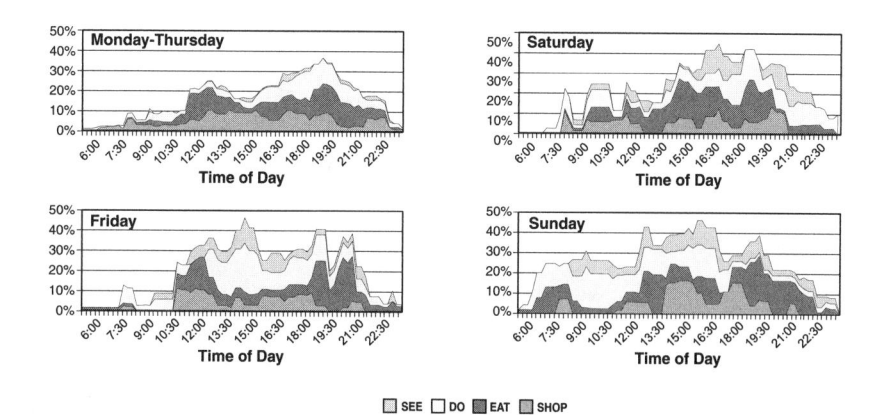

Figure 8-9 Percentage of respondents (college students in Tokyo) engaged in four different leisure activity categories on different days of the week. (Figure credit: Diane Schiano)

"I Dunno. What Do You Wanna Do?"

Short Message Service (SMS) is wildly popular among teenagers and young adults all over the world, despite the limitation of only 120- to 160-character messages (about two lines of text in a normal page). Some theories for its popularity parallel those for instant messaging: Messages can be exchanged without disrupting class, multiple non-urgent conversations can occur at once, and you can ignore messages from people you don't want to talk to!

SMS is commonly used for planning leisure outings between friends. The fieldwork in Japan suggested that these messages *might* help Magitti zero in on specific plans and be able to offer up specific, actionable information.

What was not clear, though, was how frequently planning occurred, what such plans looked like, and how a system would extract meaning from cryptic abbreviations that the short message format imposes.

Fortunately, the University of Singapore has published a research corpus of 10,000 SMS messages collected from students, a similar demographic to the Magitti target user profile. Within this, approximately 11% contain plans for leisure outings.

Consider an example of a complex message in which the person is talking about *two* possible activities after 4 PM: seeing a movie or eating dinner. This narrows the likely activities considerably.

> **tomorrow** what **time** you be in school? think me and shuhui meeting in school **around 4**. then duno still can **see movie** or not because duno if a rest want meet for **dinner**.

Understanding the whole meaning of the sentence is beyond most technologies today, but that isn't necessary. All we need to do is detect text like that in boldface and use those concepts to boost the activity predictions without necessarily having full understanding of the sentences. The Magitti recommender system is able to get plenty of information from spotting only words related to time (*tomorrow, time, around 4*) and leisure activities (*see movie, dinner*).

A possible spoiler of this approach is that the message could contain a negation of a plan. For example: "I can't go to dinner at 5. 7?" That one is easy to spot, but other negations are not as easy to spot (e.g., "dinner at 5pm is difficult"). For the most part, however, SMS messages are short, so message text generally gets right to the point.

What Do You Like?

The activity predictions determine the proportions of different types of information to present. The next stage is to determine the priority of each potential piece of information within each type. That is, among all the possible restaurants, which ones are most likely suited to your current situation and personal preferences?

This again involves multiple factors. People's preferences change depending on their mood, price, who they're with, and more. As with the activity prediction, the preference prediction combined a number of models simultaneously. The first five models are semi-static, changing infrequently, and are computed in advance.

- **General popularity:** Without any specific information about the person, the system uses the general popularity of items in each information category.

- **Stated preferences:** If they were willing to, users could explicitly state their preferences for key characteristics in each of the activity categories. For eating, the user could rate food cuisines; for shopping, they could rate product categories; for seeing, they could rate movie genres, museum types, and more; for doing, they could rate sports and physical activities; and for reading, they could rate their preference for different types of articles.

- **Learned preferences:** This model was constructed over time by recording the types of restaurants or types of stores that the person visited, which indicated preferences for cuisine, products, price range, proximity to current location, and more.

- **Content preferences:** As the user accesses web pages, videos, music, email, documents, or other content on the phone, the system learns the typical topics, genre, and so on within these content.

- **Collaborative filtering:** In this model, the system finds people with similar tastes to yours. If a large number of them have rated something highly, you probably would like it as well. This technique is commonly used in recommender systems and was described in more detail in Chapter 7, "The Soft Sell: Personalized Marketing."

The last three models depend on the user's current situation and recent actions, and are computed on the fly.

- **Distance:** Generally, people prefer destinations that are "nearby"—but what does "nearby" mean exactly? If people are walking, they likely prefer "nearby" things within walking distance, which varies among people. If they are driving, "nearby" could mean places that are in the same direction as their ultimate destination or perhaps things at the ultimate destination. If they are using public transit, "nearby" probably refers to things within the vicinity of stations they stop at along their route.

- **Recent content boosting:** Recently accessed content provides a stronger indication of current interests than the general content preferences model described earlier. If the system sees that the user has recently received a message from a friend that contains *pizza*, it will temporarily increase the person's likely preference for pizza.

- **Recommendation diversity:** Finally, a recommendation system is useful only if it is suggesting things that you wouldn't have thought of yourself. This model makes sure that the system doesn't simply recommend the same thing to you day after day.

Each of these models estimates the *utility* of each piece of information in the data repository. As with the activity prediction subsystem, the individual models' scores are weighted according to the model's influence on the final score; the weights are adjusted based on each model's success over time. The final utility score determines the order in which each item is presented within the slots allotted to its type of information, as shown in Figure 8-10.

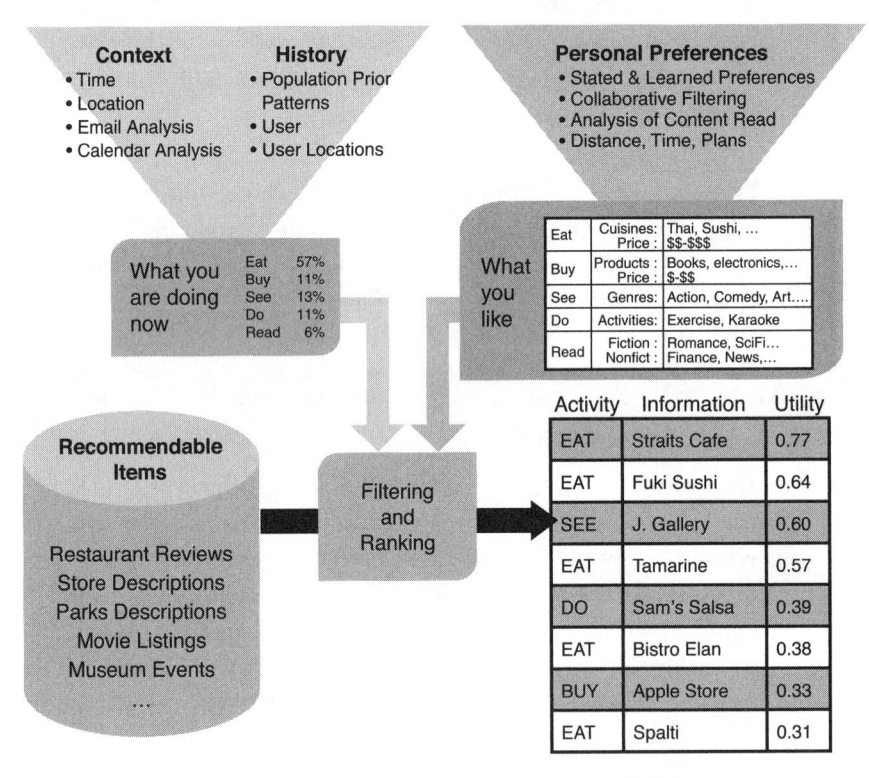

Figure 8-10 A number of preference factors combine to estimate the likely utility of each piece of information within the information categories determined previously. (Figure credit: Kurt Partridge)

Is It Worth It?

This is a fairly complex system, requiring substantial investment to pull it off correctly. If you do it wrong, you end up with a semi-intelligent system that just irritates people. (Need we be reminded of Microsoft's Clippy? "It looks like you're eating in a restaurant. Would you like help with that spaghetti?") A key question is whether the intelligence is enhancing the user's experience of the system and by how much.

Businesses can spend a lot of time and money evaluating the effectiveness and user experience of a system and still never get it completely right. Focus groups, user panels, expert walkthroughs, cognitive engineers, design consultants—it all adds up quickly. Conversely, some companies do not spend much on user experience and also never get it right—or if they do, it was a lucky shot in the dark. As always, a middle ground provides the best bang for the buck.

In the early phase of a new technology, focus on the fundamental capabilities of the system, not the details of the product design. For personalized recommendation systems, evaluate two key parts:

- Does the system guess the activity and preferences better than chance, and by how much?
- Do the recommendations provide information that people wouldn't have otherwise known?

To test these questions for the Magitti system, we conducted a small-scale study of the system with 11 people using the system for a few hours each. We had an observer follow the people as they used the system and record their actual activities and personal preferences, which we then compared to what the system guessed and recommended.

How Much Better Than a Guess?

Yes, it is possible for an "intelligent" system to do *worse* than chance. If the system is not performing better than random guessing, you can scrap all that software intelligence and just have it emit random guesses.

For the Magitti system, the problem is first to guess the person's most likely activity across five categories (Eat, Shop, See, Do, Read). We knew from the population data sets that the most common outdoor leisure activity category is eating. Without considering time, location, or individual patterns, people engage in eating 43% of the time they are outdoors. This defines the *baseline probability* against which to evaluate the intelligence of the system. In our study, if the system had used no intelligence, but simply predicted the most common activity, which is Eat, this guess would have been correct 62% of the time. That is higher than the baseline probability[14] and means the system would have been correct most of the time *without using any intelligence whatsoever.*

Figure 8-11 shows the baseline accuracy compared to gradually increased intelligence. Condition 1 is the accuracy that using the baseline activity (eating) achieved in our study (62%). Condition 2 used predictions based on activity patterns of the general population but not learned from the individual's prior visit patterns. Interestingly, the accuracy (60%) is higher than the baseline probability (43%) but is slightly lower than predictions using just the baseline activity (62%, possibly the result of small sample size). When we add the individual's patterns learned from visits of locations in the past, in Condition 3, the accuracy reaches 73%, significantly better than the baseline.

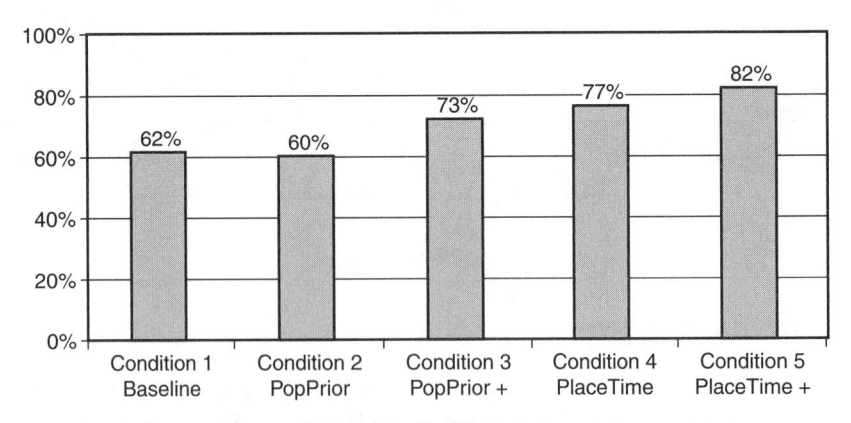

Figure 8-11 Accuracy of activity predictions in Palo Alto field trial. (Figure credit: Kurt Partridge)

In Condition 3, the individual's patterns increased the accuracy, but doing this requires recording and analyzing an individual's location history, potentially exposing personal information. Even though many people will be willing to provide a location record for better accuracy, could any other technique achieve similar accuracy without raising such concerns?

Yes. Condition 4 examines a different prediction algorithm that does not use individual data and is based on the typical activities within a geographic region at different times of day. For example a "restaurant district" in a town will have a higher proportion of Eat activity than other regions. The same is true in a "shopping district" for Shop. This is just another way of looking at the population pattern (Condition 2), but segmented by both location and time, not just time. Using this technique, the system correctly detected the user's activity 77% of the time, which is significantly better than the baseline without using individual data.

On the other hand, adding individual data improves the results further. In Condition 5, we added the individual visitation patterns on top of the place-time tendency and saw an additional boost in the accuracy to 82%. That was the *average* accuracy across participants in the study and depended on the individual person's regularity. That is, highly variable individuals show little or no improvement over Condition 4, while people with fairly regular patterns show even better performance than the 82% average.

Despite the small size of the evaluation (n=11), the differences in Figure 8-11 were statistically significant (at p=.05), meaning that there is a 95% probability that the higher scores are due to better performance thought there is still a 5% chance that the effects were due to random error[15]. These results indicate that the individualized intelligence of the system did significantly outperform population statistics and simplistic approaches.

How Much Does It Help?

This question is hard to answer. It's a subjective question that people will answer with subjective opinions. However, just because something is subjective doesn't mean it isn't measurable.

In this study, we asked people to rate how helpful the system was on a scale of 1 to 5 (5 being "very helpful" and 3 being "neutral"). The average response was 4.1 ("helpful"). People unfamiliar with the local vicinity found it particularly helpful. We heard comments such as "Cool! I like that. I would never have found that place if it wasn't for this." The system was also useful to people who were already familiar with the area, some of whom made comments such as "It makes life more interesting. It allows you to get out of your daily routine, almost as if you're going to a different city." Sometimes people get stuck going to places they already know and they forget about other options in the area. A personal recommendation system can remind them of places that might be worth a second look.

When asked to rate how "relevant and of interest" the system recommendations were, the average response was 3.8 ("usually") out of 5 ("almost always"). During the trials, more than half of the places people visited were new to them. On 69% of outings, they noticed another new place to visit later.

From these responses, it was clear that the study participants found the recommendations positively helpful, relevant, and of interest. The system provided knowledge to them that they didn't already have—or that they didn't remember they had.

Not all effects of the system were positive, however. We saw that when the system made a recommendation that the user disagreed with, for whatever reason, the user lost confidence in the system's recommendations. The system was quite engaging, and people watched it to see the list of recommendations change as they walked down the street. As a result, they paid less attention to things in the physical environment, including storefronts, walking hazards, and, most critically, their social companions.

Business Impact

Business is booming for smartphone applications, and DNP recently released a commercial version of the system in the form of an iPhone application called Machireko (*Machi* is Japanese for "town" or "area of a city," and *reko* is a contraction of the English *recommendation*). It is currently available only on the iTunes Japan store because the app serves only recommendations for certain districts of Tokyo. Machireko is more robust and has more content than the Magitti prototype we evaluated.

The potential business value of this class of system is quite high for a company such as DNP. First, it connects the company with a new form of presentation media beyond its traditional printing business. Furthermore, it invents a new form of publishing, called contextual publishing, that enhances and does not compete with their customers' content. In contextual publishing, the author not only creates the content, but also describes the situation in which the information is most useful by specifying the intended audience (tastes and preferences) and situation (time, location, activity). So far, recommender systems have had to recommend content that does *not* describe its intended audience—they expect the audience to spend the time finding what they want. Contextual publishing changes that and requires that the author not only create the content, but also specify to whom and when the content would be useful. Contextual publishing is useful not only for activity recommendations, but also for advertising, public service information, and just-in-time information delivery. DNP and the rest of the electronic media industry are just starting to exploit this power and to create tools to generate targeted content.

More content on increasingly diverse devices is trying to reach people. Currently, these recipients have to do all the work to find and pay attention to what matters. We've reached a point now that the consumers cannot manage the load. The onus of finding the target audience is starting to shift to the content authors or brokers. This nascent capability is currently largely confined to online advertising and news-filtering systems, but we will soon see its effects across other content categories: music, video, fiction, essays, opinions, everything.

Summary

The media publishing industry has been perhaps hardest hit by innovations in information technology that have made the creation and distribution of content inexpensive and reliable. Currently, the businesses at the endpoints of the supply chain are in the best positions: publishers at the content creation side and device manufacturers at the content consumption side. By leveraging some of the new capabilities that Ubiquitous Computing provides, you can shift your company's value to a different point in the industry's supply chain.

A number of methods help in identifying ways to shift position. One is to get a clear understanding of the fundamental causes behind problems that are observed and then create solutions for those root causes. Another method is to ask customers about their problems. The difficulty here is that customers can describe their problem but may not be able to envision solutions. Ethnographic methods can be employed to understand root motivations behind the methods people use. Only especially skilled ethnographers can envision solutions that still satisfy the complex needs of human practices.

Ethnographic methods were demonstrated in the case study of the Magitti prototype developed to help Dai Nippon Printing find new business opportunities outside its heritage as a printing company. The process identified a prospective market for a new rich media service for young adults in Japan.

The Magitti system provides personalized recommendations of outdoor leisure activities, such as dining, shopping, exercising, seeing movies, and others. Magitti is an example of a contextually intelligent system that combines information about physical situation (location, time, and weather) and electronic situation (recent messages, applications, web pages, and so on) to predict the probability of the user's upcoming leisure activity. The system bases its estimate on observations of past actions by this person in similar situations.

This chapter described some of the details of combining information sources and multiple computation modules to make the activity predictions and content recommendations. It also described the feedback into the system that led to more accurate personalized predictions and explained how to bootstrap the system with both publicly available data and data collected by ethnographic methods. The evaluation of the system showed that the predictions and recommendations were substantially more accurate than chance and that users considered the recommendations very useful.

The combination of ethnography and technology innovation created a new capability for DNP in the realm of contextual publishing, in which content has metadata that describes when, where, and by whom the content will be useful. This nascent capability is demonstrated by the Magitti prototype and in the recently released iPhone app Machireko. Expect to see more examples of contextual publishing services in coming years.

Endnotes

[1] Abigail Sellen and Richard Harper, *The Myth of the Paperless Office* (Cambridge, MA: MIT Press, 2001).

[2] For example, the Beatles catalog was only recently available on iTunes and other digital download merchants.

[3] Taiichi Ohno, *Toyota Production System: Beyond Large-Scale Production* (Portland, Oreg.: Productivity Press, 1988.

[4] Excerpt from Wikipedia: http://en.wikipedia.org/wiki/5_Whys.

[5] Arlene G. Fink, *How to Conduct Surveys: A Step-by-Step Guide* (Los Angeles: Sage Publications, Inc. 2008.

[6] J. Horne, "Understanding Leisure Time and Leisure Space in Contemporary Japanese Society," *Leisure Studies* 17, no. 1 (1998): 37–52.

[7] Japan Statistics Bureau, *2006 Survey on Time Use and Leisure Activities*, www.stat.go.jp/english/data/shakai/2006/pdf/koudou-a.pdf.

[8] Chaoming Song, Zehui Qu, Nicholas Blumm, Albert-László Barabási, "Limits of Predictability in Human Mobility," *Science* 327, no. 5,968 (19 February 2010): 1,018– 1,021.

[9] K. Partridge and R. Price, "Enhancing Mobile Recommender Systems with Activity Prediction," International Conference on User Modeling, Adaptation, and Personalization 2009 (UMAP), Trento, Italy, 22–26 June 2009.

[10] Japan Statistics Bureau, 2006 Survey on Time Use and Leisure Activities, www.stat.go.jp/english/data/shakai/2006/pdf/koudou-a.pdf.

[11] K. Partridge and P. Golle, "On Using Existing Time-Use Study Data for Ubiquitous Computing Applications," in *Proceedings of the 10th International Conference on Ubiquitous Computing*, Seoul, Korea, 21–24 September 2008). http://doi.acm.org/10.1145/1409635.1409655

[12] Centre for Time Use Research, information gateway: www.timeuse.org/.

[13] K. Partridge and R. Price, "Enhancing Mobile Recommender Systems with Activity Prediction," International Conference on User Modeling, Adaptation, and Personalization 2009 (UMAP); 2009 June 22–26; Trento, Italy.

[14] This is possibly due to sampling bias from the small study size. A larger study should be correct close to the baseline probability of 43%.

[15] Let's unpack the meaning of statistical significance at $p = .05$. Suppose that, in fact, the system intelligence provided no benefit. Statistical significance at $p = .05$ means that if the experiment were run 100 times, 5 of the resulting sets would show that it did make a difference due to chance, not due to an actual benefit. It is possible, therefore, that these results are one of those theoretical five incorrect runs. However, it is far more likely that these results arise from a true difference in the effectiveness of the system intelligence.

9

Discontinuous Connections

If you were to test it and it reads OL open circuit, open load. That indicates that the fuse is blown or burnt and has no conductivity, no continuity, no connection.
—Mark Blocker, *Expert Village, How to Do Fuse Visual and Continuity Tests*[1]

The value of an information device or service increases when it is compatible with others. We've already talked about Metcalfe's law of network effects (see Chapter 4, "Still Stupid After All These Years"), which states that the value of "compatible communicating devices" is roughly the square of the number of such devices. This effect has been validated in the telecommunications industry, where the value of the network grows with the number of phones or fax machines connected to it. It makes intuitive sense that the value of my telephone depends on how many other telephones it can reach. The law has also been demonstrated on data networks and the Internet, where the value of the entire network increases with each additional computer and service connection.

The benefits of network effects can be realized only by systems that *interoperate*—that exchange information and use the services of each other. If network effects are so powerful, why is it that so many devices do not easily interoperate today? Currently, interoperation can be achieved through "open" standards such as Bluetooth, ZigBee, Universal Plug and Play (UPnP), the Digital Living Network Alliance (DLNA), and others. Open standards define the media formats and encodings used across manufacturers, and they are necessary to provide consumers with the freedom to choose among compatible devices.

The two most prominent standards for media interoperation are Bluetooth and Universal Plug and Play (UPnP). Another prominent standard is the Digital Living Network Alliance (DLNA), which is based on UPnP and defines a set of media types (text, image, audio, and video) and encodings that all DLNA-certified products must understand. Consumers must understand many other data standards to interconnect devices, including multiple 802.11-something wireless network protocols; multiple high-definition video interconnection standards, including High-Definition Multimedia Interface (HDMI); Sony's HDNA (High Definition DNA); and *five different* Digital Video Interface (DVI) plug types.

Although we may understand the technical rationale behind each of these independent standards, from a consumer perspective, the existence of multiple standards that do not interoperate already breaks the promise of "standard" interoperation. The fact is, interoperation is nonstandard, and consumers have to take pains when they shop for products to ensure that the ones they buy conform to whatever sets of standards their existing products use. Caveat emptor.

We need a metastandard that bridges all the others, describing the data interchange format and protocols that each endpoint will use and providing instructions for endpoints that do not already know how to operate on those formats and protocols. Just one metastandard, please, or we're back where we started.

No More Wires

In our drive toward wireless communication, we're losing one of the advantages that wires provide: the clear definition of a *connection*. We typically think of a wire as a pipe that carries electronic signals from one end to the other. Wires get in the way, though. Any time more than a few wires are involved, they quickly get tangled and intertwined, making it nearly impossible to fix problems or reconfigure. A more critical pain, though, is that a wire constrains the distance of a connection, tethering an otherwise portable device to a confined range.

We don't need wires anymore for signal transfer—we can propagate a signal without a wire using radio, light, or other spectra. However, some other useful features of wires are difficult to replace. First, a wire is a relatively secure channel for information exchange. Fortunately, current cryptography can provide even stronger security when carefully applied. However, we have not yet found a way to replicate the *user interface* of a wire. A wire provides two fundamental user interface elements. First, a connected wire indicates the existence of a connection. Second, different types of physical connectors indicate the logically allowable connections.

Putting a wire between two endpoints creates a connection (sometimes referred to as "pairing"). How do you know what devices are connected to each other? Two ways: 1) experiment or 2) trace. The first way is to simply see whether two devices work together. For example, if you want to find out which lights a switch controls, flip the switch. This is useful only if you have some expectation that the connection does exist. If the experiment fails, you have to resort to tracing the connection. Find one endpoint of the connection and trace the wire to the other end; if the devices still do not work together, the problem is elsewhere, not in the connection.

How do you know what devices *can* be connected to each other? In some systems, such as the patch panel of early telephone switchboards, almost any connection is legitimate. In most systems, however, only certain things can be connected to each other. For example, you cannot plug an RJ-11 telephone plug into a household electricity socket, and you do not want to plug your video monitor into the audio jack of your computer. The direction of the connection can also be critical, usually to differentiate the source of a signal and the consumer of the signal, such as a video player to a monitor, an audio play to speakers, or a mouse to a computer. All sorts of physical connectors (RCA plugs, TRS connectors, RJ-11, RJ-14, RJ-25, and countless modern digital interface connectors) identify what types of endpoints can be connected to each other, sometimes including the directionality of the connection (for example, USB upstream and USB downstream connectors for hosts and clients, respectively).

These user-interface capabilities need to be replaced in an increasingly wireless world. Wireless signal propagation was the easy part, but we still have trouble detecting and creating connections between two devices (or services) and knowing what connections are allowable without wires.

Tangible Wireless

How can we make it easier to "pair" devices in a wireless world? How can your business design products to leverage network effects with mobile and ubiquitous devices without having to add a dozen different physical connectors (USB, SmartCard, Secure Digital, HDMI) or wireless radios (Bluetooth, 802.11, ZigBee), all of which are destined for rapid obsolescence? How can we re-create that physical, tangible character of a wired connection?

A wire provides continuity, an uninterrupted connection that two endpoints share. Continuity can be enabled in many ways. In wired systems, the physical continuity must persist, but in digital systems, once continuity has been shared, the devices and services can maintain the connection using digital identifiers, certificates, or other forms of credentials to perpetuate their capability to securely communicate.

Continuity can be provided in digital systems using the following techniques:

- **Shared identifiers:** The sending device identifies the recipient. A device's Internet address, media access control (MAC) address, serial number, or name are forms of identifiers that devices can share. Devices in a network can even construct identifiers on the fly, as long as they share the knowledge of which identifier corresponds to which device (or service).

- **Shared vocabulary:** Digital content does not *have* to be addressed to a particular recipient. Senders can simply push content out, and interested devices can pick it up by listening for descriptors they are interested in. The participating devices need only agree on the vocabulary they will use in the descriptors.

- **Shared physical experience:** Sensors can detect when two or more devices have experienced the same physical phenomenon, including the following. A conventional wire is a form of shared physical experience. The shared experience does not need to occur at the same time, but adding this constraint makes the sharing more secure.[2]

- **Location region:** GPS and other forms of location sensing can detect when devices or services are in a shared local region, such as local attractions, news, and weather, or for identifying devices in a building, such as printers, displays or projectors.
- **Physical proximity:** Various forms of near-field communication (NFC) can detect when two devices are in close presence of each other, without knowing their specific geographic location.
- **Sight:** Digital cameras allow devices (or services) to "see" others. The camera can see optical codes or other features that identify one of the devices and establish continuity between them.
- **Motion:** Accelerometers can detect when two devices have been moved in the same way (for example, shaking them together or being carried by the same person) or bumped[3] into each other.
- **Other senses:** Audio signatures, radio signatures, light patterns, chemical composition, and other sensing modalities can also detect when devices or services have shared a physical experience.

As mentioned, another advantage of physical wires is that they provide a level of security—only the physically connected devices can exchange information. Wireless media increase the risk of unwanted and undetectable eavesdropping. Wireless communication can be secured by using secure encryption, but setting up secure encryption involves complex installation procedures to ensure that the cryptographic keys are not intercepted; otherwise, some entity could masquerade using stolen keys.

Shared experience provides another means of ensuring that communicating devices are who they say they are. A shared experience creates a form of "location-limited channel" that can be combined with secure protocols to exchange cryptographic keys.[4]

Unexpected Data Channels

Humans exchange information across multiple sensory channels (audio, visual, and touch) whereas electronic devices primarily exchange information over electromagnetic media, converting voltage differentials to binary digits. Electronic devices actually can use any number of other sensors for transferring information, and they are incorporating more sensors for doing just that. Mobile phones, for example, contain displays and cameras that can present and read optically encoded data such as the two-dimensional bar codes called Quick Response codes (QR codes). They also contain speakers and microphones that can send and receive analog audio information that is converted to digital just like the old acoustic couplers that were once used for digital communications via modems over telephone lines. A recent example is a credit card reader, called Square, that plugs into the audio jack of an iPhone, allowing anyone to collect payment by credit card with their phone.[5]

Analog channels have much lower transfer rates than radio and conductive metal wires, so we don't think of using them. That's a mistake. Such channels provide a great way to quickly pair devices, allowing them to exchange cryptographic credentials that they can then use to communicate securely over a higher-bandwidth electromagnetic medium. In the past, a device that wanted to interoperate with others might need to carry special hardware (Bluetooth, USB ports, or infrared interchange), which added to the manufacturing cost of a device. That's no longer necessary: Many devices (digital cameras, smartphones, media players) have some kind of optical or acoustic input and/or output channel by which they can establish connections with others.

Let's look at an example of a Ubicomp prototype that incorporates these trends, enabling a new form of interoperation between a cellphone and a standard workplace printer.

Case Study: Xerox PrintTicket

Founded in 1906, Xerox has grown its core business from photographic paper manufacturing to become a globally recognized brand providing not only copier and printing equipment, but also a wide variety of document services and business process outsourcing. Despite the breadth of its offerings, though, Xerox is best known for its copiers, which are still central to much of its business.

Today's office copiers are full-service one-stop shops for office documents; they consist of a print engine, a scanner, a network connection, and a full computer inside. These "multifunction devices" (MFDs) can print, copy, scan, store, fax, send email, and process filled-out forms. New services can be added through an extensible interface platform (EIP), which can access the full power of the MFD's internal computer and connect to external, web-based services as well.

Xerox has long been aware that electronic computing technologies could one day supplant a major portion of its business in paper-based services. The company has reinvented itself several times to orient more toward information services, and not just printing. Xerox PARC was founded with the mission to create the "office of the future" (also known as the "paperless office"), which led to many digital technologies described in Chapter 1, "Introduction: Reading the Waves."

Recently, the high growth rate of smartphones and e-readers has taken another bite out of people's need to print paper. The high-resolution displays allow you to read emails, presentations, and many other kinds of documents you might have printed before. Not all printed material will be supplanted by mobile devices, though; despite decades of research, small electronic screens are not as convenient for some things or as easy to read as paper. On the other hand, some of the things people often printed in the past, such as maps or forms, are even better on smart phones than their paper counterparts because the devices provide real-time interaction and adjust output dynamically to get you where you need to go.

Nevertheless, people occasionally either need or want to print something from the phone. Frequently-asked-for capabilities include printing email attachments, presentations, brochures, and customized information sheets. People could print these before they leave the office, but it is hard to anticipate all the printed material that might be needed, and it would be wasteful to print something that ends up unneeded.

Although Xerox could easily add Bluetooth or WiFi to all its printing devices, it is not clear whether these wireless network connections would be used enough to offset the cost the hardware. However, new hardware isn't needed—most MFDs are already connected to the Internet via wired connections and secured behind firewalls, as are most handheld devices. This leads to a notion of networked print services, sometimes referred to as "cloud printing," which a number of print service vendors offer. The basic idea is that instead of requiring computers to send a document to a printer (called "push printing"), an MFD can fetch a document over the network and print it (called "pull printing"). As long as the handheld and the MFD are both sharing a secure network, pull printing is simple and easy to add to modern MFDs.[6]

Satchel

Researchers at Xerox Research Center Cambridge first envisioned pull printing in the late 1990s in a system they called Satchel.[7] At that time, handhelds did not necessarily have continuous access to the networks, and they did not have enough storage to contain the full document file. In the Satchel system, the handheld contained only an identifier called a "document token," which it could deliver securely to the printer via infrared beaming or which a person could manually enter on a keypad.

As with many innovations, Satchel was ahead of its time. Although handhelds of the time commonly used infrared for short wireless information exchange between themselves, printers did not. Since then, almost all handheld computers have a wireless radio connection; although only a fraction of printers have a wireless radio, almost all printers are directly connected to either a network or a networked computer.

Secure Optical Pairing

Two technical challenges are inherent to pull printing: 1) "pairing" the handheld with the MFD and 2) securing information if unsecure networks will be traversed. Generally, "pairing" is handled today by sending an email from the handheld to a particular email address for a network print service. Then the user goes to the printer that she wants to use and enters a code to release the print job on that printer. Entering an email address on a handheld can be awkward, but once entered, it can be stored for reuse. The security concerns are not completely solved and are typically just avoided by allowing such services to use only a secure internal network. Third-party network print service providers operate on the open Internet today, but potentially confidential documents have to be sent unencrypted to those services to be rendered for printing. Does a solution exist that provides super-simple pairing along with document security across multiple networks?

Let's start with pairing. From studies of mobile workers, we have seen that a common scenario consists of the user standing right in front of the printer she wants to use. The printer and the user's handheld are physically close, but they are unaware of each other. That's why the user has to tell the handheld what printer to use (by entering an email address) and then tell the printer what user she is by manually entering a code. However, we can circumvent all of that by using an optical code displayed on the handheld that the MFD scanner can read.

Scanning an optical code also enables a location-limited channel for securely exchanging information. Line of sight is a form of location-limited channel: If one device can "see" another, it is certain that the seen device exists physically within the line of sight. Although line of sight is potentially infinite (we can see remote galaxies within Earth's line of sight), it is also easy to block the line of sight to a very confined physical area, such as the glass platen of an MFD scanner. The scanner can retrieve an image of an optical code containing the document identifier, user identity, and cryptographic information. The user of the phone can ensure that only the MFD sees the optical code, and the MFD can then use the shared cryptographic information to decrypt the secured content it pulls from the network. Furthermore, the information exchanged between the printer and the phone is only as much as they both need to complete the task. The phone doesn't have to gain access to the printer's network, and vice versa.

These elements have been added in a prototype of a network print service called PrintTicket. In many ways, PrintTicket is an extension of the document Satchel concept (see sidebar on Satchel), but using modern technologies of high-functionality smartphones, MFDs, and optical codes. Figure 9-1 shows the high-level architecture of the PrintTicket prototype. Several variations are possible to enable different levels of security and ease of use. This approach offers the following advantages:

- Simple pairing takes place between printer and phone.
- Cryptographic material is exchanged across a location-limited channel.
- Information exchange is only as much as needed for a single purpose.

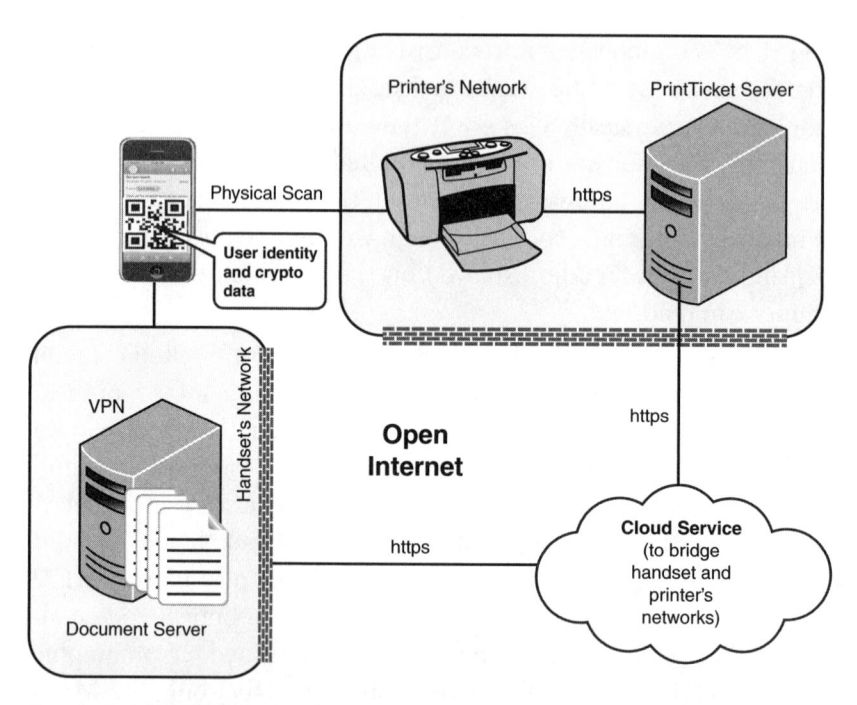

Figure 9-1 PrintTicket secure document exchange architecture. The printer's scanner can read the user identity, document location, and cryptographic information embedded in the QR code. The printer uses those credentials to retrieve, decrypt, and print the desired content.

How Well Can a Printer See?

Scanning a QR code with an MFD is a little trickier than you might expect. First of all, the scanners are tuned for reading paper, not electronic displays. Electronic displays have odd characteristics such as polarization, refresh rates, and backlighting that paper does not have, and these can throw off a scanner. In addition, the focus of a print scanner is tuned for the surface of the platen glass, whereas a phone display is often set back by a bezel surrounding the display.

9 • Discontinuous Connections

Fortunately, decoding of QR codes is fairly robust to imperfections. Images of phones such as those in Figure 9-2 can be decoded with practically 100% accuracy. A number of other practical issues could prevent this kind of solution from working on all phones, however. First, the phone has to be capable of displaying an arbitrary graphic, not just text; many phones do this, but not all. Second, phones with a clamshell design cannot be laid flat on a scanner (though some of these can still be read by a scanner). Another issue is that a button on the phone might be inadvertently pressed, or the touchscreen activated, when you place the phone on the platen glass.

Figure 9-2 Sample scans of QR codes by different models of printer/copiers and smartphones. (Image credit: Hua Liu and Arturo Lorenzo)

Any connection based on a noisy input mode, such as vision or audio, will not perform as reliably as a wired data connector. On the other hand, these kinds of noisy channels are universally available, open to any manufacturer of any device, whereas no device can offer all the possible physically wired data port specifications available.

Business Impact

The extent to which people will want to print documents off their portable devices isn't clear. After all, paper has now lost the advantage of superior portability, because electronic devices are small enough to fit in your pocket. From that respect, the business impact of mobile print solutions is uncertain. On the other hand, the major print device manufacturers do not want to be completely left out of the excitement surrounding this new wave of smartphone computing and have products or near-term plans to allow printing from mobile devices. Some of these solutions involve wireless radio technologies such as WiFi or Bluetooth, which adds cost to the hardware and complexity to the user interaction of pairing a handheld to a printer.

Almost all office printers have a physical connection to a network and usually are allowed to fetch web pages and other information residing outside a corporate firewall. Thus, no additional hardware is needed for data transfer, and only the device pairing needs a solution. PrintTicket provides a fast, simple-to-understand means of device pairing without requiring any additional hardware on a printer/scanner, providing advantages over competing cloud print solutions. At the very least, this capability increases the value of office printers as they interoperate with the new category of smartphone devices.

There is still a bit of a learning curve in North America and Europe on what an optical code means and what it is used for. Very soon, however, you could be printing from your phone as easily as you can make a photocopy today.

Summary

Interoperation is critical to adding value to services and devices and does not necessarily increase the cost of production. When people can use a product or service in combination with others, network effects occur that create an overall value that is the square of the number of interoperating devices and services.

Wireless networking has freed us from the ball-and-chain desktop computer. On the other hand, a few advantages to wires are difficult to replicate. Specifically, wires made it easy to troubleshoot connection problems because you could physically determine whether a wire was connected to the expected endpoints. Wires provided the "pairing" between devices that interoperated.

If we think of a wire as providing *continuity* between the two devices, we can identify other types of continuities that can be used instead. Continuity can be established by sharing identifiers, vocabulary, or physical experiences, such as location, proximity, sight, motion, sound, and other physical phenomena. Devices can communicate over analog media (visual and audio) other than radio frequency and wires, which opens up some unexpected ways to interoperate.

The Xerox PrintTicket prototype is an example of a novel way to easily print documents from a smartphone on a printer/scanner even if the two devices are not connected to the same network. By displaying an optical code on the smartphone, the printer/scanner can scan the code, decode the embedded document location and security information, retrieve the document, and print it. Despite the fact that printer scanners were not designed for reading smartphone screens, optical codes over the visual channel can be reliably decoded. This capability provides a new way to create value for printing services in the new business areas created by pervasive mobile computers.

Endnotes

[1] Mark Blocker, "How to Do Fuse Visual and Continuity Tests," eHow.com, www.ehow.com/video_5774048_do-fuse-visual-continuity-tests.html (accessed 20 August 2010).

[2] D.K. Smetters, D. Balfanz, G.E. Durfee, T. Smith, and K. Lee, "Instant Matchmaking: Simple, Secure Virtual Extensions to Ubiquitous Computing Environments," in *Proceedings of the 8th International Conference of Ubiquitous Computing*, Irvine, Calif., 17–21 September 2006.

[3] See http://bu.mp/ as an example.

[4] D. Balfanz, D.K. Smetters, P. Stewart, and H.C. Wong, "Talking to Strangers: Authentication in Ad-hoc Wireless Networks," Network and Distributed System Security Symposium, San Diego, Calif., 6–8 February 2002.

[5] D. Pogue, "A Simple Swipe on a Phone, and You're Paid," *New York Times*, 30 Sep 2010. www.nytimes.com/2010/09/30/technology/personaltech/30pogue.html (last accessed 10 Oct 2010)

[6]Xerox Newsroom, "New Xerox Mobile Print Solution to Allow Procter & Gamble to Print from Smartphones," 6 May 2010.

[7]M. Lamming, M. Eldridge, M. Flynn, C. Jones, and D. Pendlebury, "Satchel: Providing Access to Any Document, Any Time, Anywhere," *ACM Transactions on Computer-Human Interaction* 7, no. 3 (September 2000): 322–352. http://doi.acm.org/10.1145/355324.355326

10

Coordination

Of all the things I've done, the most vital is coordinating those who work with me and aiming their efforts at a certain goal.
—Walt Disney

How many ways do you have today of getting a message to someone? Desk phone, mobile phone, email, email groups, instant message, Skype, Facebook, LinkedIn, Twitter, YouTube, SMS, others? Too many for most of us to use effectively, but the younger generations of "digital natives" are quite adept at selecting the appropriate channel for the type of communication (social, work, or other) and the current situation (public space, classroom, private area, and so on). The growing proliferation of communication modes means more people are vying for attention, sometimes interrupting each other's activities.

The Cost of Interruptions

When you're in a social setting, interruptions are just irritating, but in the workplace, these interruptions cost real money. As mentioned in Chapter 2, "Profound Technologies," some estimates put the cost of interruptions in the workplace as high as $900 billion in the U.S. workforce[1] and state that cutting sources of overload on workers by 15% could save a company of 500 employees as much as $2 million per year.[2]

Many would agree that sources of interruption and distraction must be reduced to help people stay focused on their objectives. The problem is in determining whether something is a distraction or a necessary piece of information for accomplishing goals. We all have a hard time separating the chaff from the wheat consistently. If it's hard for humans to do, how could computers hope to do any better?

In computer research, we often use human intelligence as the "gold standard" of accuracy. We compare the results obtained by an artificial intelligence technique against those of humans performing the same function and see how well the machine can do. For mechanical tasks such as number crunching, computers excel, but for complex and subtle problems, such as making recommendations or decisions, computers often fare poorly. Is that because binary computation is inherently limited or is it because the humans who program the machines have imperfect understanding of the problem? My guess is the latter. Amazingly, we have seen examples of some problems in which computers can use machine learning techniques and outperform humans doing the same task. One such problem is in detecting whether a person is interruptible.

Case Study: Sun Microsystems, Presence and Availability Predictions

In a remarkable set of experiments conducted by Fogarty and Hudson[3] at Carnegie Mellon University, a set of participants were interrupted by a computer in their office at random points during the day. They then stated a score for how interruptible they were just before that moment, on a scale of 1 (highly interruptible) to 5 (highly non-interruptible). At the same time, a video camera in the office recorded the scene and detected the physical situation of the subject before the interruption. The video contained contextual information such as whether the participant was sitting, standing, walking, talking on the phone, using a computer, or drinking water, along with how many people were in the office and other factors.

A subset of the data containing the contextual factors and the subjects' interruptibility reports was used to train a computer to model the situations when the subjects were highly non-interruptible. Then those models were used to estimate the subjects' interruptibility on the remaining data, which the computer had not yet seen. Next, the researchers asked a set of people to watch videos and estimate how interruptible the subject was just before the recorded interruptions. Remarkably, the computer estimates were more often correct (79.5%) than the human estimates (76.9%).[4] The researchers divided the subjects into different job roles and saw that the computer's accuracy could be as high as 87.7% when assessing the interruptibility of managers. Although the computer still got it wrong 12.3% of the time, the computer error rate was almost half that of humans (23.1%) in estimating managers' levels of interruptibility.

This result is particularly impressive when you think about how difficult it is to read all the subtle clues people give off to indicate whether they are interruptible. Some indicators seem easy to read: unswerving back to the door, head down, talking to someone, concentrated expression. Even those indicators can be misleading, however, and others are more ambiguous: An office door might be closed to block outside noise or to signal that the person mustn't be interrupted, someone looking at a computer screen could be concentrating or daydreaming, and someone on the phone may be actively listening to a conference call or thinking about something else. We generally reach conclusions through a combination of cues, not just one, and that's what the machine learning techniques do as well. These studies indicate that Ubiquitous Computing technologies could reduce distractions despite the proliferation of communication tools at our disposal.

Suppose that interruptibility detection succeeds and we all suffer fewer interruptions. Would that mean others are blocked in getting their work done because they cannot interrupt you? What should they do if they cannot reach you? Should they wait for a better time or attempt to make progress through some other route? That's a common dilemma people face when they cannot reach someone they need. One of the deciding factors is how long it will take before the missing person can be reached. Along with that is the question of when the person will have enough time to deal with the issue. When people have worked together for a while in a tight-knit group, they gain an awareness of each other's patterns of comings and goings;

when others tend to start answering phone calls or email, take lunch, and leave the office; typical commute time; and general availability. Sociologist Eviatar Zerubavel discovered this kind of rhythm awareness in the 1980s. In a study of hospital nurses, physicians, and other staff, Zerubavel found that coworkers use a shared sense of temporal patterns to coordinate their work activity and form expectations of task completion, communication availability, and more. In fact, the hospital workers could practically tell what time it was simply by noticing the activities in their environment that occurred with relatively uniform rates of recurrence (medications, visits, shift changes, and so on).

Rhythm awareness is used all the time in coordinating good times to call each other, and we build this awareness over time by observing situations that turn out to have been good or bad times to call. Unfortunately, in our increasingly global workforce and society, it is more difficult to build a mental model of rhythmic patterns because we don't see each other's comings and goings on the net. We may interact with remote colleagues only over email or during prescheduled phone calls, which provide no indication of the recurring patterns of presence and availability.

However, as we've seen with the previous examples of behavioral pattern modeling, it is possible to construct a computer-based rhythm model that telecommunication systems can use for call coordination. At Sun Microsystems, I participated in a research project that collected presence data for a tight-knit workgroup with members in California, Massachusetts, and France. The periods when work time overlaps across those time zones are brief, so it is crucial to time calls appropriately. More important, perhaps, is that when a remote colleague is not in the office, the computational model can predict when the person *would* be available in the future. We saw that an online calendar is not sufficient for coordinating communication because the calendar represents only a *plan* for how time will be spent. Actual attendance at scheduled meetings differs from the plan in several respects: The person might skip the meeting, the meeting could run late, or perhaps the person will be available to communicate via email or text messaging even during a scheduled appointment. A person's actual online presence is a stronger indicator of availability than the calendar is.

To explore the effectiveness and value of computer-generated patterns for remotely collaborating teams, we recorded people's presence in an instant messaging system over a period of three months. Figure 10-1 shows the presence patterns for an individual using an instant messaging system for Mondays, logged in at the office. The activity begins as early as 9:00 AM, but only 20% of the time, usually kicking in fully before 9:30, after which time the person is present 80% of the time until about 10:30. After 11:00, the person is again very often available until lunch, from which he returns usually well before 1:00, but occasionally not until about 1:05. He's usually present for communication again until about 2:00 and then again available after 2:30 or 3:00, but with less certainty. His presence at this location usually lasts until around 5:00 and sometimes as late as 6:30. In this example, we can see the patterns and interpret some meaning as human observers. However, it is more difficult for a computer to "see" such patterns and determine whether a dip is "significant" or "noise," or uncover the likely cause of a dip.

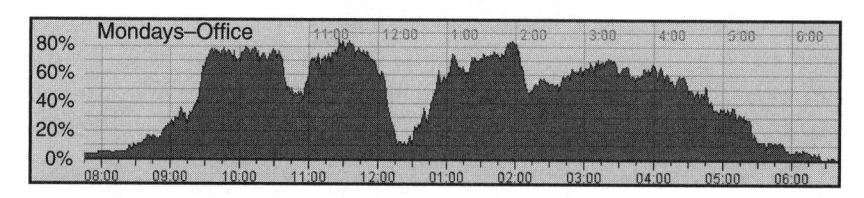

Figure 10-1 Visualization of presence history for a person on Mondays at the office. Note the typical regions of online and offline periods: start of day, lunch, end of day, and two unlabeled but often recurring periods of offline in the morning and afternoon.

Figure 10-2 shows another example of the presence history for a different person on Mondays, this time across multiple locations (home and office). The upper portion shows the historic presence probability (the white horizontal lines are threshold marks that, when crossed, indicate a *statistically significant* drop in presence). The lower portion shows the computer-generated rhythm model extracted from the presence data. Where possible, labels for the non-present periods were extracted from the user's online calendar or from self-evident characteristics of the day (start of day, end of day, changes in location, lunch).

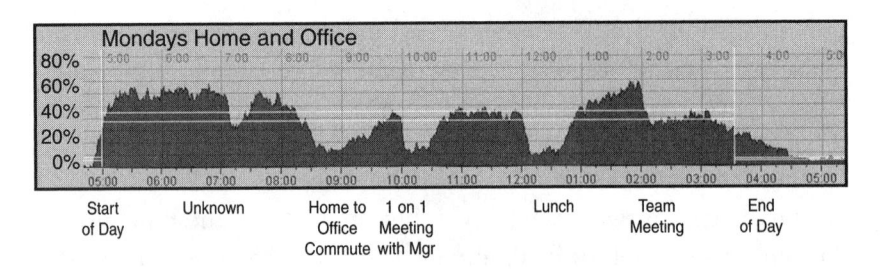

Figure 10-2 An extracted rhythm model for one person's online presence on Mondays at home and office. The graph shows the percentage of times in which this person was present in an instant messaging system over several months. Beneath the graph, the rhythm model shows the likely reasons for significant recurring periods of nonpresence.

In this example, the daily activity regularly begins around 5:00 AM (yes, one of those oddball early risers) at the person's home office. An unscheduled recurring break is detected between 7:00 and 7:30, generally lasting less than 20 minutes, on 30% of the days—this corresponds to a period when he participates in his family's morning preparations. Another unscheduled break is detected between 8:00 and 10:00 and lasts between 45 and 90 minutes. It corresponds to a location-change transition of "home to office," representing his typical commute to work.

A recurring meeting, "1 on 1 meeting with mgr," starts promptly at 10:00, lasting around 30 minutes. A lunch break is detected between about 11:40 and 1:15, generally lasting between 30 and 75 minutes, typically 45 minutes. The "Team meeting" is detected 50% of the time (a biweekly meeting), promptly starting at 2:00 and lasting between 20 and 75 minutes. The day ends with equal probability anywhere between 3:00 and 4:30, and occasionally later.

Rhythm Awareness for Distributed Teams

In the trials at Sun Microsystems, we collected presence logs for 20 people for up to ten months working in locations in California, Massachusetts, and France. The patterns we extracted from trials indicated that computers can supplement some of the knowledge that people gain intuitively. Teams of people with little or no experience working together can quickly see coworkers' patterns that would otherwise take weeks or months to learn.

Although not every person exhibits well-defined rhythms, when people do, it helps coordinate contact. In some cases, the rhythm patterns were a more accurate representation of a person's typical availability than what people listed in their online calendars because some scheduled appointments are habitually skipped and other recurring events are not scheduled at all (such as start and end of day, commute times, and lunch).

A number of messaging systems today indicate whether a person is "present" and reachable for communication. Presence information was initially seen in Instant Messaging (IM) systems and is increasingly showing up in email systems, social networks, and even voice communication systems to let you know when someone is "online." Unfortunately, if the person is not online, you're stuck. Presence information does not currently include an estimate of how long you might have to wait before you can catch that person again. Rhythm modeling makes it possible to predict when someone is likely to come back, if he or she is away, and also when someone is likely to go offline, in case you need to reach that person before the end of the day.

Figure 10-3 shows an example of integrating rhythm predictions in a presence information display. In this example, the current time is 12:14 PM on a Thursday. The system detects that Bo is away (his name is grayed out), was last seen in his office, and likely is at an appointment labeled Staff Meeting until 2:12 (the meeting officially ends at 2:00, but it always takes time to get back to his office). It predicts that John is at lunch and is expected to return by 1:07 (information not available in John's calendar). Rosco has left for the day and is expected to return around 8:42 AM the next day (his usual daily arrival time on Fridays). Jean is currently present, but the rhythm model predicts that she will depart by 4:28, in case you need to reach her before she leaves.

In general, rhythm awareness provides estimates of how much time is typical for a particular event and can be used for general planning purposes, not just finding good times to make contact. We do this already when making project plans that include estimates for how long a particular task will require. However, inaccuracies in our mental model of temporal rhythms can result in process breakdowns. Breakdowns in *plan formation* occur when the mental model has incomplete coverage of a situation and cannot provide an estimate for a particular action. Breakdowns in *plan execution* occur when the estimate is radically different than what actually occurs. Such breakdowns happen regularly among distributed teams who are unaware of the typical time spent on events at different locations. Typically, our mental models of rhythms have a personal bias that cause us to underestimate how much time other people should take in their part of the work and to overestimate the time needed to accomplish our own tasks. Computational rhythm models do not replace human mental models of temporal patterns, but they do supplement human awareness by showing actual behavior.

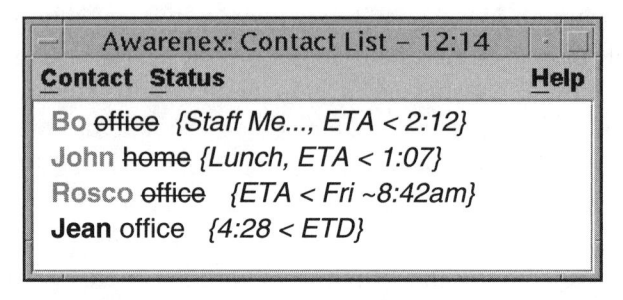

```
    Awarenex: Contact List - 12:14
Contact  Status                              Help
Bo office   {Staff Me..., ETA < 2:12}
John home   {Lunch, ETA < 1:07}
Rosco office   {ETA < Fri ~8:42am}
Jean office   {4:28 < ETD}
```

Figure 10-3 The use of rhythm predictions in an online presence system. Several people are not online, but the system shows their likely return time. One person is currently online, and the system shows her likely departure time, in case you need to reach her today.

How Is a Telephone Like a Four-Year-Old Child?

My cellphone is worse than my kids, frankly. They both interrupt when I am already talking to someone else. A child might get scolded for the interruption, but we all know that the telephone is too stupid to learn. It doesn't have to be that way, though, and emerging technologies can make devices that are as polite as Ms. Manners herself.

I previously described the experiments by Fogarty and Hudson that showed that a computer could estimate whether a person was interruptible with almost half as many errors as a human performing the same estimate. In that experiment, the sensors were simulated so the results were theoretical—would the results be true using actual physical sensors? To find out, we built a sensor system out of spare parts in the lab and simple electronics from Radio Shack that we called Lilsys. The sensors could detect four situations:

- A motion sensor detected the physical presence of a person in the office.
- A microphone detected people talking in the office.
- Use of the phone indicated that the user was in a conversation even if the microphone picked up little or no sound.
- Closing the office door indicated either a desire for privacy or simply a need to block external sounds.

The states of these sensors were combined using the same algorithms suggested by Fogarty and Hudson to determine the level of a person's availability to an interruption. Figure 10-4 indicates the information flow from the sensors to the presentation of the availability prediction, using a U.S. traffic sign metaphor to convey a sense of caution when approaching an "unavailable" recipient. The red inverted triangle Yield sign indicates that the person is *possibly* unavailable. For example, the person might have closed his or her office door or might be on the phone but not talking (such as not participating actively in a conference call). The round red Do Not Enter sign denotes a stronger indication that the user is *probably* unavailable: He or she might be involved in a conversation (on the phone or face-to-face) or might be heavily engaged in a task on the computer (editing, searching, coding, budgeting, and so on).

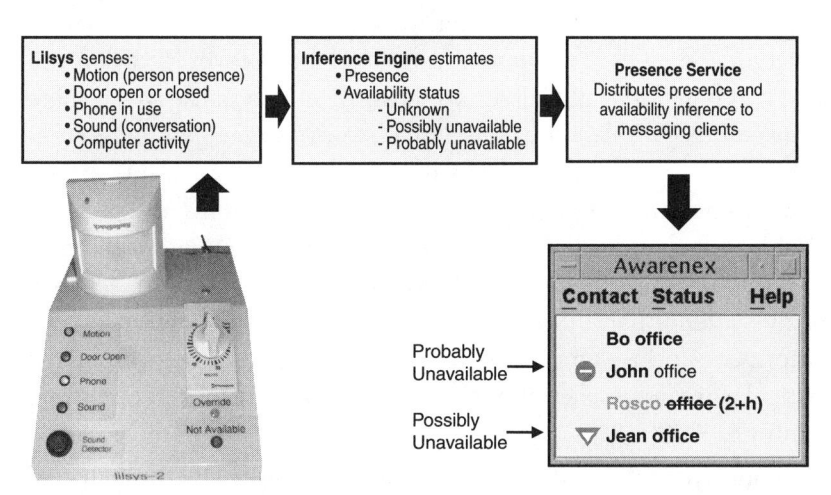

Figure 10-4 Sensors detect the physical situation and are used to infer the likelihood that a person is available, which is displayed to others via a presence service.

We constructed four of the sensor systems and deployed them in remote coworkers' offices in California, Massachusetts, and France. Another ten users had at least one of the Lilsys-enabled users on their presence contact list and could see the system's prediction of interruptibility. The system provided effective indications of remote coworkers' availability, which callers used to time their calls and to explain their disruptions in cases when they nevertheless made an interruption.

Big Brother Creepiness

Of course, these kinds of inferences raise concerns about what computers can tell and who they are telling it to. Chapter 5, "Missing Ingredients," has a section describing the core reasons for people's general concerns about technological encroachments on personal privacy. The ability to detect and describe temporal rhythms raises some unique concerns. Is the computer telling my boss that I don't usually get into the office until 10:30 AM? Is my boss also seeing the part of the pattern that shows I put in a lot of personal time at home? What impression of me are other people getting from this limited computer-generated model of my work habits?

We use a principle in human-to-human social interaction called "plausible deniability" to explain awkward social behavior, such as avoiding someone you don't want to talk to: "Oh, I didn't recognize you there!" or "Oh, I must have been out of cell coverage when you called." These kinds of excuses are possible only because we all share a sense of the unreliability of certain systems. An increase in the reliability of a technology decreases its usefulness as a plausible excuse for a miscommunication. Sensors and presence systems are generally reliable, which causes some people to dislike them. One of the nice things about the statistical model of presence rhythms is that they make evident that there is inherent variability to your presence patterns, restoring the plausibility that you might not be present at a particular moment, even if in general you tend to be present around that time.

Aside from the restoration of plausible deniability, though, the creepiness factor of a computer watching your actions can be overcome only if the benefits outweigh the risks and costs. In the examples described here, we saw that people very quickly accepted and adopted the information the systems provided into their regular practice of distributed collaboration.

Accepting these systems partly resulted from the safeguards that the systems provided. Focus group participants had said they wanted to be able to "hide" from the system anytime they wanted. To accommodate that requirement, the Lilsys sensors included a timer switch that would override the sensors for a period of time. If the user wanted to permanently opt out, she could flip another switch, which took all of the sensors offline until switched back. After trying the switches to confirm that they worked as designed, users in our trials never used them again. We should not interpret this to mean that the switches were wasted and unnecessary. In fact, users reported that they needed the reassurance that they could opt out of the system at will. This is an important lesson for context-aware systems: Give the users complete, simple, and direct control from the beginning and they may never need to use it. If you hide the controls or make them complicated, users will begin to mistrust the use of their information. Too bad Facebook didn't know about this before the furor its complex privacy interfaces caused.

Business Impact

The goal of these technologies is to increase the productivity of a workforce by making it easier to coordinate and communicate with each other. How is productivity measured? In economics, productivity is defined as the ratio of output per labor-hour. At the macroeconomic level, this can be characterized by comparing the monetary amount of goods and services produced against the number of workers employed. Unfortunately, productivity is not as easily measured at microeconomic levels because many laborers, such as managers, administrators, and other overhead job functions, do not contribute *directly* to the quantifiable goods or services of a business. Even for employees like factory line workers who are clearly contributing directly to goods and services, it is not easy to determine the amount of contribution each has made to the whole product.

As a result, most assessments of productivity at the micro level are inevitably qualitative. Nevertheless, even qualitative assessments provide an indication of positive versus negative effectiveness. In our trials of distributed group awareness technologies, we saw a number of enhancements to the groups' communication practices.

First, remote colleagues who could see visualizations of each other's rhythmic presence patterns and interruptibility found more times to talk together. Why would it make a difference? One reason is that there is a general reluctance to interrupt a person. Co-located workers tend to peer into an office to get a sense of whether a person is approachable at any given moment. When coworkers are remote and have no information to assess a remote person's interruptibility, the safest assumption is that they are busy and that an email is the best approach, which inevitably delays the remote collaboration. Also, many people have some odd times when they are available outside of the standard office hours of 9 to noon and 1 to 6. Some people arrive early to beat traffic; others stay late. Some people work during lunch or put in some time in the evenings. Unless these patterns are made apparent, there is no way for coworkers to realize when they have overlapping periods of availability outside the norm.

Second, although the interruptibility sensors did not seem to diminish the number or frequency of interruptions, users of the systems reported qualitative improvements in the character of the interruptions. Why and in what way would that improve productivity? It seems that even in physically co-located workgroups, the fact that a recipient appears *not* to be interruptible does not usually *prevent* an interruption. However, the appearance of uninterruptibility does cause the caller to approach more gradually and politely, allowing the recipient to indicate whether she can accept a long or short disruption. Restoring the sense of interruptibility for remote workgroups allows them to manage the duration of disruptions more effectively by restoring customary social cues to communication. Even though the amount of interruptions remained the same with or without interruptibility sensors, coworkers were better able to manage the character and duration of interruptions. Overall, distributed awareness technologies provide the information needed to identify more opportunities for collaborative work, generally improving workgroup effectiveness.

Summary

A rising cost of doing business is the overhead of coordination and communication among employees, groups, projects, and departments that are distributed geographically. Although people could theoretically schedule their communication more effectively, as co-located teams do, distributed teams do not have the information needed to identify better or worse times and situations. The result is interruption chaos costing U.S. business an estimated $900 billion annually.

We generally believe that we can detect whether a person is interruptible by appearance: body posture, intensity of activity, expression, engagement in conversation, and other clues. I described a remarkable set of experiments in which computer software was able to more accurately detect whether a person was interruptible than other humans looking at the same situation.

Co-located workgroups develop a sense of each other's comings and goings, developing a "rhythm awareness" of when and where coworkers are and will be. They use this to implicitly schedule face-to-face communication or to seek alternative sources of information when communication is not expected to be possible soon enough. Workgroups are increasingly geographically distributed as a result of growing globalization, telecommuting, and the economic and environmental pressures to reduce travel. Unfortunately, distributed groups have more trouble finding ways to maintain awareness of each other's activities, which is needed to form a tight-knit, high-performance team.

In prototype systems developed at Sun Microsystems and deployed across a globally distributed workgroup, we saw examples of how sensor-based information can be used to convey notions of interruptibility and rhythm awareness to distributed coworkers. The systems prudently leave the decision of whether to interrupt to the humans and merely provide analyses that augment the person's own knowledge of the situation and appropriateness of an interruption.

Concerns about invasions of personal information were mitigated by providing explicit control of the sensors, allowing people to opt in and out of the system at any moment. Despite the fact that these controls were never used, the capability was critical to acceptance of the sensors.

These distributed awareness tools allowed a globally distributed team to maintain cohesion and effective communication across distance and time zones. The systems re-created the cues that allowed effective social protocols that co-located groups use to optimize their coordination and communication.

Endnotes

[1] Jonathan Spira and David Goldes, "Information Overload: We Have Met the Enemy and He Is Us," March 2007, http://bsx.stores.yahoo.net/inovwehamete.html

[2] John Gantz, Angéle Boyd, and Seana Dowling, "Cutting the Clutter: Tackling Information Overload at the Source," an IDC whitepaper, March 2009.

[3] S. Hudson, J. Fogarty, C. Atkeson, D. Avrahami, J. Forlizzi, S. Kiesler, J. Lee, and J. Yang, "Predicting Human Interruptibility with Sensors: A Wizard of Oz Feasibility Study," in *Proceedings of the SIGCHI Conference on Human Factors in Computing Systems,* Ft. Lauderdale, Florida, 5–10 April 2003.

[4] J. Fogarty, S.E. Hudson, and J. Lai, "Examining the Robustness of Sensor-Based Statistical Models of Human Interruptibility," in *Proceedings of the SIGCHI Conference on Human Factors in Computing Systems,* Vienna, Austria, 24–29 April 2004).

11

Clear Sailing

The effect of sailing is produced by a judicious arrangement of the sails to the direction of the wind.
—William Falconer, *Universal Dictionary of the Marine*, 1784[1]

The previous chapters described ways to reduce costs through personalization, proactive information delivery, inexpensive device interoperation and efficient group coordination. Combined, these savings should free up resources for more profitable pursuits, and that's where it gets exciting. All businesspeople know that there are two ways to increase profit: reduce cost or increase revenue. Reducing cost is always painful, no matter how necessary, whereas increasing revenue is exhilarating. Instead of using the hard-bitten tactics needed to compete in existing markets by cutting and chopping costs, we want to identify new, uncharted waters for clear sailing.

Among the many books on the topic of using innovation processes to create new business, one that explores this fully is *Blue Ocean Strategy*, by Kim and Mauborgne.[2] They describe strategies at a business level for how to create a culture that seeks new markets. Here, this book explores strategies at a *product* and *technology* level for creating new value. The proliferation of Ubiquitous Computing technologies raises whole new categories of product and service categories in various industries. I start by describing some underutilized technologies and unrecognized information problems in a vertical industry, retail brick-and-mortar; then I show how that can lead to novel business opportunities.

Interactive Public Information Displays

Digital displays are quickly supplanting physical signs to push products everywhere: at the mall, in the airport, on the freeway, in taxi cabs, on theater screens, and even at the gas pump. Some of the displays are marvelous technologies—large, full color, and bright enough to see even in the glaring sun. These technologies are at the heart of a new segment of digital out of home (OOH) advertising, which is estimated at about $2.5 billion revenue in the United States in 2009;[3] that's a substantial chunk of the estimated total for outdoor advertising of $5.9 billion in 2009.[4] Nice business, but how far can digital OOH marketing go? Will it simply continue to grow by replacing physical OOH advertising, capping out once all outdoor displays are electronic? After all, outdoor advertising was estimated in 2008 to have been only about 2.8% ($4B) of the total measured marketing[5] spent in the United States ($142 billion).[6]

Some aspects of digital displays suggest that it should be possible to grow the segment. Digital displays are capable of more eye-catching animation and visual effects than static signs. Also, the content can be rotated to display multiple ads, whereas a static sign has only one fixed image. Some digital displays have motion sensors or cameras that can detect when a person comes near and can trigger the playback of an advertisement. The Reactrix digital projection system uses a camera to "see" members of the audience and provides game-like interaction with the content. These enhancements should increase the number of impressions that an ad receives, potentially raising the relative effectiveness of digital OOH advertising to capture a larger segment of overall ad spending.

Furthermore, some aspects of digital technologies should reduce costs, increasing the bottom-line profitability. Digital signs are increasingly being connected to advertising networks that update content remotely, allowing faster rotation of ad content and quick removal of unsold display inventory. Adding cameras or motion sensors to displays allows marketers to measure audience response rates, providing concrete measures of ad effectiveness analogous to those provided by web advertising. Network distribution and audience measurement should improve efficiencies, but they don't bring *new capabilities* that will increase the proportion of marketing dollars spent on OOH advertising relative to other segments.

On the other hand, audience-measurement technologies are likely to prove definitively that most people *ignore* outdoor signage. In fact, with MP3 players, digital video recorders, e-readers, portable video players, and smartphones, people today are in more control of what media they consume, not only when they're in their homes, but also when they are out and about. People riding on mass transit, waiting in airports, or riding in the back of the family minivan are no longer aimlessly staring off into space, hungry to consume any intelligible tidbit of information regardless of its worth. Rather, they are reading a pulp novel, making business plans, or watching the latest episode of a favorite television show on a portable computer.

Regardless of the eye-catching graphics, digital OOH displays are likely to remain a small segment of marketing as long as they are no more than a digital replica of static signage; in these cases, the display is simply a barker for products, broadcasting wares without regard to what the people seeing the displays care about. Sure, barking out products will sell a few more bags of peanuts at the ballpark, but it's irritating and probably puts off some segment of the audience. The bigger opportunity comes when *engaging* with customers to find out what they need and what criteria matter most, and then adopting the presentation to match. With interactive digital technologies, manufacturers now have the opportunity to engage in a *dialogue* with the customers—not in a pushy, hard-sell mode, but rather in a deeper manner where customers are finding the support they need to make purchase decisions.

Minority Report got it all wrong. In a famous scene in that movie, the hero, John Anderton, is walking briskly through an airport terminal while being inundated by holographic advertisements. The ads are annoying and clearly ineffective because, although they call him by name, the ads are not paying attention to their prospective customer. If you watch that scene, you can see clearly that John Anderton is in no mood for a new fragrance, a car, or even a refreshing beverage. The ads are simply reacting mechanically to the presence of people and blasting their message without tailoring the message to the customer. What's missing in most visions of the future of advertising is that the communication can now go both ways. The customer has something to say, and smart ads can listen.

Retail Decision Support

Making a purchase is a decision problem. Many factors influence a purchase decision, some of which are difficult to characterize and not well understood. Most marketing texts[7] describe a process in which consumers evaluate product alternatives by weighing multiple criteria and then applying a variety of decision rules to make a choice. Evaluation criteria range from basic attributes of the product, to attitudes about brand and lifestyle, as well as aesthetic factors and emotional response.

Effective salespeople read customers and shape the information to what they perceive to be most useful for them, while at the same time trying to make a sale. Sales practices have been examined in marketing and sociological research. In a deep study of sales practices from the 1980s reported in *Making Sales*,[8] sociologist Robert Prus uncovered the key elements of the face-to-face sales process:

- Promote interest
- Generate trust
- Neutralize reservations
- Obtain commitments (to purchase, lease, try, and so on)
- Manage disruptions from others
- Foster long-term relationships

During this process, the buyer's goal is to spend as little as possible and the seller wants to acquire as much as possible for the merchandise. These competing goals set the scene for a somewhat antagonistic relationship, but the buyer and seller also share an objective: satisfying the buyer's criteria with available merchandise. The buyer and seller have complementary knowledge for reaching a resolution. The buyer has at least a vague notion of what she wants but not the full range of a seller's options; the seller knows what is available but not what would optimally fit the shopper's criteria.

The sales process is a negotiation between these parties to optimize their mutual objective. From this perspective, shopping is a collaborative information-seeking process with the ultimate goal of making a mutually satisfying sales transaction. To receive effective assistance from a seller, the buyer must communicate criteria to the seller while simultaneously withholding information that could result in paying more than desired.

IT for Shopping

Reaching a purchase decision requires information about availability, cost, size, colors, texture, feel, fit, style trends, and so on. Such information needs underlie the success and continued expansion of information technology (IT) for online shopping. Using the web, shoppers can find a great deal of information about products they are interested in and they can search and compare alternative choices side by side.

In contrast to the rapid evolution of online shopping, the experience of shopping in a physical retail store has changed little during recent decades. Due to the inherent requirements of physical space, shoppers must expend more energy and time searching for products in a physical environment than when searching online. Often the full range of a merchant's inventory and product alternatives is not physically apparent (some unseen inventory might be available in the back of the store). For physical products, a shopper can compare items only by examining each one sequentially, either because products are located at different merchants or because the shopper can evaluate only one item at a time, such as when trying on clothes.

Although online shopping is used across many product categories, assessing products in certain categories, such as furniture, apparel, eyeglass frames, and jewelry products, usually includes some form of tactile and physical information: texture, fit, drape, flow, movement, light reflection, heft, and so on. These kinds of information are difficult to communicate electronically because they use human-sensing modalities that are not easily reproducible via electronic transfer and/or are based on each individual's subjective human perception. Although it is possible to simulate the look of clothing over an electronic image of a person (see Virtual Fittings sidebar), it is ultimately necessary to physically touch and *wear* the product to gauge the texture, heft, and other factors. For these reasons, electronic media cannot wholly supplant physical shopping for certain classes of products.

In addition to these tactile properties, certain intangible aspects determine how well the article *fits* the shopper. Fit is determined not only by the dimensions of the product, but also by how well suited the item is to the *presentation of self* that the shopper intends to project, sometimes referred to as *style*. Product selection also involves assessing information about the social context of products, such as style trends and the personal opinions of others, typically family and friends. Online shopping provides technologies for direct searching and even recommending items related to a focal product. However, current recommender technologies are incapable of suggesting products according to abstract characteristics such as "fashionable" because fashion is complex and subtle, varying drastically with the situation and people involved.

Social Aspects of Fashion Decisions

When buying clothes, a shopper often assesses how others would perceive a particular item—that is, the "fashion statement" she is making. Evaluating one's self-image is an important part of clothes-buying decisions, but shoppers in a store are provided very little information about what other people are wearing, other than what is presented in advertisements. Within a store, shoppers often ask companions or store assistants how they look to get this kind of feedback. Outside of the store, people find inspiration from others and from the fashion media.

Sociologists have long explored the multiple roles fashion plays in society. In a synthesis of more than 200 sources, sociologist Fred Davis examined the social construction of meaning in fashion and how an individual's choices communicate social status, gender identity, sexuality, and conformity among other subtle characteristics of self.[9] Clothing is undoubtedly used as a form of communication, conveying mood, tone, and occasionally a bold statement, but Davis describes it as a code of "low semanticity" that changes with time and trends and among different groups of individuals.[10]

Although technologies cannot interpret fashion, they can mediate human discussions of the topic. We see this happening today in online social fashion networks such as GoTryItOn.com and IQONS.com. These sites allow members to upload photographs of themselves wearing various outfits and can categorize, tag, and comment on the images. The services merely provide communication infrastructure for members to construct meaningful information through tagging and commentary. The computers in these systems are simply transporting bits, not intelligently processing information, but they are nevertheless providing critical information that the users could not otherwise obtain.

Case Study: Responsive Mirror

We look at ourselves in a mirror (or "looking glass") for many reasons, including when grooming, for personal health, during dance and athletic training, or when shopping for apparel (clothing, jewelry, hats, eyeglasses, and other accessories). In all of these situations, the mirror provides information to the observer on what they look like to others. In fact, mirrors may be the oldest information technology of all. The earliest manufactured mirrors appeared in Anatolia (modern Turkey) around 6000 B.C.; the earliest forms of writing did not appear until 4000 B.C.

Clothing stores often provide a private place to undress and try on clothes (changing room) and a private or semi-private place with a mirror to view the fit (fitting room). The fitting-room mirror is a specific point of customer interaction with products where a shopper selects items to purchase. Marketers have recognized the importance of the fitting room as a "touch point" with customers. A few prototype technologies[11] have been constructed for this domain, but rarely with the aim of supporting the decision-making process. Most often, retailers see an opportunity to up-sell or cross-sell merchandise, relegating the technologies in the fitting room to nothing more than advertising extensions.

When a shopper enters a fitting room, she has a problem to solve. She's there to decide which, if any, of the several alternatives she's selected from the sales racks will best meet her needs. That is her number one objective in the fitting room. Until she has resolved that question, technologies that are up-selling and cross-selling are wasting their electronic breath. A more effective technology would be one that helps her narrow the selection.

Selection criteria vary from one shopper to another, but two main questions are being addressed in a fitting room. One, of course, is whether the clothes fit comfortably. In a study we conducted observing men trying on casual and sports shirts, we saw a variety of behaviors to test the fit. Some participants moved very little in front of the mirror, but the majority turned to look at themselves from all sides. A few people even practiced golf swings and other sports moves to test the feel of the clothing throughout the entire range of motion.

Second is how shoppers look in the clothes. That second one is not simply a matter of looking in the mirror. Shoppers have to think not only about how much they personally like what they see, but how much *others* will like what they see. What sort of impression does this give? What kind of person would others see if I wore this? These kinds of meanings are constructed socially and depend on the individual, their companions, and the situation. Many people shop in groups so that they can ask companions for opinions. The need for social opinion is so strong that, when shopping alone, some shoppers solicit opinions from salespeople, who clearly have a conflict of interest in any opinion they express.

One last factor affects decision making for clothes shopping: comparing alternatives. Generally, people are not expecting to find the *perfect* outfit, but one that will satisfice.[12] They have a need that must be satisfied within the budget and time they are willing to expend. They make the decision by identifying alternatives within their range and narrowing the choices. Often several alternatives satisfy the goals to varying extents, and the shopper compares the relative merits and selects the few that fit her budget.

Virtual Fittings

Usually when I talk about clothes decision making, people—especially men—think about how laborious shopping is and how much they hate going through all the hassle. An immediate solution comes to mind: a virtual or augmented reality to test the alternatives and make a selection without physically trying on the clothing. Why travel to the store at all when you can shop online and see a computer-generated image of something with your body shape trying on the clothes?

Some online services, such as Intellifit and MyShape, take measurements of a customer's body and suggest clothes that will fit and provide a flattering appearance for that body shape. Other web services, such as MyVirtualModel and VirtualEShopping, provide a 3D view of a shopper's measured body that can be used to simulate fitting clothes to the body so that the shopper can view them from multiple angles. Other companies, such as Holition and Zugara, have demonstrated compelling augmented reality techniques that map an image of a garment onto a real-time image of the customer. In some systems, the clothing or accessories can move or change shape in real time as the customer moves in a virtual mirror, in others, the virtual overlay is static. With current technology, even the best overlaid virtual clothing appear somewhat artificial, but the images are becoming more realistic and will soon effectively emulate the shading, drape, and movement of fabrics.

As visually compelling as they are, though, virtual fittings are little more than paper dolls: It isn't really you wearing the clothing—it is an image of you. There's no way to *feel* the fit of the garment, especially as you move. Projecting a 3D image of a watch onto someone's wrist is straightforward, but how does the watchband feel? Is it too loose? Do the links pinch the skin? Does it rattle when you move? How heavy is it? You can't get that information from a virtual fitting. The best you can do is get a rough sense of how the garment would look on you.

> In many ways, virtual fittings are little more than a personalized digital mannequin, except that you can change its clothes quickly. On the other hand, virtual fittings provide even less than an old-fashioned physical mannequin that can show off a wide range of ways to wear a garment. A buttoned-down shirt, for example, can be worn buttoned or unbuttoned, collar up or down, pulled tight or baggy, tucked or untucked, tied at the bottom, and with sleeves rolled to different lengths. In sum, virtual fittings can be a great first filter for narrowing selections faster and with less effort but ultimately, before the purchase decision is final, you still need to try it on.

Digital Fitting Rooms

Retail space designers know that you can increase sales lift by making the retail space more pleasant and that the fitting room is a key place to target the experience. In 2008, Ken Nisch, chairman of JGA, Inc., a retail design firm, said, "When customers try something on and have a pleasant experience, it increases the likelihood that they will buy the item three or four times." Toward that, several attempts at creating "Fitting Room 2.0" have been made.

In 2001, Prada opened a flagship store in Manhattan, where it conducted a trial of many technologies designed and constructed by Ideo and IconNicholson, including a sophisticated dressing room with a variety of capabilities.[13] A scanner identified each garment as the shopper took it in, providing additional information about the garment's price and alternate colors and sizes—the kind of information shoppers can find when browsing products online. The fitting room also contained a "Magic Mirror" with a motion-triggered video camera that recorded the shopper and played back a video loop after a pause. The room also provided the ability for a person trying on clothes to send video of himself to friends, who could send back comments and vote (thumbs up/down). The system could also project a static image of a garment onto the mirror, providing a basic "virtual fitting" capability. Unfortunately, the trials of these technologies in the flagship store were not successful. A report in *Business 2.0* describes the dramatic mismatch between expectations of the technology designers and the impracticalities of using the technologies in regular store operations due to overflow traffic, technical failures, and non-intuitive controllers (such as floor pedals to set the opacity of a glass wall through which shoppers could be seen if not set to opaque).

Similar systems have been created and deployed for market evaluation in a number of other retailers. The Gardeur Shop in Essen Germany created a radio-frequency identity (RFID)–based system that provided product information, including price, available sizes and colors, material, and care instructions. Warnaco created a system to show fitting information for women's brassieres. Other digital technologies have been deployed in dressing rooms by companies such as Metropark, Bloomindales, Nordstrom, Kira Plastinina, and Macy's.

Responsive Mirror

Let's step back a moment and think about all the information needs of someone trying to decide among clothes. He needs to compare how well different articles feel and look. Virtual fittings can help compare how things look, but not how they feel. Another missing ingredient in today's physical retail environment is some support for the comparison that shoppers need to perform to reach a decision. Some *online* retail stores have support for this in terms of feature-comparison tables, but these are most effective for feature-rich product categories such as electronics, housewares, and tools. Feature comparisons are less valuable for product categories in which the decisions are based on subjective assessments such as fashion and decor.

If comparing features is not useful for clothing, what other support can we provide? One problem is that, with so many options, it can be hard to remember what you thought of each one, especially when trying on clothing. How can you remember how the first shirt felt by the time you've reached the seventh try-on? In these situations, you need to bring a friend to supplement your memory. Another way is to use electronic recordings to review prior fittings, as in the concept for trying on garments illustrated in Figure 11-1 called the Responsive Mirror.

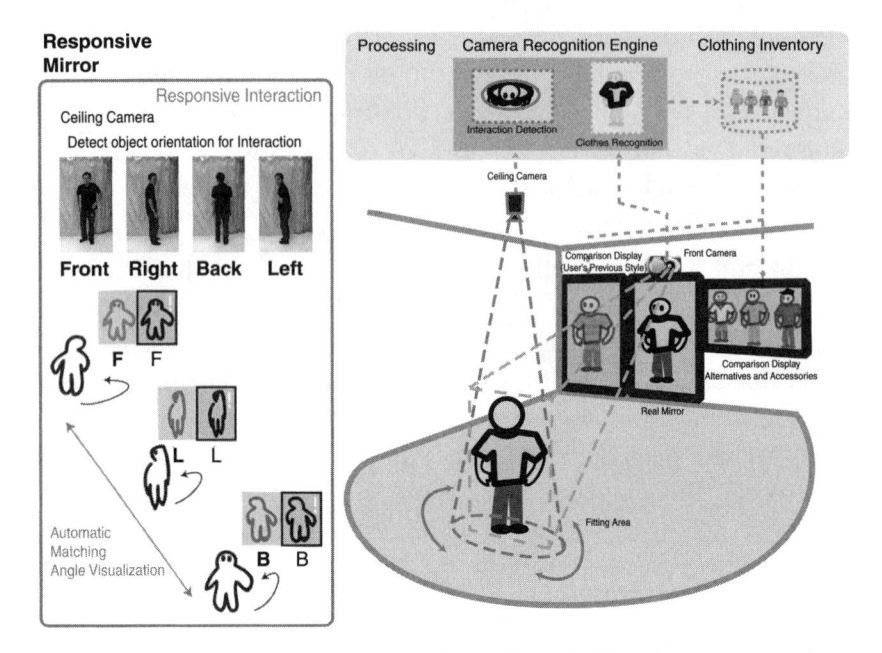

Figure 11-1 Responsive Mirror concept diagram. The shopper uses the conventional mirror to try on clothing. A front camera captures each trial and replays previous trials in the electronic display to the left, while similar clothing styles are shown in the display on the right. The overhead camera captures the shopper's orientation as she turns from side to side, and the electronic images are turned to match the same pose as the shopper. (Figure credit: Takashi Matsumoto)

Figure 11-2 shows a photograph of a Responsive Mirror prototype system. As a customer interacts with a conventional mirror, cameras record the trial and detect his pose and the style of the garment being worn. A display on the left of the mirror shows the shopper in the previously worn garment, matching the pose of the image to the pose of the shopper as he moves. This allows the shopper to compare his current garment directly to a previous item he tried on. The display on the right of the mirror shows images of people wearing similar styles (or different styles to the clothes he is considering).

When a person interacts with a fitting room mirror, he gives off implicit cues about the information he is seeking. When he turns his body, he is observing how the clothes look from different angles.

11 • Clear Sailing

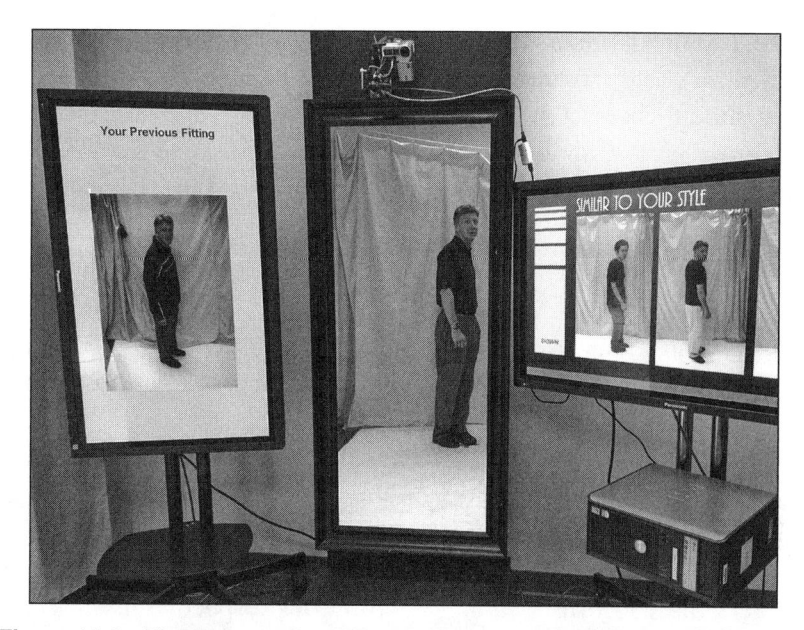

Figure 11-2 The Responsive Mirror prototype. The images in the left display show previous clothing trials matching the same pose in real time as the person turns in the mirror. The images in the right display also match the pose but show other clothing similar to what the shopper is trying on.

This kind of implicit information-seeking behavior can be detected using sensors, and supplemental information can be provided. Users of this kind of system do not need to be taught how to use the system—they simply behave naturally. This style of interaction is an example of "invisible computing" from the early visions of Ubiquitous Computing.

Cameras in a Fitting Room? You've Got to Be Joking.

A common concern that sensor technologies and Ubicomp systems face is how they impact a user's sense of personal privacy. We have carefully made sure that the camera is not in the same room where shoppers change clothes, but is instead in the public fitting area where shoppers can share the look with companions. Nevertheless, even in the public fitting area, cameras are traditionally absent. Will customers accept a camera in such a semi-private space as a fitting area? What concerns would they have and what measures should the system incorporate to mitigate such concerns? In the press articles about fitting-room technologies, privacy concerns either are completely avoided[14] or are stressed to a sometimes alarming level.

People are subjected to video capture on a daily basis, sometimes happily (home movies, videoconferencing, camera-based game controllers) and sometimes without much choice (store surveillance, toll collection, traffic cameras). Cameras used for these purposes have achieved at least some level of tolerance, yet debate continues about the overall effects of sensing technologies on the long-term health of our society. In Chapter 5, "Missing Ingredients," I described a set of guidelines for best practices to mitigate privacy concerns. When deploying sensing technologies in public places, those guidelines will address the concerns of a large portion of prospective users. However, when a camera is introduced into a semi-private space such as a fitting room, we need to examine its potential impact on privacy more deeply.

What boundaries of personal information will be changed by cameras and sensing technologies in a fitting room? Let's return to the findings of sociologist Irwin Altman, mentioned in Chapter 5, from his studies of people managing the seeming contradiction of wanting to publicize some characteristics and protect others. Altman found that people actively manage three aspects of personal information: disclosure of information, social identity, and timing. Let's examine the potential encroachments across these boundaries that camera technologies create.

Disclosure

People naturally have an expectation that a fitting room is a private place where they can change clothes without being seen. The Responsive Mirror cameras do not capture images of people *changing* clothes in the changing area itself—only after they are re-clothed and moved to the fitting area outside. Nevertheless, there is still a potential for concern from capturing the interaction with the mirror. In addition to the awkward poses that a shopper may take to test the fit of clothing, a shopper naturally expects that she can experiment with clothes styles in which she might not like to be seen for any number of reasons: fit, style, status, expressiveness, and so on. On the other hand, a shopper interacting with the Responsive Mirror may not want the fittings to be completely *un*disclosed either. She may want to show clothes to her friends or publish them to a social fashion network. Maintaining control of the disclosure is critical.

Social Identity

We all have a range of identities that we maintain across different social relations: familial, communal, political, religious, business, hobbies, and others. The clothes we choose are generally intended to reinforce our identities. As we are experimenting with alternatives in a fitting room, we may find that a particular choice undermines some aspect of our persona. This boundary can be managed by the same mechanisms used to control disclosure.

Timing

Shoppers today expect that an experimental fitting is transient, not lasting for others to see at another time. In addition to the obvious concern about recording images of an embarrassing outfit, even images of currently flattering outfits could become embarrassing in the future as style and tastes change (Guys, raise your hand if you've thought about throwing out a picture of yourself in a leisure suit. Gals, where do we start?) A flattering garment may be an excellent choice at the moment, but it could come to represent something contrary to the shopper's style in the future. This concern can be mitigated by providing the ability to delete regrettable images, but the damage cannot be wholly undone, as the images may have been stored in an Internet archive. Furthermore, simple deletion is possibly more drastic than people want. The temporal boundary is one that has a varying permeability over time and that people might prefer simply to have it become more difficult, but not impossible, to see older images.

Public Trials

It's important to uncover the fundamental concerns people have about private information and give them complete control over the disclosure, identity, and temporal boundaries. Unfortunately, you cannot simply ask people about their concerns. When faced with a hypothetical question about sharing private information, people may be either more cautious or more cavalier than in real practice. A public trial is needed to find out the tradeoffs that *real* people make in *real* situations with *real* personal information.

To achieve that, we designed a version of the Responsive Mirror for countertop usage, for products such as eyeglass frames, hats, and jewelry. The selection problem with these kinds of apparel products is similar to that of clothing—you need to select from several options and it is difficult to recall how each item looked on you. For eyeglass frames, the problem is exacerbated because the trial frames do not have your prescription lenses installed so you cannot see yourself well in the mirror. Generally, shoppers want to know how the frames, hat or jewelry look from multiple angles, just as with clothing, but the kinds of poses in a smaller mirror differ from full-body twist and rotation in front of a full-length mirror. For glasses, hats, and jewelry, people turn and tilt their heads, look up and down, and move forward and back in front of the mirror.

Although the countertop mirror was designed to handle multiple product categories, we paid special attention to support the practices of an expanding market in South Asian retail jewelry. Due to cultural history and the emerging middle class in India, retail jewelry is a $13 billion dollar industry with projected annual growth of 8.7% through 2025.[15] The market is deeply mature in many ways, due to centuries of practice, and, at the same time, it is open to new innovations.

South Asian Retail Jewelry Shopping

Apart from being decorative, jewelry is often purchased in India for special occasions: to celebrate annual spring and autumn festivals, the birth of newborns, marriages, and birthdays. The purchase of 22- and 24-carat gold and diamonds is also seen as a long-term investment.

Indian jewelry ensembles are often elaborate combinations of large necklaces with matching earpieces, along with a variety of bangles, rings, forehead pieces, and more. Figure 11-3 shows a magazine cover with a photograph of a woman in a typically elaborate ensemble. Shoppers spend considerable time examining and selecting such items before purchasing.

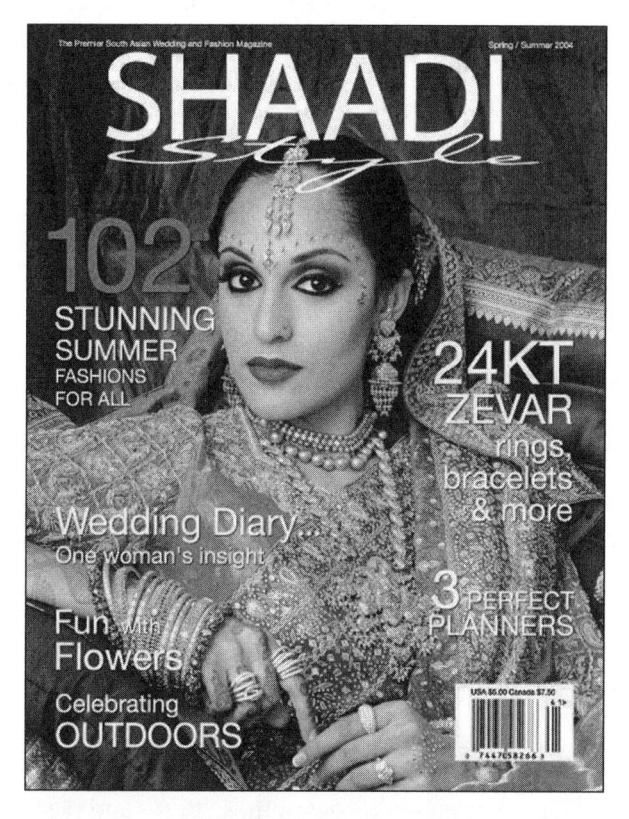

Figure 11-3 Cover of spring 2004 Shaadi Style Magazine. © 2004 Shaadi Style Magazine, Inc. Included here by permission.

A typical Indian jewelry store is laid out similarly to jewelry stores in other parts of the world, but with a few significant differences. Jewelry items are often laid out on velvet trays, either placed in glass counters that are about midtorso height and run the circumference of the room, or decoratively placed on shelves on the walls. Items are often grouped by type, with necklaces, bands, rings, and other pieces clustered together. Several small, portable mirrors sit on glass counters, and large mirrors are installed on the walls as well. A significant variation from other types of jewelry store layout is that matching sets of elaborate neck and earpieces are often placed prominently at eye level, on the wall.

The buyer–seller relationship in Indian jewelry stores is even more important than in Western-style retail. In India, families buy from the same jeweler across multiple generations. Furthermore, shoppers expect in all cases to be served by a salesperson, not left simply to browse on their own. Generally, an Indian jewelry store has enough sales staff to serve each shopper individually, and shoppers expect to have personal service even in less expensive stores.

Salespeople assist customers by standing behind the counters across from the customers. The salesperson retrieves an item of interest and hands it to the shopper to try on. If a mirror is not nearby, the salesperson brings the nearest mirror. The shopper then tries on the jewelry and looks in the countertop mirror for close-up views and looks in the mirrors on the walls to evaluate the whole look.

Shoppers usually come with their friends or family, in larger groups than typical in Western jewelry stores, so the process is a social one that involves looking in the mirror, posing for companions, and exchanging feedback. Shoppers sometimes get feedback from the salespeople, who use this time as an opportunity to suggest similar items to try on. Also, shoppers bring in clothing for which they want to buy matching jewelry so that they can see the jewelry in the context of the clothing they will be wearing.

After trying on several items, the shopper may ask to see a few of them again. The salesperson retrieves those items and places them on a tray in front of the shopper. Many Indian jewelry items are larger than Western counterparts, and the tray is compartmented into five or six segments to hold the matching elements of ensembles. The shopper then compares the jewelry items against the others with far more scrutiny than before and tries on the items again, if desired. A mirror is brought over to help the shopper make a decision, and the shopper's friends and families give feedback to help evaluate the jewelry in more detail.

The mirror is one of two common points of interaction between the buyer and seller, and also between the buyer and her companions. In addition, sellers typically arrange the customer's preferred jewelry pieces on a light and portable tray so that the shopper can compare items side by side, which provides the second most commonly used interaction point. The following observations of interactions among the seller, the buyer, and their companions suggest that a Ubicomp system could address unsatisfied needs.

- Mirrors provide an opportunity for salespeople to give feedback to the shopper and offer recommendations.
- The shopper's companions also engage with the shopper through use of the mirror, holding items up to the shopper's face to simulate wearing the items.
- During the final decision, trays containing the top selected jewelry items are provided to the shopper for detailed evaluation and comparison. To see how each jewelry item looks on the shopper, she would need to try it on again but usually does not.
- Sellers typically leave out only a few items at a time, for security and because shoppers sometimes ask them to retrieve items that have been put away.

To accommodate and enhance the existing uses of the mirror and tray, we designed the countertop Responsive Mirror to consist of two components: one for "capture" and one for "access." The capture component is shown on the top of Figure 11-4 and consists of a half-silvered mirror with an embedded camera. The associated silver-colored knob serves as a recording button that the shopper can use to capture a sequence of images. An embedded LCD monitor is visible behind the mirror (not visible in the photograph in Figure 11-4), giving feedback to the shopper when recording is occurring, along with how many sessions have been recorded. The "access" component, taking the place of the comparison tray in conventional buyer–seller interaction, is a graphical user interface shown on the bottom of Figure 11-4 and accessed via a tablet-sized touchscreen display. The interface lets shoppers view and compare their recorded sessions two at a time. Below the two large panels is a single slider that gives the user control of which pair of images from the two sessions to show.

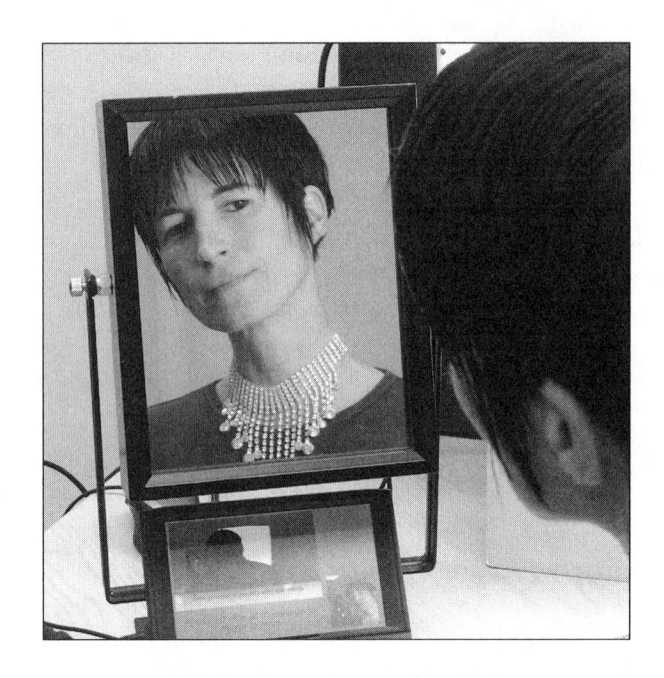

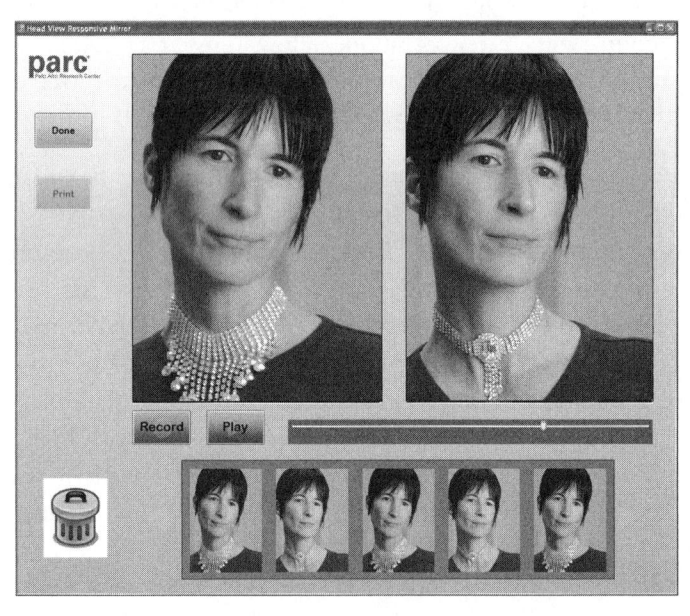

Figure 11-4 The countertop Responsive Mirror prototype consists of a "capture" component using a camera behind a half-silvered mirror (top, image retouched for clarity) and an "access" component (bottom) that emulates the functionality of the jewelry tray for reviewing multiple pieces of jewelry side by side. (Figure Credit: Victoria Bellotti)

The comparison is enhanced by showing the closest matching poses of the shopper wearing two different articles. Moving the slider controls which frame in the sequence of images in one recording will be shown, and the closest matching pose from the second recording is shown at the same time. This lets the shopper see how the two items looked in the same pose side by side. For example, in Figure 11-5, the column of images on the left displays one session in which the customer is trying on a long necklace. Accordingly, in the right column, the Image Matching engine has selected and displayed poses from a second session that most closely match those of the customer looking to the left, to the right, and straight on. Note that the images in the second panel do not necessarily show the entire set of captured images from the second session and are not presented in the same sequence in which they were acquired. This "matched access" capability enables shoppers to compare how two items look in similar poses.

If the user presses the Play button, the frames in the recorded session advance automatically and appear videolike, although the matched "video" may be playing frames out of sequence. Shoppers can use the slider to scan the images in a session and select particular images to view in detail. Tapping either image automatically zooms both for comparison.

The rationale for creating this countertop version of the Responsive Mirror was to explore real-world issues that might arise. We conducted four trial deployments of the system in two local jewelry stores in the San Francisco Bay area that specialize in South Asian jewelry, along with two focus group trials.[16]

Among the many responses we heard, generally people confirmed the expected value of the system: It helped them recall what they had tried on. For example, when people tried on four or six items over the course of 20 minutes, they often had trouble recalling the appearance of the first few items. The system provided a convenient inventory of recordings well after the salesperson had put items away.

Across all deployments, the image-matching capability caused the most excitement among shoppers. The slider was the single most used interface element, promoting a good deal of interaction among shoppers and their companions. The image-matching capability was

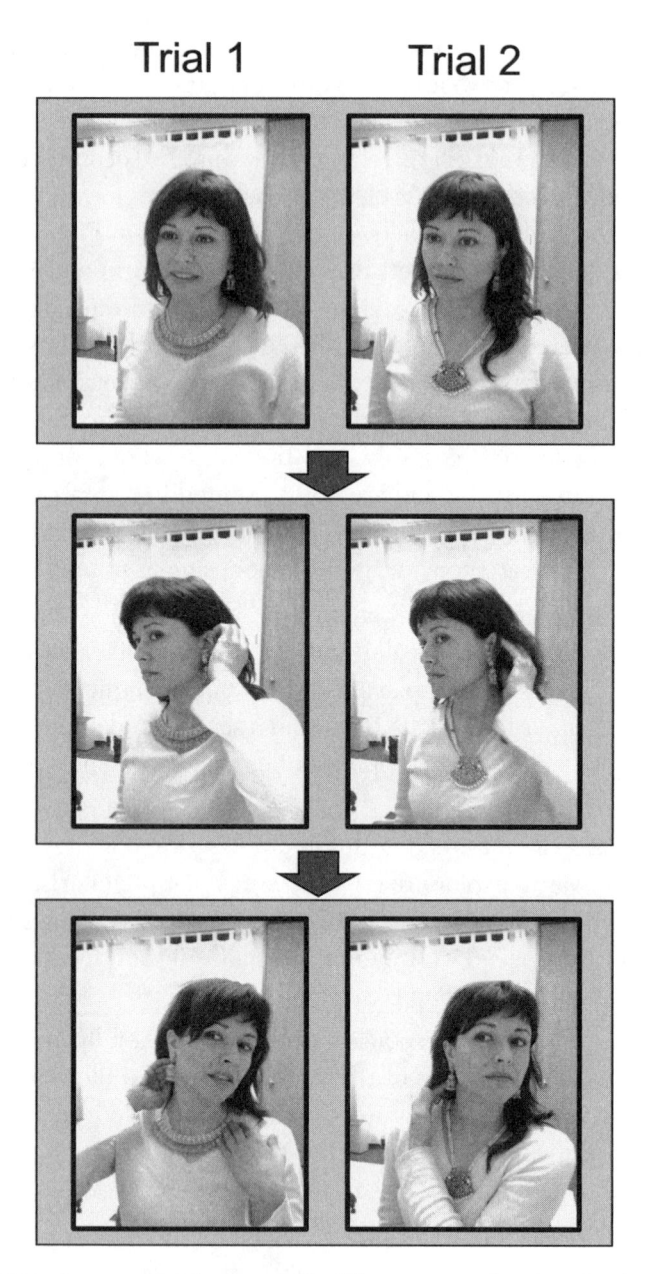

Figure 11-5 Pose-matching example. When comparing jewelry (or apparel of any kind), a shopper usually prefers to see herself from the same angle to compare the items side by side. The images of poses in trial 2 were captured in a different order than those in trial 1, but the poses are matched when shown on the Responsive Mirror system. (Figure credit: Maurice Chu and Brinda Dalal)

viewed as a "cool" capability and provided a high degree of interactivity to quickly make a comment about the appearance of an item in a particular image; this was true both for salespeople and for their customers.

Participants particularly liked the image-matching capability as they watched multiple frames because it showed the "personality" or "flair" given off by the shopper's movements in the jewelry. Shoppers generally preferred to see the fluid motions over static images so that they could see this kind of personality.

Looking at recorded images of themselves helped people get a stronger sense of third-person perspective than they got from using a conventional mirror alone. That was a little surprising, because the photographed images are nearly identical to what is in the mirror; if anything, the fidelity of the sharpness and colors is worse in the images than in the mirror. Nevertheless, shoppers felt that somehow looking at the images allowed them to make a more objective assessment of how they looked to others.

With regard to privacy, customers generally wanted to have images available beyond store boundaries so that they could obtain family members' opinions about items, especially if their spouse was unable to accompany them to the store and wanted to be consulted on the purchase decision. In contrast, store owners and managers, cautious about designs being shared and copied by competitors, did not like the idea that customers could send images of proprietary designs outside the store.

Digital media enables whole new classes of systems that support both senses of the word *reflection*: (1) the projection of an image representing objects outside of one's direct field of view, such as seeing oneself in a looking glass, and (2) the contemplation of past events.

Business Impact

The Responsive Mirrors are still undergoing refinement and trials at the time of this writing, and their ultimate impact has yet to be proven. The point of this case study is to show an example of an information *need* that exists today but for which there is no information technology support. The example we have used is supporting shoppers in making decisions by providing them the information that *they* use to make a judgment. Too often, merchants think only of their own information needs, which is generally that they need to get marketing information out to customers. As a result, information technologies are bombarding us with messaging that is not helping us accomplish goals and is, at best, a distraction.

Instead, I've tried to illustrate examples that start with finding out about an existing information problem. Then I described some of the steps taken to design Ubicomp systems that can alleviate that problem. *Customers come first.* Once their fundamental information problem is satisfied, customers will be more receptive to hearing other marketing messages.

Summary

Ubiquitous Computing technologies not only displace conventional business, add value to existing products, or increase efficiencies across operations, as described in previous chapters; they also create new capabilities that can generate whole new business capabilities. Ubicomp is encroaching on a variety of domains, most notably in retail settings where digital displays are replacing conventional signage.

Shopping is an information-seeking problem where shoppers are identifying alternatives and comparing them to find the product or service that most closely matches their needs and constraints. Currently, technologies in physical retail are simply pushing unwanted (and unheeded) advertising to customers as they struggle with their shopping decisions. By first understanding and providing the information shoppers need to make their decisions, they will have enough capacity to see and consider additional offerings.

In a series of Ubicomp prototypes called Responsive Mirrors, we explored decision support for retail clothes fitting and for retail jewelry (and eyeglasses and other head-worn garments). The Responsive

Mirrors use embedded cameras to record the trial wearing of garments in the mirror. As each new garment is worn and seen in the mirror, prior trials are displayed in adjacent electronic displays. The orientation of the person to the mirror is detected using computer vision, and the closest matching pose is shown in the electronic image. The system is implicitly controlled by the person's body movement and does not require him to learn how to operate the computer.

The system was designed with particular sensitivity to the privacy of users, by analyzing the impact on Irwin Altman's boundaries of personal privacy: disclosure, social identity, and timing.

The Responsive Mirror systems allow people to directly compare alternatives and quickly narrow their selections. The images also provide new ways for salespeople, shoppers, and companions to interact and communicate about the options. Instead of simply using public information displays to hawk wares, retailers can provide information that helps shoppers make decisions, making them more receptive to subsequent offerings.

Endnotes

[1] William Falconer, *Universal Dictionary of the Marine*, 1784. Available at http://books.google.com/books?id=3pVAAAAAYAAJ&dq=falconer%27s%20marine%20dictionary&pg=PT282#v=onepage&q&f=false (accessed 30 August 2010).

[2] W. Chan Kim and Renée Mauborgne, *Blue Ocean Strategy: How to Create Uncontested Market Space and Make Competition Irrelevant* (Boston: Harvard Business Press, 2005).

[3] Andrew Hampp, "Digital Marketing Guide: Out of Home," *Advertising Age*, 22 February 2010, v. 81, no. 8. http://adage.com/mediamarketingguide2010/article?article_id=146098 (accessed 16 Oct 2010)

[4] Outdoor Advertising Association of America, "Facts & Figures," accessed 6 June 2010.

[5] Includes all forms of media advertising except paid search and broadband video

[6] Advertising Age, U.S. Ad Spend Trends: 2008, 22 June 2009. http://adage.com/images/random/datacenter/2009/spendtrends09.pdf (accessed 16 Oct 2010)

[7] A. Chaudhuri, *Emotion and Reason in Consumer Behavior* (Oxford: Elsevier, 2006).

See also P. Danziger, *Why People Buy Things They Don't Need* (Chicago: Dearborn Trade Publishing, 2004).

See also D. Hawkins, R. J. Best, D. L. Mothersbaugh, *Consumer Behavior: Building Marketing Strategy*, 10th ed. (New York: McGraw-Hill Companies, 2007).

See also P. Underhill, *Why We Buy* (New York: Simon & Shuster, 1999).

[8]R.C. Prus, *Making Sales: Influence as Interpersonal Accomplishment* (Newbury Park California): Sage Publishing, 1989).

[9]F. Davis, Fashion, *Culture and Identity* (Chicago: University of Chicago Press, 1994).

[10]A. Lurie, *The Language of Clothes* (New York: Random House, 1981).

See also M. Barnard, *Fashion as Communication*, 2nd ed. (London: Routledge, 2002).

[11]Jeanine Poggi, "Dressing Rooms of the Future," Forbes.com, 22 July 2008.

[12]To satisfice is to satisfy sufficiently. The term was coined in H. A. Simon, "Rational choice and the structure of the environment." *Psychological Review*, 1956. Vol. 63 No. 2, 129-138.

[13]G. Lindsay, "Prada's High-Tech Misstep," *Business 2.0* 1 (March 2004). http://money.cnn.com/magazines/business2/business2_archive/2004/03/01/363574/index.htm.

[14]Reports of the Magic Mirror refer to the camera as "infrared technology," presumably to avoid triggering knee-jerk negative reactions.

[15]Commodity Online, "India's Gems and Jewelry Market Is Glittering," 20 August 2007. www.resourceinvestor.com/pebble.asp?relid=34936. Accessed 8 January 2010.

See also McKinsey Global Institute, The 'Bird of Gold': The Rise of India's Consumer Market, May 2007.

[16]M. Chu, B. Dalal, A. Walendowski, and B. Begole, "Countertop Responsive Mirror: Supporting Physical Retail Shopping for Sellers, Buyers, and Companions," in *Proceedings of the 28th international Conference on Human Factors in Computing Systems,* New York, 2010. http://doi.acm.org/10.1145/1753326.1753711.

12

Ubiquitous Business

He has a great knack for picking the right wave and he's a really smart competitor. He might even bust out a superman air. He has a few tricks up his sleeve. He always pulls reverses and airs that other people don't.
—Kelly Slater, nine-time World Champion, Association of Surfing Professionals

It's been twenty years since the potentials of Ubiquitous Computing were first articulated. Innovators at the time thought the Ubicomp wave would be the next big surge, and it might have been, but the industry was soon washed over by the World Wide Web. In the interim, Ubicomp inventors have occasionally despaired that perhaps Ubicomp benefits were somehow not as valuable as the scientists had imagined. An apocryphal story in the research community is that sometime around 2000, one of the leading visionaries said at a conference "We've had Ubicomp for ten years now and no one wants it." However, just as the birth of Ubicomp had been prematurely forecast, so was its death. Today, as the business potential of the Internet has reached maturity, sensor-enabled smartphones are becoming widely adopted, and wireless broadband networking is pervasively available, we have reached a point where the essential elements to realize the Ubicomp vision are in place.

Just as business opportunities propelled the World Wide Web to incredible heights, so too will business opportunities drive the adoption of Ubiquitous Computing throughout societies globally. There are two sides to this business opportunity. First is that businesses' reach to customers has expanded, through massive adoption of broadband and wireless networking accessed via portable and handheld computers, along with sensors and displays embedded throughout the environment. Second is that Ubicomp technologies extend a business workforce's abilities to operate in a variety of settings (in the office, at a customer site, at home, while traveling, at a worksite) across distance and time to increase operational efficiencies. Such ubiquity of information technologies to increase reach was a key objective of the initial visions of Ubiquitous Computing. Having achieved that objective, we now need to tackle *new* problems and exploit new opportunities that Ubicomp has created.

The second stage of the Ubiquitous Computing vision was the goal of having the technologies become so reliable, personal, and easy to use that their presence would become less noticed and less disruptive. Toward that objective of "calm" computing, this book has focused not on the fact that technologies are ubiquitous, but on what is enabled by the ability to capture and access information ubiquitously. Not only do these technologies reduce drag of some existing problems, such as information overload, but they create *new* capabilities in ways to capture and exchange information, simplify interaction, anticipate and respond to goals, and generally enhance our ability to engage in life across both physical and digital environments.

On one hand, the increasing diversity and pervasiveness creates new complications. We now have to learn to operate multiple classes of digital devices, manage networks of them in our homes, exchange information across distrusted networks, and fend off intrusions to our personal space. Yet at the same time, the interconnected complexity can be harnessed. Our interactions in physical and digital space can be used to learn the relationships among people, places, things, and information without requiring people to explicitly state such relationships. Contextual intelligence leverages such a personal semantic network that it can personalize our views and find information that is more pertinent and actionable. Contextually intelligent systems observe the context of actions in the past to predict needs in the future.

Contextually intelligent services use estimates and probabilities, meaning that the predictions are never 100% accurate. The same is true of human estimates and predictions, which are nevertheless useful in many situations. Surprisingly, machine predictions can sometimes *outperform* human estimates using the same information.

We deeply explored the issue of privacy raised by sensing technologies, identifying some of the root causes of people's concern: economic risk, security, and personal relations. The very nature of learning enough about an individual to personalize technologies makes it impossible to completely avoid these issues, but I explained several steps that can alleviate some of the concerns while keeping the user in control.

Part II, "Business Opportunities," examined the concrete impact of Ubicomp technologies across industries and suggested strategies to find your business opportunities. The most obvious application of personalization today is in advertising and marketing. Ubiquitous computing technologies enable far better targeting of information than previous approaches, including optimizing the timing of delivery, not just the content, to moments when people are more receptive and the information is more actionable. Cameras and vision technologies provide new information about a person's preferences and tastes (psychographics) that are far more telling than the basic demographic segmentation used in marketing until now.

We took a deep look at the media industry, arguably the one industry that has been most broadly transformed by ubiquitous information technologies. Some of that transformation has been anticipated, and some companies are strategically repositioning themselves by developing novel services that leverage contextual intelligence to provide media at the moment it is most valuable.

Another strategy is to enhance the value of your existing products and services by making the functionality accessible to other products and services. Interoperation does not necessarily require electronic data interchange over wired or wireless links, which might increase the production cost of a product; the necessary information to establish a "continuity" between devices can be exchanged over physical media channels (such as optical and audio channels), allowing even inert objects such as paper to share digital information.

As coworkers become more physically remote from each other, they lose some of the information needed for effective coordination and communication. They lose an awareness of each others' patterns and paces, making it difficult to effectively coordinate work and hand off tasks. Contextual intelligence can reconstruct patterns, augmenting a distributed team's coordination and effectiveness even across time zones.

Chapter 11 "Clear Sailing," examined methods for identifying completely un-served information problems and designing new products and services for new business opportunities. We saw some of the insights of ethnographic investigations of retail apparel and jewelry shopping that led to the creation of image- and video-based decision support tools. Similar methods in other domains can identify un-served information problems as well.

Future Ubiquitous Businesses

It has taken 20 years for the initial visions of Ubiquitous Computing that emerged from the world's leading research laboratories to find preliminary commercial success. The delay resulted largely from the slower-than-expected adoption of wireless, handheld computing and large displays. At this point, the necessary hardware has nearly reached critical mass of adoption. In the intervening years, innovation has continued in the research labs, and we should see accelerated adoption of Ubicomp systems now that the infrastructure exists.

It is always dangerous to predict the future from the past, but it is less dangerous than predicting the future from nothing. Innovations in Ubicomp have advanced in research institutions around the globe. The following innovations should quickly become commercially viable in coming years, not necessarily in this order or appearance.

- **Indoor location detection:** The initial context-aware services at PARC were based on indoor location technologies. Since those prototypes, however, we have not yet seen a widely available indoor location technology. I don't expect that a standard will be settled on soon, but many technologies are being tested (ultra-wideband radio, television radio, WiFi signal mapping, GPS repeaters), and eventually location sensing will be as ubiquitous indoors as GPS is outdoors.

- **Electronic memories and activity-based information retrieval:** In addition to organizing information according to topics and folders, people find it convenient to associate information with places, people, times, projects, and events. Early prototypes in the 1990s at Xerox Research Center Cambridge, U.K., and elsewhere provided hooks to remember and retrieve information according such contextual factors. New context-aware information-management systems are starting to let us capture and organize around contextual factors,[1] but not yet to the same degree as the earlier visions.

- **Contextual intelligence middleware and infrastructures:** Following the emergence of context-aware applications, context-aware middleware infrastructures have been developed to make accessing context easier for developers. We are already seeing some of this in the form of location-sensing aggregators such as Google Latitude[2] and Yahoo! FireEagle.[3] We will see more that aggregate multiple sources of contextual information, perhaps providing plug-in APIs to mine the data and infer higher-level meaning.

- **Location prediction (and other context predictions):** Currently, almost all commercial location-based services are based on detecting your *current* presence in a location. Research projects have shown that it is possible to predict future location with relatively high reliability, to help anticipate your needs and proactively provide suggestions or reminders about things you need to do in those locations.

- **Personalized smart homes and buildings:** About once a year, an announcement comes for a "home of the future" concept that uses sensing and intelligence to conserve energy by managing heating and cooling and lighting, to set appropriate entertainment options, and to provide more comfort with less effort. In the past, such visions were merely added convenience, but with increasing energy costs, smart services will become a necessity. In addition, homeowners are increasingly accepting sensors in homes for security and games. By deploying technologies for these needs, additional services will become possible, including assisted cooking, elder care monitoring, and other telehealth services.

- **Personal service assistants:** We perform a variety of routine, mundane tasks that could be personalized and (semi-)automated. Current examples include booking a table at a nearby restaurant and arranging travel.[4] As this capability demonstrates success, more is expected from it. The ultimate assistant may never be *completely* attained, but we will see more intelligent personalized services in coming years.
- **Meeting capture and summarization:** Mobile video and audio recording of an entire day's worth of meetings is possible on data storage devices today, but the challenge is in summarizing the event for later reference—you don't want to have to sit through the same meeting twice to find the part you're interested in. Summarization and indexing is a complex problem, but some progress has been made to extract the important cues from a recording.[5]
- **Automated workflow services:** A variety of business process software exists for handling common workflows such as expense reporting, contract management, field service reporting, and sales force automation. Instead of depending on error-prone manual input of outdated data, these systems will achieve their full potential when they are populated with accurate up-to-date information collected from contextual sensors.
- **Lifestyle coaching:** As a constant companion, smartphones and smart environments are capable of reminding us to engage in healthy habits and behaviors. In addition, they can identify opportunities to present instructional material in context, such as teaching language phrases according to the current situation.
- **Mobile payment:** A 2008 IDC report found that most people would choose their mobile phone over their wallet, laptop, or keys if they could take with them only one object for 24 hours.[6] We are already seeing progress on a number of fronts to allow people to transfer money to a merchant using just their mobile phone via NFC and optical codes, as well as to receive payment from others using portable magnetic-strip card readers that plug into a smartphone's audio jack.[7]
- **Real-time language translation:** Translation services already exist for text on web pages and for images of signs, menus, and other text. Audio translation utilities also work for verbal language translation, but the translations incur some

delay because the computational complexity and databases used require sending audio to back-end servers. Increasingly powerful handheld processors will make such services available on the devices for real-time responsiveness.
- **Rich telepresence (robots, 3D avatars, or other):** Ubicomp technologies enable a wide array of ways to keep remote friends and colleagues aware of each other's ongoing activities. Video telepresence is increasingly common and available even on handheld smartphones. Future forms of telepresence will use sensors that detect and distill one's activities to others without necessarily pointing a camera at what you are doing or otherwise exposing potentially private information.

The existing and future contextually intelligent services will become even more insightful as they are fed with additional sources of information such as medical devices, on-body biometric monitors, vehicle telematics, access of devices and information services, social network services, and other as-yet-unforeseen information technologies. The amount of personal information that will be (and already is) available warrants continued introspection and caution to ensure that appropriate controls are enabled and enforced. Nevertheless, when the use of such information *benefits the person who generates the data,* not solely marketers and businesses, people increasingly choose to provide it.

Riding the Wave

At this point, you probably have some great ideas for how to tap into the capabilities of Ubiquitous Computing for your own business. Great! Or maybe you've thought of some information problems that information technologies do not currently address. Even better! Beyond giving you ideas of what the future will hold, I want to provide you with actionable information and suggestions for how to prepare your business to benefit from your ideas.

Technological innovation is no longer primarily about making devices faster, smaller, and cheaper. Successful innovations today reduce complexity. As the variety of solutions described in Part II indicates, constructing a solution is application specific, influenced by multiple considerations. Think about your ideas in the following contexts and identify the situations that customers of your solutions will be in. What compromises will a technology have to make to operate in these situations? What tradeoffs can your business afford to make in each of these?

- **Physical activity:** Unlike desktop or laptop computing, in which the user can be assumed to be sitting stationary in front of the computer, Ubiquitous Computing can be conducted while sitting, standing, walking, driving, or riding; while indoors, outdoors, on an airplane, or in a store; and while talking to strangers or arguing with family members. The activity in which it will be used constrains not only the form factor, but also the attention resources that the user can afford to operate a product or service.

- **Physical space:** Again, whereas desktop computing implies an officelike space and laptop computing implies at least a lap to rest on, Ubiquitous Computing can occur in any kind of space: hallway, retail store, airport, urban street, rural settlement, or back-country wilderness. The space constraints influence whether Ubicomp technologies need to be carried with the user or possibly embedded in the environment.

- **Varying network connectivity:** Portable devices typically have only intermittent connectivity, which varies with where the systems will be deployed. Sensors and displays in smart homes and buildings have more reliable connection to a network but are not as constantly available to a user who roams outside such smart spaces.

- **Varying input/output capabilities:** Ubicomp devices vary in their input/output capabilities. Smart pens, wireless headsets, smartphones, media players, and cameras have variously capable microphones, speakers, displays, buttons, and sensors. Systems can also interact with non-electronic devices, such as paper, which may be able to display only static information (text, images, and optical codes).

Evaluating Opportunities

I assume that you and your business already employee some methodology for evaluating the business viability of an opportunity,[8] but what about the technical viability? What criteria should you use to examine the technical risk of a Ubicomp solution? The following are practices that we use at PARC to ensure value while also creating novel, differentiable technologies.

- Start with the application goal. Conduct observational studies to find insights that aren't obvious. Surveys are okay for a first step, but they provide only a rough "order of magnitude" metric. The rationale behind responses is hard to interpret. Interviews and ethnographic studies take longer but provide more insight about the details of the problem, giving ideas of what specific problems to solve or processes to streamline along with the resources and constraints the customers have.
- Characterize the value if the technology is successful. Find out *before* taking on development and addressing hard problems such as privacy. Do this through mockups, storyboards, and scenarios with prospective customers. Find out the negative impact as well as the positive, and calculate a net value based on the customer's perception of the positive and negative tradeoffs.
- Find sources of labeled behavioral data. If the solution involves some kind of prediction or statistical learning, you need enough real-world data to determine whether the approach is feasible. The best place to start is government data sets (usually free!), followed by experience sampling methods to capture data from prospective customers in their real lives.
- Create a computational model that fits the application. Use off-the-shelf modeling tools when possible, but there are predictive problems for which existing methods either are overkill or are imprecise. In particular, if the customers need to be able to see and edit the models, off-the-shelf statistical packages are too complex to interpret. Simpler, more direct methods are often easier to understand.

- Mitigate privacy concerns.
  - Accept only opt-in users. To motivate people to opt in, the service must provide some direct benefit to that person.
  - Provide temporary opt-out and override capability.
  - Allow people to permanently opt out and destroy their personal information at will (at the risk of having to start over if they want the service again later).
  - Show users what the system is saying about them and to whom.

Conclusion

We're free, no longer chained to a desk to use a computer. Increasingly, information and content are available in our daily surroundings. Generally, we manually seek information and services, but in many cases they are offered automatically through location-based services or sensor-triggered digital displays, for instance. We no longer need to deliberately instruct machines to the very smallest detail because they can fill in some of the blanks by learning how similar things were done before.

I want to emphasize that the goal of Ubiquitous Computing is not to create *The Matrix,* with people simply plugging in and disengaging from life's realities. Ubiquitous Computing is about living and working via technologies that allow people to focus on their higher goals of achievement. Many of the technological building blocks exist already but require too much manual integration. If our technological environment is not meeting our needs today, we have only ourselves to blame. It is within our collective power to create products and services that fit our goals and natural behaviors.

Born around 1973, the Internet reached its full potential for business value approximately 20 years later, during the mid-1990s, following mass adoption of broadband networking and the simplicity of web technologies. With this mass adoption, a variety of new business opportunities were enabled, including online retail shopping, product auctioning, news aggregation, online advertising, B2B operations, and other services. Now again, approximately 20 years since the initial visions of Ubiquitous Computing were articulated, we have arrived at critical mass penetration of the enabling technologies. *Ubiquitous Computing for Business* is not simply about the pervasiveness of technologies in our lives, but about the new capabilities that such technologies enable for businesses to connect to customers and improve operating efficiencies through personalization, massive contextual interlinking, and bridging between digital and physical environments.

Ubiquitous Business is no longer a dream from the 1990s—*that future is now.*

Endnotes

[1] For example, Evernote.com's tagline is "Remember everything."

[2] See Google Latitude at www.google.com/latitude/intro.html.

[3] See Yahoo! Fire Eagle at http://fireeagle.yahoo.net/.

[4] See Siri at http://siri.com/.

[5] P. Hsueh and J.D. Moore, "Improving Meeting Summarization by Focusing on User Needs: A Task-Oriented Evaluation," in *Proceedings of the 13th International Conference on Intelligent User Interfaces,* New York, 2009. http://doi.acm.org/10.1145/1502650.1502657.

See also S. Basu, S. Gupta, M. Mahajan, P. Nguyen, and J. C. Platt, "Scalable Summaries of Spoken Conversations," in *Proceedings of the 13th International Conference on Intelligent User Interfaces,* New York, 2008. http://doi.acm.org/10.1145/1378773.1378809.

[6] IDC, "The Hyperconnected: Here They Come!" May 2008. www.nortel.com/promotions/idc_paper/index.html.

[7] See Square at https://squareup.com/.

[8] In case not, here are a few references that provide techniques for evaluating investments in innovation:

Alexander B. van Putten and Ian C. MacMillan, "Making Real Options Really Work," *Harvard Business Review* (December 2004): 134-141. http://hbr.org/2004/12/making-real-options-really-work/ar/1.

Scott Mathews, "Valuing Risky Projects with Real Options," *Research-Technology Management* 52, no. 5 (September/October 2009): 32–41. www.iriweb.org/Public_Site/RTM/Volume_52_Year_2009/September-October2009RTM/Valuing_Risky_Projects_with_Real_Options.aspx.

Appendix

Further Reading

I've given only the most cursory overview of the scope and history of Ubiquitous Computing. Consider this list of additional resources on the topic for further reading.

Magazines that publish leading-edge topics in Ubiquitous Computing:

- *IEEE Pervasive Computing*, www.computer.org/portal/web/pervasive/home

Conferences at which to find research and inventions on technology, applications, user experience, and interaction techniques of Ubiquitous Computing:

- ACM International Conference on Ubiquitous Computing, www.ubicomp.org
- International Conference on Pervasive Computing, www.pervasive2010.org/
- IEEE International Conference on Pervasive Computing and Communications, www.percom.org/

Books that describe the vision and social implications of Ubiquitous Computing:

- *Everyware: The Dawning Age of Ubiquitous Computing*, by Adam Greenfield (New Riders Publishing, 2006)

- *World Without Secrets: Business, Crime, and Privacy in the Age of Ubiquitous Computing,* by Richard Hunter (Wiley, 2002)

Technical books, to learn the theory, methods, and metrics for designing, constructing, and evaluating Ubicomp systems:

- *Smart Things: Ubiquitous Computing User Experience Design,* by Mike Kuniavsky (Morgan Kaufmann, 2010)
- *Ubiquitous Computing Fundamentals,* by John Krumm (Chapman and Hall/CRC, 2009)
- *Advances in Ubiquitous Computing: Future Paradigms and Directions,* by Soraya Kouadri Mostefaoui, Zakaria Maamar, and George M. Giaglis (IGI Publishing, 2008)
- *Security for Ubiquitous Computing,* by Frank Stajano (Wiley, 2002)
- *Context-Aware Mobile and Ubiquitous Computing for Enhanced Usability: Adaptive Technologies and Applications,* by Dragan Stojanovic (Information Science Reference, 2009)
- *Security and Cooperation in Wireless Networks: Thwarting Malicious and Selfish Behavior in the Age of Ubiquitous Computing,* by Levente Buttyan and Jean-Pierre Hubaux (Cambridge University Press, 2007)

Academic journals, to find more thorough research on particular topics in Ubicomp:

- *Pervasive & Mobile Computing,* ISSN 1574-1192 (Imprint: Elsevier)
- *International Journal of Pervasive Computing and Communications,* ISSN 1742-7371 (Imprint: Emerald)
- *Personal and Ubiquitous Computing,* ISSN 1617-4909 (print) and 1617-4917 (online) (Imprint: Springer)

Web sites for historic information:

- Mark Weiser's Ubiquitous Computing program at Xerox PARC, www.ubiq.com/hypertext/weiser/UbiHome.html (last updated in 1996)
- Wikipedia: Ubiquitous computing, http://en.wikipedia.org/wiki/Ubiquitous_computing

INDEX

A

accuracy of prediction models, 165-167
actionable information, 71-72
   for individuals, 72-74
   process for determining, 74
actionable receptivity, 130
Active Badge Location System, 14
activity awareness, 65
activity detection, 49
activity prediction model, 154-160
   accuracy of, 165-167
   effectiveness of, 165
   helpfulness of, 167-168
activity-aware systems, 69
activity-based advertising
   effectiveness of, 130-131
   testing, 132-133
Activity-based Information Retrieval (AIR), 49, 231
activity-targeted advertising, 128-129
advertising industry
   information overload from, 111-112
   interactive displays, 202-204
   positive value of, 112-115
   targeted advertising, 115-116
   characteristic-based filtering, 116-117
   collaborative filtering, 117-120
   computer vision technologies, 120-122
   effective advertising, types of, 129-130
   effectiveness of activity-based advertising, 130-131
   pervasive advertising, 124-129
   testing activity-based advertising, 132-133
   Ubiquitous Computing in, 105
Agent-based Interaction, 46-47
AIR (Activity-based Information Retrieval), 49, 231
airline industry, Ubiquitous Computing in, 106
Altman, Irwin, 93, 214
Amazon (publishing industry supply chain example), 140-141
American Time-Use Survey (ATUS), 158-159
analytical intelligence, 60
Anderson, Chris, 58
application overload, 57
artificial intelligence, simulating, 132

241

ATUS (American Time-Use Survey), 158-159
Augmented Reality, Ubiquitous Computing versus, 27-28
automated workflow services, 232
availability prediction models, 188-192
   business impact, 197-198
   estimates of interruptibility, 194-196
   privacy concerns, 196-197
   rhythm awareness, 190-194
awareness
   relationship-aware systems, 66-67
   types of, 65

B

balancing privacy concerns, 91-94
Barnes & Noble (publishing industry supply chain example), 141
behavior models, 76-77
behavior-aware systems, 69
behavioral context, 63
behavioral targeting, privacy concerns, 87-88. *See also* targeted advertising
   balancing, 91-94
   best practices for mitigating, 95
   criminal activity risk, 89-91
   economic risk, 88-89
best practices, mitigating privacy concerns, 95
BI (business intelligence) systems, actionable information, 71-72
Blocker, Mark, 173
Blue Ocean Strategy (Kim and Mauborgne), 201

brand awareness, 129-130
Burma-Shave advertising example, 111
business impact
   personalized leisure activity guide case study, 168-169
   presence and availability prediction, 197-198
   Responsive Mirror case study, 223
   Ubiquitous Computing, 229-230
   Xerox PrintTicket case study, 184
business intelligence (BI) systems, actionable information, 71-72
business strategies for commercialization of Ubiquitous Computing, 107-108
business value, relationship with innovation, 101-104
By Design (Caplan), 7

C

"calm computing," 12
CALO (Cognitive Assitant that Learns and Organizes), 48
cameras in fitting rooms, 213-215
Caplan, Ralph, 7
case studies
   Dai Nippon Printing (DNP), 146-148
      identifying opportunities, 148-151
   Magitti (personalized leisure activity guide), 151-153
      accuracy of prediction model, 165-167
      activity prediction model, 154-160

Index

business impact of, 168-169
"contextual intelligence," 153-154
effectiveness of prediction model, 165
helpfulness of prediction model, 167-168
preference prediction model, 162-164
Responsive Mirror, 211-213
  business impact, 223
  privacy concerns, 213-215
  public trials, 216-223
Sun Microsystems, 188-192
  business impact, 197-198
  estimates of interruptibility, 194-196
  privacy concerns, 196-197
  rhythm awareness, 190-194
change latency, 86
characteristic-based filtering, 58, 116-117
clothes shopping
  digital fitting rooms, 210-211
  purchase decision factors, 207-208
  Responsive Mirror case study, 211-213
    business impact, 223
    privacy concerns, 213-215
    public trials, 216-223
  social aspects of, 206-207
  virtual fittings, 209-210
cloud printing, 179
Cognitive Assistant that Learns and Organizes (CALO), 48
collaborative filtering, 58, 117-120
commercialization of Ubiquitous Computing, business strategies for, 107-108
communication, implicit, 42
communication channels, number of, 25-26

communication modalities, 41
communication overload, 56-57
complexities of Ubiquitous Computing, 21-23
  devices, number of, 23
  networks, number of, 26-27
  nonstructured versus structured information, 23-25
  social connections, number of, 25-26
computation. *See* Ubiquitous Computing
computer interaction
  Agent-based Interaction, 46-47
  proactive interaction, 39
    activity detection, 49
    communication modalities, 41
    context-aware systems, 44-45, 49
    direct manipulation, 41-43
    as natural interaction, 40
    proactive systems, 44
computer vision technologies, 120-123
computers, exponential growth of, 53-55
connections
  controlling, 36-37
  determining, 174-175
content context, 63
context
  semantic networks, 63-65
  types of, 62-63
context-aware services, 44-45, 49, 61-62. *See also* personalization
  activity-based information retrieval, 231
  automated workflow, 232
  indoor location detection, 230
  information inaccuracy, 83-85
  location prediction, 231
  prototypes of, 12

context-filtered systems, 67
context-triggered systems, 68
contextual intelligence, 59-61, 153-154
   actionable information
      for BI (business intelligence) systems, 71-72
      for individuals, 72-74
      process for determining, 74
   awareness, types of, 65
   benefits of, 60-61
   context-filtered systems, 67
   middleware and infrastructures with, 231
   proactive systems, 68-70
   progress in, 228
   real-time language translation, 232
   relationship-aware systems, 66-67
   Semantic Web versus, 67
   telepresence, 233
   unstructured information, 66
   user models, 76-79
continuity, enabling, 176-177
controlling connections, 36-37
cost of interruptions, 187-188
creative intelligence, 60
criminal activity risk, as privacy concern, 89-91
customers
   studying via ethnography, 145-146
   surveying, 144-145

D

Dai Nippon Printing (DNP) case study, 146-148
   identifying opportunities, 148-151
Davis, Fred, 206

decision-making process, 204-205
   digital fitting rooms, 210-211
   factors when clothes shopping, 207-208
   IT (information technology) and, 205-206
   Responsive Mirror case study, 211-213
      business impact, 223
      privacy concerns, 213-215
      public trials, 216-223
   social aspects of, 206-207
   virtual fittings, 209-210
deleting fitting room images, 215
demographic segmentation, 117-120
detection latency, 87
devices
   number of, 23
   for Ubiquitous Computing, 33
Dick, Philip K., 31
digital fitting rooms, 210-211
digital information displays, 202-204
digital out-of-home (OOH) advertising, 124, 202
digital personal assistants, 45
direct manipulation, 41-43
dislosure of images, control over, 214
Disney, Walt, 187
disruptive technologies, precursors to, 1
distribution in publishing industry supply chains, 139-140
DNP (Dai Nippon Printing) case study, 146-148
   identifying opportunities, 148-151
Drucker, Peter, 111

E

economic risk, as privacy concern, 88-89
economic value of advertising, 112-115
effective advertising, types of, 129-130
effectiveness of activity-based advertising, 130-131
electronic devices, exponential growth of, 53-55
electronic memories, 231
embedding information technologies. *See* Ubiquitous Computing
energy industry, Ubiquitous Computing in, 106
entertainment media, value added by, 139
ethnography, studying customers, 145-146
Europe, Ubiquitous Computing in, 21
evaluating Ubiquitous Computing opportunities, 235-236
event capture/summarization, 232

F

face work, 92
Falconer, William, 201
fashion shopping
  digital fitting rooms, 210-211
  purchase decision factors, 207-208
  Responsive Mirror case study, 211-213
    business impact, 223
    privacy concerns, 213-215
    public trials, 216-223
  social aspects of, 206-207
  virtual fittings, 209-210
feedback loop for actionable information, 74
filtering
  characteristic-based filtering, 58, 116-117
  collaborative filtering, 58, 117-120
  with computer vision technologies, 120-122
  context-filtered systems, 67
finance industry, Ubiquitous Computing in, 104
fitting rooms. *See* clothes shopping
"5 Whys" method, 142-143
future
  of pervasive advertising, 125-126
  of Ubiquitous Computing, 230-233

G

The Gardeur Shop, digital fitting rooms, 211
geographic segmentation, 119
goal awareness, 65
goal-aware systems, 70
Goffman, Erving, 92
Golle, Philippe, 90, 158
González, Victor, 56
Google
  innovation and business value example, 102
  personal profiling on, 93
  problem-solving example, 148
government, role in Ubiquitous Computing, 18-21

H

hardware for Ubiquitous Computing, 33
healthcare industry, Ubiquitous Computing in, 107
helpfulness of prediction models, 167-168
history of Ubiquitous Computing
 in Japan, 14
 in United Kingdom, 14
 Xerox PARC research, 9-14
hospitality industry, Ubiquitous Computing in, 106
human limitations in information problems, 8
hype curve, 2

I

identifying factors for individuals, 89-91
Illuminating Clay, 41
image parsing, 25
implicit communication, 42
inaccuracy of information, 83-85
indexing of events, 232
individuals
 actionable information for, 72-74
 identifying factors for, 89-91
indoor location detection, 230
Industrial TRON (ITRON), 14
industry segments, impact of Ubiquitous Computing on, 104-107
inferences, effect of information inaccuracy on, 83-85
information
 inaccuracy, 83-85
 interoperability barrier for, 33-35
 latency, 86-87
 structured versus nonstructured, 23-25

information overload, 55-57, 111-112, 150
information problems
 current types of, 8-9
 historical problems, types of, 8
information technology (IT)
 embedded technologies. *See* Ubiquitous Computing
 facilitating clothes shopping, 206-207
 in purchase decisions, 205-206
infrastructures with contextual intelligence, 231
innovation, relationship with business value, 101-104
insurance industry, Ubiquitous Computing in, 105
insurance premiums, behavioral targeting and, 88
intelligence
 BI (business intelligence) systems, actionable information, 71-72
 contextual intelligence, 59-61, 153-154
  actionable information, 71-74
  awareness, types of, 65
  benefits of, 60-61
  context-filtered systems, 67
  middleware and infrastructures with, 231
  proactive systems, 68-70
  progress in, 228
  real-time language translation, 232
  relationship-aware systems, 66-67
  Semantic Web versus, 67
  telepresence, 233
  unstructured information, 66
  user models, 76-79
intelligent agents, Ubiquitous Computing versus, 46-47

interaction
   Agent-based Interaction, 46-47
   proactive interaction, 39
      activity detection, 49
      communication modalities, 41
      context-aware systems, 44-45, 49
      direct manipulation, 41-43
      as natural interaction, 40
      proactive systems, 44
interactive public information displays, 202-204
interest models, 76
interoperation, 173-174
   barriers to, 33-35
   connections, determining, 174-175
   continuity, enabling, 176-177
   sensors for, 177-178
   standards for, 174
   Xerox PrintTicket case study, 178-180
      business impact of, 184
      secure optical pairing, 180-183
interruptions
   cost of, 187-188
   effect of, 56-57
   Sun Microsystems case study, 188-192
      business impact, 197-198
      estimates of interruptibility, 194-196
      privacy concerns, 196-197
      rhythm awareness, 190-194
IT (information technology)
   embedded technologies. *See* Ubiquitous Computing
   facilitating clothes shopping, 206-207
   in purchase decisions, 205-206
ITRON (Industrial TRON), 14

J–K

Japan, Ubiquitous Computing in, 14, 19-20
jewelry shopping, Responsive Mirror case study, 216-223
k-anonymity scores, 90-91
Korea, Ubiquitous Computing in, 20
Krumm, John, 124

L

latency of information, 86-87
Lean Manufacturing, 142
learned behavior models, 77
leisure activity guide case study, 151-153
   accuracy of prediction model, 165-167
   activity prediction model, 154-160
   business impact of, 168-169
   "contextual intelligence," 153-154
   effectiveness of prediction model, 165
   helpfulness of prediction model, 167-168
   preference prediction model, 162-164
lifestyle coaching, 232
lifestyle overload, 57
lifestyle-based segmentation, 58, 117-120
Lilsys system, 91, 194-195
location prediction, 231
location-based devices, 44-45, 49, 61-62. *See also* personalization
   activity-based information retrieval, 231

automated workflow, 232
indoor location detection, 230
information inaccuracy, 83-85
location prediction, 231
prototypes of, 12
The Long Tail: Why the Future of Business Is Selling Less of More (Anderson), 58

M

Magitti case study, 49, 151-153
  accuracy of prediction model, 165-167
  activity prediction model, 154-160
  business impact of, 168-169
  "contextual intelligence," 153-154
  effectiveness of prediction model, 165
  helpfulness of prediction model, 167-168
  preference prediction model, 162-164
Making Sales (Prus), 204
manufacturing industry, Ubiquitous Computing in, 106
Mark, Gloria, 56
marketing industry
  information overload from, 111-112
  interactive displays, 202-204
  positive value of, 112-115
  targeted advertising, 115-116
    characteristic-based filtering, 116-117
    collaborative filtering, 117-120
    computer vision technologies, 120-122
    effective advertising, types of, 129-130
    effectiveness of activity-based advertising, 130-131
    pervasive advertising, 124-129
    testing activity-based advertising, 132-133
  Ubiquitous Computing in, 105
media publishing industry
  Dai Nippon Printing (DNP) case study, 146-148
    identifying opportunities, 148-151
  supply chain in, 139-142
  Ubiquitous Computing in, 105
meeting capture/summarization, 232
Metcalfe, Bob, 55
middleware with contextual intelligence, 231
Minority Report (film), 203
mirrors
  Responsive Mirror case study, 211-213
    business impact, 223
    privacy concerns, 213-215
    public trials, 216-223
  role in clothes shopping, 207-208
mobile advertising, 124
mobile payments, 232
Moore's law, 10
Morris, Jim, 112
motivations, understanding
  asking customers, 144-145
  ethnography, 145-146
  "5 Whys" method, 142-143
multimedia information, interoperability barrier for, 33-35
multimedia services, prototypes for, 15
The Myth of the Paperless Office (Sellen and Harper), 10

N

natural interaction, 40
near-field communication (NFC) systems, 19
networks
  number of, 26-27
  semantic networks, 63-65
news media, value added by, 139
NFC (near-field communication) systems, 19
Noland, Kenneth, 53
nonstructured information, structured information versus, 23-25

O

Obje interoperability framework, 35, 37-39
Olivetti, 14
online shopping, physical stores versus, 205-206
OOH (out of home) digital advertising, 202-203
open demand, 130
opportunities
  evaluating, 235-236
  identifying, 148-151
optical pairing in Xerox PrintTicket case study, 180-183
origins of Ubiquitous Computing
  in Japan, 14
  in United Kingdom, 14
  Xerox PARC research, 9-14

P

pairing in Xerox PrintTicket case study, 180-183
Pandora, 15
PARC Pad (tablet computer), 12
PARC Responsive Mirror, 42
PARC Tab (handheld computer), 12
PARC, Inc., 35
parsing information, 24-25
Partridge, Kurt, 90, 158
pattern detection, 86
payments, mobile payments, 232
personal assistants, 45
personal computing, exponential growth of, 53-55
personalization. *See also* context-aware services
  information inaccuracy, 83-85
  information latency, 86-87
  lifestyle coaching, 232
  of service assistants, 232
  of services, 57-58
  smart homes/buildings, 231
personalized advertising, 115-116
  activity-based advertising
    effectiveness of, 130-131
    testing, 132-133
  characteristic-based filtering, 116-117
  collaborative filtering, 117-120
  computer vision technologies, 120-122
  effective advertising, types of, 129-130
  pervasive advertising, 124-129
personalized leisure activity guide case study, 151-153
  accuracy of prediction model, 165-167
  activity prediction model, 154-160
  business impact of, 168-169
  "contextual intelligence," 153-154
  effectiveness of prediction model, 165
  helpfulness of prediction model, 167-168

preference prediction model, 162-164
pervasive advertising, 124-129
physical awareness, 65
physical context, 63
physical distribution in publishing industry supply chains, 139-140
physical stores, online shopping versus, 205-206
plausible deniability, 196
Porter, Michael, 101
positive value of advertising, 112-115
Prada, digital fitting rooms, 210
precursors to disruptive technologies, 1
predicting
  activities, 154-160
    accuracy of, 165-167
    effectiveness of, 165
    helpfulness of, 167-168
  locations, 231
  preferences, 162-164, 188-192
    accuracy of, 165-167
    business impact, 197-198
    effectiveness of, 165
    estimates of interruptibility, 194-196
    helpfulness of, 167-168
    privacy concerns, 196-197
    rhythm awareness, 190-194
    technology needed for, 127
  presence and availability, 188-192
    business impact, 197-198
    estimates of interruptibility, 194-196
    privacy concerns, 196-197
    rhythm awareness, 190-194
preference awareness, 65
preference prediction model, 162-164, 188-192
  accuracy of, 165-167
  business impact, 197-198
  effectiveness of, 165
  estimates of interruptibility, 194-196
  helpfulness of, 167-168
  privacy concerns, 196-197
  rhythm awareness, 190-194
  technology needed for, 127
printing (Xerox PrintTicket case study), 178-180
  business impact of, 184
  secure optical pairing, 180-183
privacy
  in behavioral targeting, 87-88
    balancing, 91-94
    best practices for mitigating, 95
    criminal activity risk, 89-91
    economic risk, 88-89
  in presence and availability prediction, 196-197
  Responsive Mirror case study, 213-215
proactive interaction, 39
  activity detection, 49
  communication modalities, 41
  context-aware systems, 44-45, 49
  direct manipulation, 41-43
  as natural interaction, 40
  proactive systems, 44
proactive systems, 44, 68-70
problem-solving (Google example), 148
Prus, Robert, 204
psychographic segmentation, 118
public information displays, 202-204
public relations, balancing privacy concerns, 91-94
public trials (Responsive Mirror case study), 216-223
publishing industry
  Dai Nippon Printing (DNP) case study, 146-148
    identifying opportunities, 148-151

supply chain in, 139-142
Ubiquitous Computing in, 105
pull printing, 180
purchase decisions, 204-205
   digital fitting rooms, 210-211
   factors when clothes shopping, 207-208
   IT (information technology) and, 205-206
   Responsive Mirror case study, 211-213
      business impact, 223
      privacy concerns, 213-215
      public trials, 216-223
   social aspects of, 206-207
   virtual fittings, 209-210
push printing, 180

Q-R

QR codes, 182-183

RBI (Reality-Based Interaction), 42
real-time language translation, 232
The Real-time Operating System Nucleus (TRON) project, 14
receptivity awareness, 65
recognition techniques, 122-123
recommendation systems case study, 151-153
   accuracy of prediction model, 165-167
   activity prediction model, 154-160
   business impact of, 168-169
   "contextual intelligence," 153-154
   effectiveness of prediction model, 165
   helpfulness of prediction model, 167-168

   preference prediction model, 162-164
reflection, 223
relationship awareness, 65
relationship-aware systems, 66-67
relevance of advertising, 113-114
Responsive Mirror case study, 42, 207-213
   business impact, 223
   countertop, 219-221
   privacy concerns, 213-215
   public trials, 216-223
restaurant industry, Ubiquitous Computing in, 106
retail industry, Ubiquitous Computing in, 107
revenue, role in commercial innovation, 103
rhythm awareness, 65, 190-194
rich telepresence, 233

S

Sakamura, Ken, 14
sales process, 204-205
Satchel (printer connections), 180
scattershot advertising, 114
search-based advertising, 114
   characteristics of, 131
secure optical pairing in Xerox PrintTicket case study, 180-183
security of wireless communication, 177
semantic networks, 63-65
Semantic Web, 63-65
   contextual intelligence versus, 67
sensors for interoperation, 177-178, 194-196
services
   context-aware services, 61-62
   personalization of, 57-58
shared identifiers for continuity, 176

shared physical experience for continuity, 176
shared vocabulary for continuity, 176
shopping decisions, 204-205
   digital fitting rooms, 210-211
   factors when clothes shopping, 207-208
   IT (information technology) and, 205-206
   Responsive Mirror case study, 211-213
     business impact, 223
     privacy concerns, 213-215
     public trials, 216-223
   social aspects of, 206-207
   virtual fittings, 209-210
Short Message Service (SMS), 161-162
simplified computing, 12
simulating artificial intelligence, 132
skipping supply chain links, 137-138
Slater, Kelly, 227
smart homes/buildings, 231
SMS (Short Message Service), 161-162
social aspects of fashion shopping, 206-207
social connections, number of, 25-26
social context, 63
social identity, maintaining, 215
Songdo International City, 20
South Asian retail jewelry shopping (Responsive Mirror case study), 216-223
South Korea, Ubiquitous Computing in, 20
spyware, 87

standards
   interoperability barriers and, 34
   for interoperation, 174
statistically learned classification, 122-123
statistics
   amount of information, 55
   cost of interruptions, 187
   growth of personal computing, 53-55
   interruptions, effect of, 56-57
Sternberg, Robert, 60
streamlining supply chains
   Dai Nippon Printing (DNP), 146-148
   "5 Whys" method, 142-143
   identifying opportunities, 148-151
   in publishing industry, 139-142
   by skipping links, 137-138
structured data, unstructured data versus, 63-65
structured information, nonstructured information versus, 23-25
structured recognition, 122-123
Suica (Super Urban Intelligent Card) system, 19
summarization of events, 232
Sun Microsystems case study, 188-192
   business impact, 197-198
   estimates of interruptibility, 194-196
   privacy concerns, 196-197
   rhythm awareness, 190-194
Super Urban Intelligent Card (Suica) system, 19
supply chains, streamlining
   Dai Nippon Printing (DNP) case study, 146-148

"5 Whys" method, 142-143
  identifying opportunities,
    148-151
  in publishing industry, 139-142
  by skipping links, 137-138
  surveying customers, 144-145
Sweeny, Latanya, 89

T

tangible user interfaces (TUI), 41
targeted advertising, 115-116
  activity-based advertising
    effectiveness of, 130-131
    testing, 132-133
  characteristic-based filtering,
    116-117
  collaborative filtering, 117-120
  computer vision technologies,
    120-122
  effective advertising, types of,
    129-130
  pervasive advertising, 124-129
task overload, 57
technology transfer, 103
telecommunications industry,
  Ubiquitous Computing in, 106
telepresence, 233
testing activity-bsed advertising,
  132-133
text messaging, 161-162
text parsing, 24-25
tools, role in work, 11
Toyoda, Sakichi, 142
Toyota Production System
  (TPS), 142
transactional advertising, 129-130
translation services, real-time
  language translation, 232
transportation industry,
  Ubiquitous Computing in, 106
trigger-action pairs, 77

TRON (The Real-time Operating
  System Nucleus) project, 14
TUI (tangible user interfaces), 41

U

Ubicomp. *See* Ubiquitous
  Computing
Ubidocs, 49
Ubik (Dick), 31
Ubiquitous Computing
  Augmented Reality versus, 27-28
  business impact of, 229-230
  characteristic technologies in, 50
  commercialization of, business
    strategies for, 107-108
  complexities of, 21-23
    devices, number of, 23
    networks, number of, 26-27
    *nonstructured versus
      structured information*,
      23-25
    *social connections, number
      of*, 25-26
  components of, 31-32
  controlling connections, 36-37
  definitions of, 15-16
  description of, 3, 7
  evaluating opportunities,
    235-236
  future of, 230-233
  hardware devices for, 33
  industry segments, impact on,
    104-107
  intelligent agents versus, 46-47
  interoperability barrier, 33-35
  objective of, 44
  origins of
    in Japan, 14
    in United Kingdom, 14
    Xerox PARC research, 9-14
  proactive interaction, 39
    activity detection, 49
    *communication
      modalities*, 41

context-aware systems,
  44-45, 49
 direct manipulation, 41-43
 as natural interaction, 40
 proactive systems, 44
 progress in, 227-230
 in publishing industry
  supply chain, 140
 suggestions for utilizing, 233-234
 in United States versus Japan, Korea, and Europe, 18-21
 World Wide Web, effect of, 16-18
United Kingdom, Ubiquitous Computing research in, 14
United States, Ubiquitous Computing in, versus Japan, Korea, and Europe, 18-21
universal controllers, 36-37
unstructured data, structured data versus, 63-65
unstructured information, 66
usefulness of advertising, 113-114
user models for contextual intelligence, 76-79
user preference model, technology needed for, 127
utilities, Ubiquitous Computing in, 106

V

value added in publishing industry supply chains, 139
virtual fittings, 209-210
virtual reality, 17
visual recognition, 120-122
 techniques for, 122-123
Voltaire, 137

W

Wanamaker, John, 129
Warnaco, digital fitting rooms, 211
web sites, personalization, 57-58
web-based advertising, 130
Weiser, Mark, 11, 15-18, 47
wireless communication
 connections, determining, 174-175
 continuity, enabling, 176-177
 security of, 177
wireless connections, controlling, 36-37
World Wide Web, effect on Ubiquitous Computing, 16-18

X–Z

Xerox PARC
 current projects, 35
 origins of Ubiquitous Computing, 9-14
Xerox PrintTicket case study, 178-180
 business impact of, 184
 secure optical pairing, 180-183
Yeager, Chuck, 83
Zerubavel, Eviatar, 190
zip codes, identifying individuals by, 90-91